rightsizing your life

Simplifying Your Surroundings While Keeping What Matters Most

Ciji Ware

SPRINGBOARD PRESS

NEW YORK BOSTON

Springboard Press
Hachette Book Group USA
1271 Avenue of the Americas, New York, NY 10020
Visit our Web site at www.HachetteBookGroupUSA.com

Springboard Press is an imprint of Warner Books, Inc. The Springboard name and logo are trademarks of Hachette Book Group USA.

First Edition: January 2007

Library of Congress Cataloging-in-Publication data

Ware, Ciji.
Rightsizing your life : simplifying your surroundings while keeping what matters most / Ciji Ware.
p. cm.
Includes bibliographical references and index.
ISBN-13: 978-0-8212-5813-2 (alk. paper)
ISBN-10: 0-8212-5813-3 (alk. paper)
1. Simplicity. 2. Conduct of life. 3. Storage in the home.
4. House cleaning. I.Title.
BJ1496.W37 2006
646.7—dc22 2006013416

10 9 8 7 6 5 4 3 2 1

Printed in the United States of America

This book is dedicated to Tony Cook,
my husband of three decades with whom
I have shared the partnership of a lifetime.
We did, indeed, get it "right."

Contents

Foreword

Gail Sheehy

A dozen years ago, when my husband and I graduated into the vagabond years, I wish we'd had Ciji Ware's book. We were bare-nesters, neither of us tethered to a nine-to-five job, but shaken by a battle with serious illness into thinking about how to pursue our passions.

Lifelong New Yorkers, we sold our Manhattan apartment and lit out for a sojourn on the opposite coast, where my husband started a new career as a teacher at the University of California, Berkeley. We bought a house in the Berkeley hills and felt our vistas stretch across the Bay to the Atlantis of San Francisco as it arose from the foggy sea each morning. We could see all the way to the vast Pacific. It felt like a rebirth.

Like many in our circle, we graduated within the next ten years into the more-life-left-to-live-than-you-saved-for stage. For people like us — over fifty, with most of our equity tied up in a home we love — there comes a sober moment when we have to get real.

Ciji Ware describes many recognizable variations on that moment. It may never come for the superrich, unless they have their nest egg sliced up by a divorce or death taxes, but it comes for most of us in the shrinking middle and working class. Conventionally, it has been described as downsizing. But by viewing it through that dark lens, we set ourselves up for feeling like victims or failures or the unlucky ones. Couples seek relief in playing the blame game: "Why didn't you sell the Lucent stock before it tanked?" "You were the one who fell for that interest-only mortgage loan and got us sucked into rising rates six months later."

There is another way to look at making necessary changes in our lifestyle in our seasoned years. By the time we are moving into our Second Adulthood (and today that age varies widely, depending on how old we are when our little darlings move out), we have often reached a point of exhaustion. So much effort has gone into operating the incredibly complex switches of that instrument called family life, into building careers, expanding homes, proliferating possessions, we just want to take a deep breath. And if we allow ourselves to breathe awhile, we'll probably feel the counter-urge to pare down, simplify, consolidate, and lighten up.

It's not a question of giving up a way of life. We are now graduating to a stage that allows us to pull free from the maintenance work of holding on to a past stage. For women, in particular, reaching the age fifty peak can feel like standing on top of a mountain with a 360 degree view in all directions. We can look back and see the steps we have taken — when we were on the right road, when we veered off-track. Looking ahead, we see a vista more lengthy than any generation has ever known. It's time to pursue a more passionate life. And that is only possible once we are willing to change.

For my husband and me, one bright light that illuminated our changing priorities came with the birth of our second grandchild. But how will we be able to help our adult children tend to our grandchildren if we're not prepared to finance our own extended life spans?

So, like legions of boomers who will follow us, we had to consider cashing in our greatest equity — the house — and paring down on the costs of maintenance. It took us two or three years of hand-wringing and inner and outer conflict before we bit the bullet.

So here we are, as I write this, sitting outdoors on our patio while the prospective buyer makes her fourth excursion through our house over a holiday weekend. Our houseguests and we have been living as if in boot camp, mitering the corners of our bedclothes and using only the corners of our towels, in order to keep the house showable. I'm feeling a combination of sad and mad — why should somebody else have the home I have spent thirty years nurturing into our ideal nest?

I feel better when I anticipate the weightlessness of not carrying the small army of tree pruners and pool cleaners and gutter muckrakers and grass mowers and mole/vole catchers and on and on. We have begun nursing a brand-new fragile-as-a-bubble dream of buying a little dock on the bay, with a smaller house, and a lot less land. We both love looking out at the water. And you don't have to mow water. I could have a rowboat and a kayak to entertain my grandchildren.

Still, I'm fighting clingitis. The house has never looked so close to perfect, but I can't leave it alone. I'm constantly shifting throw pillows and turning the comforters and cutting flowers for every room, despite nature's chandeliers of white wisteria just outside the windows and bouquets of rhododendron pushing over the sills. I'm like a mother overdressing her children for the holidays.

I want to be a cool and collected rightsizer instead.

When my stomach knots is when I look at all the furnishings and books and chotchkes we've collected over three decades. Where to stash it all while we're in between? And once the artifacts of our life are in cold storage, will we ever have the energy to sort through it all again?

These are exactly the fears and frustrations that Ciji Ware unravels in her book. She takes us by the hand and leads us through the cascade of predictable emotions. By breaking down the planning and timing of a rightsizing move, she gives us the practical help that makes it all seem quite doable.

Making any major life passage is hard. I know it, I write about it, but writing about it and actually living it are two different things. A writer is in control of the story. The sojourner midway through a major life passage is in disequilibrium. Suspended in midair. Not knowing when or where she will touch ground again.

What I do know, from making many passages, is that taking action to resolve an inner conflict is a great deal better than digging in one's heels and resisting change. And having attempted a few bold passages in previous stages, I know in my heart as well as my head how to get over the hump. I remind myself that once having set the wheels in motion, then is the time to sit back and pray, take walks, talk to my soulmate, meditate, and try to go to sleep at night — not planning or panicking about the future, but thinking only of what I can do to be fully present in the next day.

I also believe that the greatest harmony in marriage comes from seeking and finding a creative resolution to a major life passage, together.

We are not about to "lose our home," we are about to gain our freedom. We are plants whose roots have grown gnarly and cramped and need repotting in fresh soil. And won't it be fun to find a romantic nest where we can play newlyweds again, designing our new surroundings, even as we remind ourselves that to arrive at this stage still full of zest for life is an incredible gift.

We have enough.

PART I

Time for a Change

THE CASE FOR RIGHTSIZING

Chapter 1

What Is Rightsizing?

Why rightsizing is becoming our new way of life

TIME FOR A CHANGE

There comes a moment when you pass the half-century mark that is hard to pinpoint or even predict, but you know intuitively when it has occurred. It's a flash of recognition, an instant when you realize something important has changed and that it is time *for* a change. Your old life just doesn't fit anymore.

Maybe it's the day you put your youngest child on the plane for college. The day you sign a divorce decree or your beloved family dog dies. It could be the week you witness a parent pass away, your spouse is scheduled for open-heart surgery, or the company that's employed you for decades is sold to a competitor and your job is handed to a twenty-five-year-old.

It's that first Thanksgiving you don't cook the turkey, but your daughter-in-law does. It's the winter you swear off downhill skiing and decide cross-country might make more sense. And when that feels like too much work, you opt for a cup of hot chocolate and a good book in front of the fire.

The signal that change is in the wind might even be made of lighter stuff: a nanosecond of exasperation when you haul a pile of folded laundry up two flights of stairs. A moment when you realize you're not much interested in working in your wood shop anymore, or the bridge club is starting to be a bore, or you'd rather take a class in memoir writing than teach another year of third grade or continue as CEO of your company.

lay is usually bittersweet, and yet strangely full of promise. s if a generation that is forecast to live longer, in better alth than anyone in the history of our planet is about to walk down a totally new path no one has ever trod before.

The road that presently stretches in front of our "baby boomer" generation — the estimated seventy-seven million Americans born between the end of World War II and the beginning of the Vietnam War — is uncharted territory. Indeed it's fraught with uncertainty and, for some, no small amount of anxiety about what this "third act" will bring to a generation expected to live a very long time.

Some of the questions prompted by the coming new phase are seriously unsettling. Where will I live? What will my environment look like? What will it be like? Who will I be living with, spending time with, and ultimately depending upon?

RIGHTSIZING DEFINED

I've come to think of this transition for baby boomers and the generations that bookend them as "rightsizing your life." In contrast to downsizing it is a process, not an event, and its outcome has more to do with the "right" of the equation than "size." It involves not just the square footage of a person's living quarters but an approach to all aspects of living, holding out the opportunity "to get it right, once and for all."

Rightsizing in this context is a conscious, practical, and psychological evolution in the way one lives one's life, a process that enables people to create new surroundings that will profoundly impact the way they feel and behave. It leads to simplifying, decluttering, perhaps even redesigning one's environment. It may even prompt a move — either to smaller, more practical quarters or to a home (or homes) that could be larger, but more suited to your needs. The transition will, if executed properly, liberate you from many real-life burdens and free you in ways you cannot now imagine.

For many, the rightsizing process will certainly involve physical and emotional upheaval and could even result in a total reinvention of your personal ecosystem. For the resilient, however, these major life changes provide an opportunity for discovering the truest sense of home you may ever have known.

That being said, I suppose this is as good a time as any to tell you my story.

A RIGHTSIZING TALE

For me the moment it became clear that a major change in my life was under way was quite vivid. On an early Saturday morning one raw March day, my husband and I stood shivering on the loading dock at Nor-Cal Moving and Storage Company in San Jose, California. We watched as a forklift operator lined up *five* ten-foot-square wooden containers, all overflowing with the accumulated possessions of twenty-five years of marriage.

We were sorting through our possessions after a move from a large and reasonably luxurious family home in Los Angeles, where my family had lived for twenty-two years. My husband had been recruited to join a Silicon Valley company — a great professional move for him. But what in God's name had made us think it was a good idea to decamp to a smaller home (a mere 1,200 square feet, as compared to our roomy 4,000 square feet of living space in southern California)? Somehow we needed to make our life fit into a much smaller San Francisco apartment . . . and I was just starting to realize what a challenge this was going to be.

The first object to emerge from the packing crates was a child-size rocking chair with a petit point seat cover that I had crafted during my first and only pregnancy, decades earlier. My husband picked up the little chair and swiftly consigned it to a pile next to a sign we'd scrawled that read: "Throw Away."

I reacted with tears and a sudden urge to kill. How dare my husband consign this sentimental trophy to the trash! How had it come to this? What had possessed us to abandon our beautiful home in Southern California for a tiny urban apartment, stashing most of our worldly goods into off-site storage?

This entire upheaval was suddenly too painful. Why did we have to dispose of the things we didn't have room for anymore? And while we were on the subject, why did I have to go through this process of domestic downsizing anyway?

True, our only child was now grown and self-supporting; our beloved, fourteen-year-old English setter, Chelsea, had died before we had exited LA; and a number of our close friends had moved to the beach or far away. Okay, so my job of sixteen years as a radio commentator had melted away in the wake of the station's budget cutting and desire for something "edgier" in the manner of a female Howard Stern.

My sense of bereavement over our domestic downsizing was visceral. "Is this the way I'll feel when they cart us off to the nursing home?" I lamented to no one in particular on that frigid landing dock. And I have to be honest — it was hard to let go of all those things I'd spent a lifetime accumulating. I felt naked without my belongings, poorer somehow. And what would our friends think when they saw the return address on our Christmas card had an apartment number listed, not a house?

Appallingly superficial of me? Disgustingly bourgeois? All right, I admit it probably was, but I'm trying to be honest here. I felt absolutely wretched that day.

Then it hit me. My emotional reaction probably paralleled the feelings that everyone "of a certain age" must confront eventually. My husband and I were only in our mid-fifties, but the fact was our needs had changed, become simpler. As a practical matter we couldn't carry all this baggage into the next chapter of our lives — nor, in truth, did we really want to.

So the question remained: how in the world were we going to sort through all this stuff? I became exhausted just looking at all the clutter and dreaded the notion of culling through it. Why wasn't there some rescuing angel who would magically appear and just deal with it?

And what about our memories, the fabric of our lives pictured in the photo albums and the contents stashed in scores of file boxes filled with the detritus of our professional lives? Where would we put our outsize family "heirlooms," our wicker porch furniture that seated ten, and a soup pot that could hold seafood gumbo for forty? There had to be a sensible, systematic way to deal with the practical and emotional aspects of this domestic winnowing process — a way to "rightsize" one's life without the emotional trauma and the angst. My quest to figure out this process had begun.

WHO IS RIGHTSIZING?

As I started to look into what's happening to other midlife people, I found that my husband and I were not alone. Huge numbers of people fifty-plus are moving, relocating far and wide, and continuing their consumerist ways (and debt accumulation), as witnessed by the remarkable expansion of the self-storage business and the popularity of unloading household goods at weekend flea markets. And one need only look around to observe the mass disposal of personal items on eBay — or at city dumps — every day. Looking ahead at the incipient wave of millions of boomers, I saw that my "war baby" husband and I were living witnesses to their future: we had too much stuff and not enough room for it.

Our experience began to serve as an early warning system for our younger friends. What we discovered — and what they all wanted to learn about — was how the experience of paring down to *only* the possessions we loved and actually *used* had ultimately brought us relief . . . and even elation.

Rightsizers truly come in a "variety pak": they include empty nesters, the widowed, the newly divorced, the never married, the early retired, the unwillingly retired, the second-and-third marriage set, the elderly, the financially strapped, the physically impaired, and finally, a group I call "the highly adventurous."

For all these groups, however, it's definitely not the Age of Aquarius anymore. America's approximately fourteen million war babies and some seventy-seven million boomers are getting older by the minute — and living longer. As a result an American woman reaching age sixty-five today can plan on living nearly twenty more years, while men can expect more than fifteen years of continued life, most of it in reasonably good health. The collection of centenarians is also growing by leaps and bounds. There are forty thousand currently alive in America, and the number of our citizens living to one hundred is expected to increase to eight hundred thousand by the midcentury mark.

Ask the silver foxes in skintight Nike warm-up suits striding briskly on the treadmill at the gym or the sinewy sixty-year-old specimens taking off on the seven-day, four-hundred-mile San Francisco to LA AIDS bicycle ride each year how long they expect to live. True, they may not say "forever," but they will cheerfully tell you they're assuming advances in medicine and genetic research will enable them to make it to one hundred or more.

This "graying of America" (though many in this group wouldn't be caught dead without coloring their hair!) is spawning many trends, but one of the largest certainly involves mobility. A survey by the Del Webb Corporation, a developer of active-adult communities, indicates that nearly 60 percent of those age forty to sixty will move to at least one new home in their lives. That, dear reader, probably means *you* will soon — or will eventually — hit the road.

Some studies show that the number of households without children will increase dramatically as the boomers' kids fly the coop. Meanwhile the National Directory of Lifestyle Communities database claims *six times* as many new active-adult community building projects — where children need not apply — went up for sale in 2004 compared with a decade earlier. And the CEO of Pulte Homes, America's largest builder of active-adult housing for people fifty-five and over, says, "We don't see any end to the active-adult boom in sight."

For most of us the transition to new housing will mean scaling back to a simpler, more streamlined lifestyle, but for those fifty-plus the research predicts their future plans do not include checking into the "foyer-to-the-tomb" type retirement facilities populated by their parents and grandparents. Not if they can help it, that is.

Take Cris and Linda Hammond, a couple in their late fifties who made a well-deliberated decision to sell their hyperinflated "trophy house" on a hill overlooking San Francisco Bay, move into a 950-square-foot rental cottage they owned, and purchase a 55-foot canal barge, on which they spend several months a year cruising around France.

Linda continues to work as a real-estate agent *and* a national sales manager for an artisan Bay Area bakery, while Captain Cris, having abandoned the executive world, has gone back to painting landscapes full time, the fruits of which he sells to his American clients when he returns from his adventures abroad. We'll hear more about the Hammonds later in this book. How do they feel after making such a radical change in housing and lifestyle? "*Magnifique!*"

Another example of the late-life moving trend are Amos and Sylvia Spady, now in their seventies. When Amos was fifty-five, he and his wife, Sylvia, sold their 3,000-square-foot family home in Yorktown, Virginia, banked most of the money, moved to an 1,800-square-foot condo in Newport News, and took up *serious* ballroom dancing three or four nights a week — a hobby they've pursued with enthusiasm ever since.

It should be noted that not everybody scales down when rightsizing. A couple I once visited outside of Jackson Hole, Wyoming, added on to their log cabin vacation home that had become their permanent residence in retirement, a common occurrence among the more affluent, second-home boomer brigade. Their idea of rightsized bliss was a "playroom/bunk room" 400-square-foot extension with six pull-down Murphy beds to lure their adult children and young grandchildren for frequent visits.

And then there is the single professional woman in her late fifties who bought a derelict "landed ark," a one-hundred-year-old house built on stilts over Richardson Bay, near my home in Marin County, California, across the Golden Gate Bridge from San Francisco. She bailed out of her corporate PR job and carved out a studio rental unit within the existing layout to help pay her mortgage. Then, within the remaining square footage, she created a charming two-bedroom home for herself that was elegant enough to merit a color spread in *Coastal Living* magazine. When she wants a change of scene, she rents out the "big house" and heads for San Miguel d'Allende, Mexico.

As I mentioned earlier, to rightsizers it's more about "right" than "size" when it comes to fashioning surroundings that make sense for one's age, stage, and situation in later life. And it's probably clear by now that merely knowing the number of rings on someone's tree doesn't tell you very much about them these days. According to boomer marketing guru Matt Thornhill, people born around the middle of the twentieth century are tending to "reinvent themselves every three to five years" in ways that are both surprising and inspiring.

Exhibit A: In May 1998, when Rob Gomersall and Wendy Catlin were in their late fifties, they departed Airlie Beach, Queensland,

Australia, to begin a four-year world sailing cruise on their forty-foot sloop, *Sea Fever.* "We love our new home," says Wendy. "We decided to just take off'til we stopped . . . meaning if we ran out of money, our health wasn't good, or it wasn't fun anymore." Seven years later they are still heading for new harbors. They love "the challenge and adventure of sea travel" while living aboard their boat.

The downside? Admits Wendy, "I don't like being so distant from my family." But thanks to e-mail and international cell phones, they stay in touch, and a grandchild recently sailed one leg of their journey with them.

And then there are the homebodies like my widowed sister Joy, who declares her traveling days are at an end, though she walks a good mile and a half each day in her town of five thousand. A retired schoolteacher in her late sixties, she returned to the coastal village of her youth, Carmel-by-the-Sea. She'd sold her family home before the California real-estate market went insane in the late 1990s and missed the home-equity bonanza that so many of her friends have enjoyed. She now lives "on a *very* fixed income" in a 420-square-foot rental cottage, writing for pleasure, knitting professionally in the evenings, and serving as a part-time, paid companion for a woman fifteen years her senior.

"I have never been happier! My cottage is so cozy, everyone I know wants to come by for tea at four. I can walk to the beach, walk to town, church, the grocery store, and the post office! What else would I need?"

What's the secret of these contented people living such a variety of lifestyles after turning fifty?

Regardless of their income level or tastes for adventure, they "rightsized" their lives in the strong belief that they still had years of good living left. They had figured out their "core passion," as author and cultural observer Gail Sheehy recently described it to me, and have found exciting interests to pursue and new reasons to get up every morning.

Happy rightsizers also have made a conscious commitment to the principle of simplicity, surrounding themselves with only the people, possessions, and activities they love. They didn't just downsize, they made mindful choices about the who, what, where, when, and why of the places they considered — and ultimately selected — to live during their "third age." They gave considerable thought to the kind of people they still aspired to be and weren't shy about striking out in directions that excited them — even if it meant sailing the seas or simply knitting in front of a fire. For many the paradigm shift that is occurring is a move away from the notion of "aging in place" to aging in a community of kindred spirits with fewer material possessions, yet plenty of time for sharing activities and pursuits that have meaning in their lives as currently constituted.

Amazingly enough, my family's own personal rightsizing miracle began as a painful (and pain-in-the-ass) process that slowly shifted into something astonishingly *positive* — at times even joyful. With each item sold or given away, with every trip to Goodwill or the dump, we began to feel . . . *lighter* . . . freer, unburdened — almost buoyant!

We even began to feel strangely youthful as we deep-sixed worn croquet mallets, outdated clothing, rusted weed whackers, magazine back issues, and untold objects that no longer had use in our current lives. Gone were the physical and psychological albatrosses we'd been carrying (and had paid good money to maintain) for far too long.

That's not to say there weren't potholes along the way, including the purchase of a low-ceilinged, 950-square-foot condo we hated and sold four months later and culling our possessions not once, but four different times. But in the process of discovering which of our worldly goods actually meant something to us and were useful in our lives *now*, we learned to reach out to a new community, be more flexible, be open to change, and admit to ourselves this would be a process of trial and error. We suddenly felt as if we'd liberated ourselves from an outmoded way of living that had been weighing us down in more ways than mere bulk.

It was a year or so after that miserable rainy morning when I'd wept at the sight of my grown son's little rocking chair that I realized my husband and I had taken a course of action I ultimately dubbed *rightsizing* our lives. Not merely "downsizing" to fit into a smaller living space, with fewer physical possessions, but taking positive steps to create a living environment filled only with the household goods — as well as people and activities — that we love, along with surroundings that suit our stage in life to a T. We had discovered that we didn't merely want "smaller," we wanted "better," and we achieved our goal the rightsizing way.

This book is intended to make a potentially bumpy transition to smaller — or larger — scale living a lot smoother by fully preparing you for it emotionally as well as practically. The goal is to help people begin to liberate themselves from their "stuff" so that they can enjoy a precious time of life surrounded by the people and possessions that give them joy in a place where they feel fulfilled.

We did it, and so can you.

WHAT'S SO "RIGHT" ABOUT RIGHTSIZING?

Dominique Browning, editor of *House & Garden* magazine, is a woman I admire tremendously for her stylish writing, her talent for articulating the beauty to be found in our surroundings, and her searing honesty. Contemplating the sale of her exquisite home, she writes, "It is a house I love. It has sheltered me through the end of love and the beginning of love. It has been home to two boys . . . [yet] there is liberation in recognizing what you don't need, as well as understanding what you want."

Perfectly put! The rightsizing of Browning's world already appears under way. It consists of understanding what you want your environment to look like as your needs change with age. It is also about being spunky enough to embark on a journey to *discover* just exactly what those needs might be.

Some rightsizers will, indeed, choose to "age in place," adapting their own homes to be safer, more secure places in which to grow older. Others will opt for a series of homes that meet the criteria of their evolving stages and situations as they continue to age. And still others will seek out the "perfect place" they hope to live in until they die, a home that fulfills longings they've sublimated for too long.

In this journey we move away from the idea that "we are what we have" and that if we have fewer things, we amount to less. Rightsizing your life examines these superficial judgments and celebrates our lives through thoughtful selection of the environment, possessions, and people that resonate for us.

Rightsizing is also a way to rescue you from being a *prisoner* of your possessions. It examines some of the emotional and psychological ties we have to material things and suggests ways to free ourselves from here on out so we can travel more lightly and revel in surroundings that speak to us in ways we never imagined.

Rightsizing lays out lifestyle preferences and encourages out-of-the-box fantasies. It starts by imagining what you've always dreamed about — the cottage by the sea . . . the cabin on the lake . . . the condo on the links . . . the sophisticated city apartment . . . the vagabond life on the road or the high seas. The truly adventurous sign up for activities like Habitat for Humanity's Care-A-Vanners, hundreds of older adults in recreational vehicles who build houses for the poor all over the country. Everything and anything is acceptable when you're conjuring visions of the ideal rightsizing scenario, for it just might lead you to a totally new world.

Diane Barr and Ken Young were both challenged by several health problems and concerns that they might outlive their nest egg. For years they'd been drawn to the romantic rolling hills and magical lure of California's wine country, but there was no way they could buy into the area's million-dollar lifestyle, given their financial constraints.

After several fits and starts, they ultimately sold their family home in California's Central Valley and scaled down to a two-bedroom, two-bath modular home in the small town of St. Helena in Napa Valley, with a spectacular slice of the vineyards out their back window. They're both continuing to work as long they can, they say, "loving each and every day of our new lives in such a beautiful place."

But wasn't it hard for them to move into a much more modest home? Some might call their neighborhood a "trailer park," but "the word 'trailer park' never passes our lips," she says. "We call where we live now a 'cottage community.' After all, there are no *wheels* on our new home! It looks darling inside and out. We searched and searched until we found the perfect spot featuring this unique kind of housing." The price? Less than $200,000.

Was the transition for the Barr-Youngs easy? Diane offers a rueful laugh.

"Frankly, while it was happening, it was one of the most traumatic things I've ever gone through; paring down and repurposing many of our things, while getting rid of tons in order to fit into this smaller home. What I discovered, though, is how we live now is a lot less work to keep up, and I just love everything about St. Helena — the beauty of our surroundings, the wonderful restaurants, the culture of wine making. For us the move was well worth it."

On the other hand, the Mathers-Rotella clan four hundred miles to the south in Thousand Oaks, outside Los Angeles, had to scale *up* in order to rightsize their lives. Laurie Rotella Mathers, in her mid-fifties, wasn't necessarily ready to make a move, but when her mother, Gloria Rotella, eighty-four, fell several times in her own home, Laurie and her brother, Tom, decided to take action.

"I was in a panic when Mom called to tell me she'd slipped in her bedroom and lay there on the floor from two until seven at night," remembers Laurie. "That's when Tom said, 'We've got to take this out of Mom's hands.'"

None of the Mathers-Rotellas wanted their mother to be confined to a nursing home or even an assisted-living facility. After all, they joke, "We're Italian!" Instead the family pooled its financial resources and built an 800-square-foot addition to Laurie and Larry Mathers's house. "Upsizing" was their rightsizing solution.

"We didn't dare call it a 'Granny Unit,' though. It's called 'Mother's Suite.' She's picked out the furniture and the things from her other home she wants to bring with her, and she can shut the door to her own section of the house whenever she likes."

The money from the sale of Gloria Rotella's house went into building the addition at the Matherses', as well as a pool of funds that pays Laurie — who retired as a bookkeeper when her mother moved into her home — to be her mother's companion. Brother Tom agreed this was the wisest use of his mother's money. When Laurie and her husband eventually sell the house years down the road, Tom will then receive his share of the family inheritance.

The point is that rightsizing isn't necessarily about shrinking your living space, although for the generations now in their seventies and eighties that may come to pass. It's more about stepping back at around age fifty and beyond, taking serious account of your future finances, analyzing the particulars of your family situation, your likes, dislikes, and best choices among several nice-to-haves. It's a process by which you learn to evaluate people, places, and possessions according to how they make you *feel*, choosing to live with the material things that truly have meaning because of their sentiment or utility — and preferably both.

Rightsizing is also a method for drilling below the surface to examine what your life is like now — not a year ago or ten years ago. It also suggests you "play it forward" and think about likely scenarios in the future. The exercise involves both the *emotional* and the *practical* aspects of making a change in your living quarters and your way of life.

Take Susan Peck in Cincinnati, Ohio, who was divorced in her forties. She continued to rattle around in her 5,200-square-foot family home while her son and his wife and a growing family were squeezed into their cute but tiny "starter home" nearby. Their rightsizing solution? Trade houses. Mom moved into the starter home, and her son took over the larger house.

As you can probably surmise by now, the process of rightsizing your life will be stimulating, sometimes aggravating, sometimes upsetting and exhausting (especially if you're helping someone else go through the exercise), but with the proper approach, solutions exist to every problem. The best news is that coming to grips with the issues and solving them can be downright exhilarating.

As Diane Barr in Vineyard Valley and hundreds of fellow rightsizers have told me, "Despite the exertion involved, it's ultimately well worth the effort."

So here's my motto for people like us: don't just move to somewhere new . . . *rightsize your life!* This book will show you how.

Chapter 2

Am I Ready to Rightsize?

How to deal with the hurdles that stand in your way

DEALING WITH CHANGE

Since you are holding this book in your hands, it's probably reasonable to assume that you have been *considering* making some changes in your current living arrangements, either by retooling your existing home to make it work better for your present lifestyle or by thinking about — or actively planning — a move out of your current abode.

Any change, even one eagerly embraced, can give a person pause — or result in sleepless nights. That's perfectly normal, as are the fears that factor into the decision of where to make your home. See if any of the following concerns resonate with you and add your own remedies to those listed below.

Top Ten Fears about Rightsizing

1. **Fear:** I dread being forced to deal with the contents of my home, especially the (attic, basement, garage, workshop, storage room, etc.).

   Antidote: Trust the wisdom of those who have gone down this road ahead of you: whether you move, or merely adapt where you are to suit the next phase of your life, getting rid of clutter is liberating!

2. **Fear:** I feel really sad about letting go of big chunks of my past.

Antidote: Accept that the past *is* past. Letting go of it, while acknowledging feeling sad about it, can lead to closing the book gently on a previous phase of life. This acceptance, in turn, can open doors to new worlds, along with an appreciation for the advantages of the age you are *now*.

3. **Fear:** I'm afraid my kids would be upset if we changed or altered the family home.

   Antidote: Discussing future housing scenarios with grown children can lead to surprisingly positive results.

4. **Fear:** I'm worried that any change I make might be the wrong one financially.

   Antidote: Nothing is certain in life, but examining one's options usually leads to *better* financial decisions.

5. **Fear:** I'm afraid that any change I make might produce a worse result than the way I'm living currently.

   Antidote: Carefully considered choices generally result in a better outcome, not a worse one.

6. **Fear:** I'm afraid that any change I would like to make will upset my spouse, sibling, parent, etc. and cause conflicts between us.

   Antidote: Conflicts with loved ones are inevitable; openly discussing possible changes and options can lead to compromise and consensus.

7. **Fear:** I don't like change because the unknown frightens me.

   Antidote: The one constant in life *is* change. It's okay to be frightened, but seek out better solutions anyway!

8. **Fear:** I'm worried that if I bring up the subject of making a change in our living situation I'll end up being forced into doing something I don't want to do.

   Antidote: Slavery has been abolished. No one can make anyone else do something they don't want to do unless they give their permission.

9. **Fear:** I'm afraid what other people will think if we move to something smaller.

   Antidote: Some 60 percent of seventy-seven million baby boomers are expected to make at least one more move, so the people whose opinions you're worrying about are likely to be envious of the well-ordered life you've created for yourself!

10. **Fear:** I'm worried that making these changes means facing up to my own mortality.

    Antidote: As one wag puts it, "Nobody gets outta here alive!" We're born; we eventually die. Rightsizing will help us make the most of what we have *now!*

YOU KNOW YOU'RE READY TO RIGHTSIZE WHEN . . .

If you're one of those people who have experienced that moment of truth, that tipping point that tells you that it's probably — or definitely — time for a change in your living arrangements, you'll be able to see yourself in the following scenarios:

- You're sick of putting up storm windows or mowing the lawn.
- You've occasionally wondered how many sets of dishes a person can eat off at one time or how many Beanie Babies constitutes a collection.
- The family pet has passed away.
- Your last child has gone to college — and your home feels empty.
- Your kids are grown and have moved into their own places; your home feels quiet and dull.
- Your spouse has passed away (or asked for a divorce) and your home feels too big and probably costs too much financially or emotionally to maintain.
- You've at last met the love of your life and are combining households.
- You're moving in with a friend or family member and are combining households.

- Half your friends have left town — permanently.
- You have an unrequited yen to get out and see more of the world before you die.
- The thrill is gone from the way you've made your living all these years.
- Your company gave you a gold watch and declared you retired.
- You didn't get the gold watch, but your full-time job has gone bye-bye.
- You've survived a crisis — a serious illness, death or abandonment of a spouse, a natural disaster like Hurricane Katrina, or a reversal of financial fortune — and are forced to make a change.
- Your elderly parents or siblings are failing and need your help.
- You're not as spry as you once were and *you* need help.
- You are an incredible, forward-thinking person who never lets any grass grow under your feet and are planning ahead!

IMAGINING THE "PERFECT" RIGHTSIZED LIFE

It's one thing to sense that the time has come to consider your options as circumstances in your life alter but quite another to declare yourself ready to rightsize, sort through those options, and pick the right choice in housing and lifestyle just for *you*.

Perhaps you and those in your family circle already know exactly where you're headed (or where an elderly relative is slated to reside) and have purchased this book because you want to know what steps are necessary to rightsize yourself *out* of where you are currently and *into* the predetermined new location you've already chosen. If that's the case you may wish to skip directly to chapter 4 to estimate how long you might expect the rightsizing process to take and then proceed to Part II, which describes rightsizing in seven simple steps.

On the other hand if you're still in the throes of trying to figure out your next — or perhaps first — step, and you're trying to determine the type of place you'll eventually call home, I want you to hear more about the Hammonds, a couple we discussed in the last chapter, who split their time between a 950-square-foot cottage in California and a 55-foot, well-appointed barge on the canals of France. Their rightsizing story is certainly not the norm, but it may be highly instructive when it comes to understanding how the act of paying close attention to what feels "right" can result in creating a life that suits you perfectly.

A while back I wondered how Linda and Cris Hammond, whom I knew casually around town, were able to switch gears and make such radical changes in their lives. Cris had once been a painter of marine landscapes and had owned an art gallery in Tiburon, California, before getting embedded in the high-flying corporate world of human-resources management. Approaching sixty, he realized that the business environment he'd ridden to success during his fifties was starting to grate on his nerves.

As he tells it, "I'd go to corporate events in Silicon Valley and realize I was an *artist* at heart. It occurred to me one day that we'd bought our big house mostly to solve a tax problem."

As for Linda Hammond, she could look back on raising two daughters, along with a successful career selling software to banks, serving as a specialty food broker for eighteen years in the rarified world of smoked salmon and caviar, and more recently, peddling high-end real estate to twenty-seven-year-olds with fists full of New Economy cash.

Both Cris and Linda had a palpable feeling of time passing without experiencing much excitement and pleasure in their daily routine. The go-go nineties were over, and the Hammonds began to sense that the party was, too.

"My fifty-fifth birthday was approaching," recalls Linda. "My daughters were launched. We'd gone to France for years and loved it — the food, wine . . . everything! Suddenly, I spotted an ad in a boat magazine for a barge that was tied up somewhere in Burgundy. I circled the ad and left it in the bathroom for Cris." He took the bait, she says with a laugh. "By the end of the day, he was on the computer and had brokers looking for barges all over France."

Before long, though, Linda had reservations. "Cris was much more of a boat guy than I, and I'd never been barging. My dream had been to have a little place . . . a cottage in France someday with my favorite things *in* it."

Neither of them felt it was the moment to retire in the classic mode, but they definitely sensed it was time for a mini upheaval.

What ultimately became their "rightsized" lifestyle turned out to be the perfect compromise: a small cottage in their old Sausalito neighborhood "and a moveable cottage on a French canal!" Linda says, delighted.

The Hammonds' 575-square-foot new "home" in Europe had three staterooms with built-in beds, drawers, and closets, a charming galley (kitchen), bikes stashed forward near the second stateroom, and plenty of lounging room on the deck.

How, you ask, could the Hammonds afford this radical change in lifestyle, and what was the sequence of steps that brought about their satisfying shift? Well, they were certainly blessed with adequate financial resources. But trust me, this change wasn't financed by stock options. The price tag for their French houseboat? About $110,000 — the same cost as a used mobile home.

What the Hammonds possessed is what I've come to label an *attitude of intention.*

DECLARE YOUR INTENTIONS

We'll talk about declaring your intentions again when it comes to editing your possessions to suit whatever surroundings you select for the next chapters of your life. For now, we're adding another query to the simple question, "Am I *ready* to rightsize?" and that is, "What are your *intentions* about the way you'd like to live the rest of your life?"

In other words, what are you going to rightsize *to?*

This is a very important part of the rightsizing process for, as organizing coach Michi Blake of Santa Barbara says, "unless you have a really clear view of yourself — your likes and dislikes . . . who you really are [as you make life-changing decisions] — you'll tend to fulfill other people's expectations. For example, if you're unconsciously trying to please your dead mother's ghost and end up with a life she'd approve of (including her gold-rimmed chinaware that you've never really liked), you'll never know why the end result doesn't quite sit right."

Another aspect of your readiness to rightsize will depend on what problems you are currently trying to solve.

Where Am I?

Put a check mark next to the following situations that reflect your current status:

- Pressing circumstances dictate a need to make a change in living situations as soon as possible.
- I/We know change is in the offing in the next year or so.
- I am/We're merely approaching the planning stage of designing a future that won't arrive for a few more years.

Rightsizers need to assess if a major shift is comfortably far off or looming just around the corner — but they haven't forced themselves to face it yet.

Where you are in the process of determining a major life transition dictates what actions you will (or won't yet) take. People make decisions about where they should live right up till the day they die, but Cris and Linda Hammond's tale is a good example of increasing the odds you'll be happy with your new surroundings if you do some long-term thinking as soon as there are signs that a major life transition is looming.

Says Linda, her eyes alight, "We [always] loved France. To us it represented escape. And besides, we always thought 'someday' we'll do something crazy!"

Before the moment Linda spotted the magazine ad for the barge, the couple had had children to raise and educate, salaries to earn, in short, the usual life-as-a-three-ring-circus to support.

But as my friend author Gail Sheehy wrote in *New Passages*, the lengthening life expectancy of aging boomers means that "profound changes in lifestyle are to be expected and planned for." Sheehy follows this with *the* central question for those who now expect to live into their eighties and beyond: "What do I do with this 'Leftover Life?' "

And in *Sex and the Seasoned Woman*, Sheehy cautions, "The increased life span alone, of course, does not promise a rich Second Adulthood. The added years are merely a blank slate; it's what we write on them that makes the difference."

What Does That Little Voice Say?

The key to figuring out what your intentions are is to ask yourself: what is it *you* love?

- What activities do you enjoy pursuing?
- Where are the places that make you feel wonderful when you wake up in the morning?
- Who are the people you like being around?
- How does your life work for you *now*, as opposed to in the past?
- What were the peak times in your life where you had a sense of joy?

So what about it?

One way to sort out thoughts and feelings is to purchase a lined notebook that will also have other uses in later chapters of this book. In your rightsizing notebook, jot down the questions listed above and spend some time thinking about them. Later, you can write down your answers.

Successful rightsizers like the Hammonds discover that developing an attitude of intention encourages you to ignore opinions of the Joneses in your life and listen to your own sensibilities and inner voice.

SO WHAT'S STOPPING YOU?

There's a line supposedly uttered by Ernest Hemingway about the difficulty writers sometimes have forcing themselves to sit down and do their work.

"The hardest part of the job," this genius of fiction is reputed to have said, "is that, *first*, you have to defrost the refrigerator!"

No doubt about it, even when we want to, moving forward and making substantial changes in our lives can be hard. We have habits, ways of doing things, ways of being in our environment that feel familiar and even comforting, despite a voice inside that may be telling us our surroundings aren't working as well for us as they have in the past — or have never worked well for us, period.

So if that's true, what do you suppose is holding us back from doing something that the "sane" part of our brain tells us is necessary and is ultimately going to be positive? Why do we often say that we want to do a thing and yet allow a million reasons to creep in that distract us from obtaining our stated goal? Why is it that we'd even do some *distasteful* task — such as defrost the refrigerator, or continue to live in chaotic surroundings, or remain where it hurts your knees every time you walk up the stairs or annoys you each Saturday you have to mow the lawn — rather than just get on with what our stated intentions are: make a change in our living arrangements that we think, in the end, will be good for us?

The hardest part about making a substantial transition in life is that *first* you have to figure out what may be standing in your way of making that change and *why*. Those schooled in human behavior tell us that there are several reasons we sometimes sabotage ourselves when poised to launch into something that ostensibly is in our best interest. Boiled down to its essence, the hurdles generally fall into two categories: practical and emotional.

In the practical realm many things can put a damper on making a life change:

- timing
- finances
- unexpected events
- illness

It's the emotional side of things, however, that generally turns out to be the principal factor blocking our paths. That's because most humans tend to:

- fear what change might bring
- say one thing, but actually want something else because of hidden psychological agendas sometimes unknown even to themselves

When you add to this equation the desires of two or more individuals who are part of the decision-making process, you've got a complicated mix, ripe for either misunderstanding or paralysis. So how do you get two or more people on the same page about rightsizing their lives?

Owning a barge in France is obviously not a lifestyle choice that everyone could or *would* make, but the point of the Hammonds' saga is that they spent considerable time figuring out what suited *them*, not their neighbors and not other family members or former business associates. Once they homed in on the life each could envision, they didn't let outside influences sway them from pursuing the goal they imagined as they headed into their sixties.

So the question arises: why don't more people at these obvious crossroads that predictably occur during midlife and beyond simply sit down, consider their options, and make a sensible decision to rightsize their lives?

Because often it's just not that easy. Those practical and psychological hurdles already mentioned must be taken seriously into account.

The good news is that, as the Hammonds discovered, there are steps to take and techniques to learn that will help you power through very real problems and uncertainties, fears and fantasies that have stood in the way until now. Through the process that follows, you can arrive at a place where you're *ready* to make life-changing decisions that feel solid and result in tailor-made surroundings that suit the age, stage, and situation you're in, as well as prepare you to segue into the future.

But first, let's consider any personal obstacles that may impede your readiness to *begin* rightsizing your life. This is another opportunity to jot down your answers in your rightsizing notebook.

Quiz

WHERE DO YOU SEE YOURSELF . . . TOMORROW?

Take this quickie quiz:

1. Currently I'm living in (describe in some detail the place and style of your dwelling)_____, spending my days doing mostly (list your profession in and out of the home, your hobbies, any volunteer work, ongoing family obligations, etc.) _____.

2. In a year I expect to be living in (describe the physical environment and location) _____.

3. Five (or ten or fifteen) years from today, I could see myself living (describe in as much imaginative detail as you can)_____.
4. At age eighty I imagine I will be living in (describe in your physical surroundings) _____.

If you are drawing a blank on questions 2–4, don't worry about it. Just continue to the next section.

Quiz
WHAT WORK/PLAY ACTIVITIES SUIT YOU BEST?

Ask yourself these questions about how you expect to be spending the majority of your time as you grow older.

- A year from today I expect to be spending most of my time doing _____.
- Five years from today I expect to be engaging in such activities as _____.
- When I'm eighty I expect to spend my days doing (work) _____ and (play) _____.

Again, if you're having difficulty answering any of these questions, it just means you may be considering them seriously for the first time. The next quiz is the most fun!

Quiz
WHAT WOULD YOUR IDEAL LIFESTYLE LOOK LIKE?

Excluding all other considerations but your own dreams and fantasies of what *might be* possible for you, what would your ideal life look like? Think in terms of where you'd like to be living, what type of dwelling and atmosphere (house, cabin, condo, boat, cottage, city, countryside, climate, scenery, etc.) you would love to live in, and what activities you would find most engaging. One way to approach this is to recall the most enjoyable vacation or adventure you ever experienced or the best hotel room you ever slept in. On this questionnaire consider only your *own* needs and desires. Try not to censor yourself in any way!

A year from today I would love to be living in a _____ in the (town, region; more than one is fine!) of _____, spending my days involved in doing the things I enjoy most, which include (list work or retirement, hobbies or volunteers activities, ongoing family responsibilities) _____.

Five (or ten or fifteen) years from today, I would love to be living in (town, region) _____, spending my days doing the things I love most, which include _____.

When I'm eighty (same question; answer as imaginatively as you would like your life to be as an octogenarian) _____.

We will deal with issues relating to the others in your life who are involved in the decision-making process in the next chapter, but as a preview, go back over the previous three quizzes and answer the questions *as if* you were in the head of the other person or persons who are part of the rightsizing equation.

The results should be interesting . . .

CALCULATE THE REWARDS OF CHANGING YOUR LIFE

Back to the fascinating subject of *you!* Ask yourself this: what are the *benefits* you might derive if you chose to adapt your living situation to match the preferences that you've described in the three quizzes above? List what you would gain (or lose) by selecting any of the lifestyles you imagined for yourself. Here you go:

Quiz

THE REWARDS OF A RIGHTSIZED LIFE — THE SIX FS

If I "rightsized" my surroundings by doing _____, I would gain (or lose) the following benefits in terms of the Six Fs:

1. Financial security: _____
2. Flexibility in daily living: _____
3. Freedom to do the things I've always dreamed about: _____
4. Family near (or far away):_____
5. Friends nearby:_____
6. Facilities close by for health care, recreation, spiritual and intellectual stimulation:_____

Substitute various lifestyle scenarios, for instance, a condo near your current residence, a townhouse in an urban setting, a modular home community adjacent to a park or a lake, a small farm or vineyard, a place in a golfing or senior cohousing community in the sunshine of Arizona or Florida, an adobe casita in New Mexico — or in Mexico itself!

Don't be afraid to be grandiose. Calculate the rewards to your psyche and pocketbook assuming you were to move to an ideal home in your version of paradise, a dream retirement place that you build to suit your tastes from the foundation up (with — or without — room for adult children and grandchildren). Or imagine your current abode, retrofitted for safety, security, and even elegance as you age, or a small apartment building with your favorite friends as coresidents.

You supply the details and measure a particular, appealing scenario in terms of what you would gain or lose as measured against the Six Fs. If you find it difficult to come up with answers that resonate, go back and again consider other choices you *could* make in the previous assessment sections. This may take you a couple of days, weeks, or even months of concentration and weighing your alternatives, your likes and dislikes. Keep evaluating your evolving choices against the Six Fs — which stand for a fabulous third act that may be just over the horizon . . . or a lot closer than you think.

GETTING REAL

Okay, you pragmatists. No more of this fantasizing. You want to deal with reality, don't you? A lot of people experience discomfort when they think in expansive terms about their own needs and desires. It's "selfish" or "indulgent" or "totally unrealistic" to think these unfamiliar thoughts.

Contemplating your own preferences also involves laying claim to boundaries and stating opinions about your place in the world. When you clearly declare your predilections, you run the risk of offending people in your close circle of friends or family. Any prospective changes could even be interpreted by them as "abandonment."

Initiating any major lifestyle change, whether it's by the book or off the charts, can be daunting when confronting the needs and desires of the *other* people who also may be part of the rightsizing equation.

And there's no denying that unexpected hurdles can put a damper on dreams. These sorts of roadblocks include serious health issues; an unanticipated, negative change in finances; or a rupture in a relationship.

Even so, it "won't hurt," as the saying goes, to spend at least *some* time and effort thinking about your own dreams and desires. In the next chapter we will tackle the issue of integrating your personal vision of a rightsizing scenario that suits you well with the preferred circumstances envisioned by your nearest and dearest, the people who might wield influence in your world.

For now, though, let's stay focused on the person reading this book.

You will hear a few themes repeatedly throughout this book, and one of them is: do *not* discount the importance of the emotional side of your endeavor to adapt to changes as you grow older. "Getting real" about rightsizing is partly about recognizing that sometimes there *are* hard-to-recognize psychological hurdles blocking your personal path. Certainly one major roadblock for many people is a squeamishness about the confrontations that can result from proposing major life changes.

WHY CHANGE IS HARD

Even though many of us are loath to admit it, change can be upsetting, unsettling, and downright scary. It can bring to the surface long-dormant conflicts. It means doing things differently. It means a new routine. It means letting go of the familiar and leaping off a cliff into the unknown.

Who would want to do *that?*

As we saw earlier in this chapter, there are often compelling reasons to make a shift in one's life after age fifty. But it can feel overwhelming to be pressured by circumstances to make a transition we're not convinced we want.

At the same time change can bring liberation. The Hammonds discovered the major shifts they made in lifestyle lightened the financial and psychological burdens they had been carrying as the owners of a big, beautiful, but demanding house. Change also brought them daily and much-welcomed stimulation and a chance to ply both new and well-loved skills, all of which gave them a renewed zest for life.

The good news is that brain scientists tell us that each of us can learn to think differently about embracing change and lifelong learning. In other words, humans, old dogs, and even laboratory rats can be taught new tricks!

Studies performed at the University of California at San Francisco have demonstrated the brain's "plasticity." Scientists demonstrated that rodents — including older ones — could be taught new skills. What they found was that success depends on the rewards doled out to the animals as they were taught these new tricks. Solve the puzzle, and the rat got a delicious morsel of food. As the rat recognized the reward, he was prompted to repeat the behavior, and as the behavior was repeated over time, doing a particular task became a habit. After a while, the rewards for following through on a task became self-evident, and you got a cage full of fat and happy rats!

Remember the rewards identified in the Six Fs? For the Hammonds the benefits that flowed from the major life decisions they made and the skills they continue to acquire match up almost perfectly with the six categories on the list. They reduced the **financial** burdens that were destined to ensue if Cris and Linda had kept the big house. They gained the **flexibility** to spend time doing activities they like and still earn incomes from professions they enjoy. They gained the **freedom** to try new things, such as learning French or trying travel writing while being stimulated by the dynamic scene they witness both in Europe and America. They have **friends** on two continents — yet remain close to their **family** when in the States and in rendezvous with kin abroad. They have access to excellent healthcare **facilities** near their home in California and can use the national health system in France, should there be an emergency during the three to five months they spend on the barge.

As Linda discovered in the months leading up to the sale of the larger of their two homes, making such major decisions about surroundings and the resulting changes in lifestyle can render any of us uneasy because it requires a shift in our normal way of life — and there is often resistance to that. It's that old bromide: sometimes we prefer the devil we know (even if it doesn't feel good) to the devil we don't know (fearing that something new might be even worse!).

That being said, there is no risk in merely letting your imagination run wild as you think about these questions: "Am I ready to rightsize?" and "Do I know what I want to rightsize *to?*" All you need to do when considering your options is give yourself the gift of dreaming — and writing down — the things that have been important to you over the years.

Take a moment to ask yourself what has inspired you in the past? What has "floated your boat"? What activities have you participated in that made you feel jazzed about getting up in the morning? Where are the places you've been where you felt as if you'd suddenly "come home"?

It doesn't cost a cent to think in semiextravagant terms about these subjects, and the answers could guide your choices and save you from wandering down the wrong — and perhaps expensive — path as you consider decisions about the next decades of your life. Assessing your readiness for rightsizing can be an exhilarating exercise, opening doors you never even dreamed were right there in front of you.

WHAT SPECIFIC HURDLES STAND IN YOUR WAY?

We're talking *personal* hurdles here, not the roadblocks put there by others. Personal, as in, "I open the door to my basement, look at all that stuff that I'd have to deal with, close the door, go make a peanut butter-and-jelly sandwich and forget about it!"

Personal, as in, "I lost my spouse and half my income. I'm stuck . . . and I'm scared." Or maybe the biggest hurdle of all: "I don't want to face that I'm getting older and I'm gonna die one day."

Even scarier than death can be the thought of entering the last phase of your life alone. "I can't deal with the thought of being on my own when I'm old" or "I'm questioning my thirty-year marriage, not to mention my entire life, so what's the purpose of such an exercise? What's the *point?*"

Dr. John Grenner, a marriage and family therapist in Southern California, says he's now seeing retirees who are coming in with all sorts of emotional problems. He reports, "Couples, especially, can go straight into crisis with all their deferred issues bubbling to the surface. There are suddenly no distractions provided by kids and jobs, and one says to the other, 'You and I are now going to be home together all the time in a *smaller* house? Yikes!' " Adds the therapist, "The issues are either dealt with or there's a divorce — even after forty years of marriage."

Many in this group need professional help reassessing where they are, says Grenner, because some problems, papered over by the couple, can go back a long way. And besides, there's no reliable blueprint for dealing with problems in marriages of long duration.

"No population in the history of mankind has ever lived this long," notes Grenner. "Many will be living together for *years* in relatively good health. We have to create new lives as we go along." That, in-turn, requires us to invent what to do with the "Leftover Life" as the years unfold.

PRACTICAL VERSUS EMOTIONAL BARRIERS TO RIGHTSIZING

Before we can invent what happens in our own third act, we need to look squarely at the things that could be blocking our path. See if you can quickly fill in the blanks.

Quiz

WHAT ARE THE HURDLES?

1. The **practical** hurdles I might personally have that stand in the way of rightsizing can be summed up as _____.

2. The **emotional** hurdles I might personally have standing in the way of rightsizing can be summed up as _____.

Many people — and you may be one of them — don't have anything seriously holding them back from rightsizing their lives, and in fact, they're raring to launch the editing, winnowing, and jettisoning process.

Not so fast! Is everybody involved in this major lifestyle shift on the same page with you? If so, terrific! Skip to chapter 4. If not, let's find out if your family members are ready to rightsize along with you.

Chapter 3

Is My Family Ready to Rightsize?

Why it's important to get everybody on board

WHO'S IN YOUR BOAT?

Each person poised to rightsize his or her life needs to appreciate how other people in their immediate circle will be influenced by a change in surroundings. This impacted group can be divided into two categories: those who will actually make this transition with you and those who will be directly or indirectly affected by it.

Sara Yogev, a Chicago psychologist, believes that the turmoil brought about by major life transitions like moving is akin to the tumult of adolescence. "Psychological security is just as important as financial security," she says. "Yet so many people fail to prepare and plan for the psychological component of these shifts."

Much of the research on human behavior indicates that the psychological factors are often missing in discussions about third-act planning, so anyone who feels ready to rightsize would do well to recognize that other family members may not yet be on the same page with you. What this means is that it's important to recognize whether the other people in your family circle have achieved, as you may have, a certain "psychological security" about your decision to make a change. If they feel *in*secure about it, your first task will be to take this into account and begin to work through the issues troubling them. Should you ignore this emotional component, your nearest and dearest may be thrown into a state of elevated anxiety or agitation if prodded into a major life transition they may not be ready to make.

A sense of security consists of feeling safe in one's environment.

Usually the familiar feels safe; the unfamiliar can be scary until it becomes familiar. Applying undue pressure or making the wrong moves at this delicate time by disregarding the feelings and emotions of family members on the fence can backfire. The unhappy result is that you unwittingly erect barriers blocking the very path you are hoping to travel.

A better plan is to stand back for a bit and make an honest effort to understand "how the other half feels."

CALLING ALL DIPLOMATS

A crucial thing to keep in mind is the importance of understanding *why* a person affected by a proposed move may be adamantly opposed, or is offering passive resistance, or is just plain dragging his or her feet. This can require some diplomacy, which means adopting the skills of a mediator and asking nonthreatening questions when you sense a pullback about your proposal from a key player. Ignore at your peril that unmistakable chill pervading the discussion whenever you attempt to address later-life issues or the specifics of making a move or major change in lifestyle.

I met a woman from Chicago who was attending a rightsizing workshop in Tampa Bay, Florida. In the middle of the session, she suddenly stood up; her voice was quavering, and she was close to tears.

"What do you do when your husband comes home one day and announces he's fed up at work, has put in for retirement, and without even discussing it, has decided you're moving to the Carolina coast? Just like that! He's had a busy, active life outside our home, but my life has been *in* our home, and he completely disregarded that when he suggested we just pack up and leave!"

The woman described the early days of her thirty-seven-year marriage when, on an intern's salary, she and her physician husband scraped together a down payment on an architecturally significant but derelict home in a run-down section of town near his hospital. During the subsequent years, as the neighborhood slowly gentrified, she put all her energy, heart, and soul into restoring the place.

"Every single piece of furniture meant something to me, every object on a shelf, every restored wood panel, every hand-rubbed finish on the floor." Thanks to years of hard work, the house became a veritable showplace, admired by all the neighbors. "My job was perfecting this house, just as his job was working in the operating room, but on that day he came home and announced he wanted to sell, I felt as if my whole life meant nothing to him!"

Was this woman ready to rightsize? Not on your life; and who could blame her?

It's not just husbands who can have tin ears and the diplomatic skills of Attila the Hun. In my own family, when suggestions were floated by my husband that it was time to consider selling our commodious four-level home in Southern California, I adamantly opposed the idea. I was of the opinion it was too disruptive to my teenage son for us to cash out of the place we'd lived in for twenty-two years while he was still in high school.

Did we consult him about our choices?

No.

In fact, I righteously demanded that my husband not even bring up the subject until after our boy had taken his SAT exams and written his college applications.

Long after he'd graduated from both high school and college, I mentioned to him in passing that we'd considered selling the family house much earlier than we ultimately did to take advantage of a hot real-estate market and had contemplated moving into an apartment near the high school while he finished his last two years of secondary education.

"Why didn't you do that, Mom?" he asked with a puzzled look. "It would have been cool to live in one of those places across the street from school. It sure would have made it a lot easier to get to track practice at the crack of dawn."

Oh.

I guess I should have asked him how he felt about it way back when and not presumed to feel his feelings for him.

HONE YOUR COMMUNICATION SKILLS

The lesson is simple: be sure you know as much about the wishes of your family members as you do about your own. You'll be treading in dangerous waters if you *assume* you know what the other person is thinking unless you've had a good heart-to-heart talk about your choices *and* you've listened as much as talked.

It's even riskier if you adopt the attitude, "Well, this is what we're doing, so you'd better get used to it!"

A psychologist friend specializing in couples' therapy once told me about a high-powered duo that ran into trouble as soon as the husband, a business executive, announced he wanted to slow down and buy a smaller place out in the countryside somewhere. The wife, who was a businesswoman in her own right, immediately balked.

Explains the therapist, "She had felt very unappreciated by her husband during the course of the marriage and declared she wouldn't leave her friends for all the tea in China. Her women pals had been her life raft. They had given her comfort and nourishment, which she hadn't gotten from the husband, who'd been consumed for years by his work. This outside support had allowed the marriage relationship to go forward. The wife felt that if she lost that life preserver and went with him to a small town, she'd drown."

The shrink can't predict whether the issues between couples like this are likely to be resolved. It's often at the moment of decision about their future together when many couples go into crisis mode, and all their buried disagreements come screaming to the surface. Bad stuff that happened twenty-five years earlier comes up, and these bones of contention are either dealt with or there's a divorce — even after marriages of long duration. In Japan there's a clinical name for these problems: RHS — Retired Husband Syndrome. Support groups for both men and women number in the thousands there.

It's not only *couples* that can run into snags when it comes to getting everybody on board for a major change in living circumstances. Remember Laurie Rotella Mathers, whose mother took a serious fall and lay in her bedroom until help came five hours later?

Laurie had promised her father on his deathbed that she would "take care of Mom." What that meant was that she and her husband were pondering whether they should buy a new, larger house for the three of them or add on to their 1,610-square-foot ranch house so eighty-four-year-old Gloria Rotella would have a safe place with them.

The plans went forward to buy a new, more spacious house, says Laurie. "Contracts were signed and everything, and then Mom got cold feet. I guess she felt that leaving the house where she and Dad had lived all those years was like losing him all over again. She obviously wasn't ready. She looked at me tearfully and said, 'I just can't do this.' "

It was another year before Gloria was ready to commit to building "Mother's Suite" onto Laurie's existing house.

HOW LOSS PLAYS A PART

Clearly the anticipated loss of a home and a familiar environment that represent stability is one of the major stumbling blocks to making significant changes in people's lives after fifty, even if it might be "good for them."

A key skill required here, grief counselors say, is for everyone in the family to have — and show — compassion for the turmoil that one of their members may be going through at any particular time. The ability to recognize the pain of loss that others may be feeling without judging or belittling the person suffering will go a long way to helping them resolve it, experts say.

Interestingly, some people who suffer losses find a way to heal *themselves*. The Chicago surgeon's wife who felt tremendous pride and personal achievement in having restored her home so magnificently (and terrible grief at the thought of giving it up) searched for a way to deal with the resentment and bitterness she felt over the high-handed way her husband had announced their incipient move.

Granted, the good doctor in her life lacked a bedside manner. He didn't appear to be sensitive to the fact that, while he built his career as a celebrated heart surgeon in the public arena, she'd spent her adult life in her own orbit, raising their children and working tirelessly in their private realm to make their home a warm and welcoming showplace.

"That house was my identity!" she declared with understandable anger.

She was left with few choices.

- She could refuse to move, divorce him despite three decades of marriage, and make peace with the financial and emotional repercussions of such a radical move.

- She could sign on to the move without protest and attempt to deal with her boiling resentments during the years that followed.
- She could listen to his point of view and put forth some suggestions that would make such a move more palatable to her.
- She could seek a way to grieve over the loss of her beautiful house and gain the emotional strength to move on.

I asked what she had finally decided to do and was impressed by her method of coping with the upheaval foisted upon her by her husband's abrupt declaration.

"After I got over the shock, I could see that my husband wasn't being a complete ogre. Our house was large. Our children were long gone. The Chicago winters were tough on us both. Then, one day, I had the most marvelous idea. I called up a wedding videographer I found in the Yellow Pages and told him I wanted to pretend I was Jackie Kennedy, showing off the White House. He came over, and we planned out how he'd photograph me walking through my house explaining to the camera what changes I'd made, where each family heirloom came from and what it meant to me, and why I thought various objects in the house were an important part of our family's legacy."

When the video session was complete, she supervised the editing of all the footage they'd shot. For a couple hundred bucks, she says proudly, "I made thirty DVDs and gave each family member, my close friends, and the local historical society a copy."

Did her family ever sit down and watch it, I wondered?

"I didn't care if they did or they didn't. At least there was a *record* of what my last thirty years had been about. From then on I could leave it behind and feel proud of what I'd accomplished."

Did her husband ever acknowledge he'd been pretty ham-fisted in the way he'd initiated the subject of leaving Chicago?

The woman offered a faint smile. "Well, we're still married."

GETTING TO "YES" — NOW OR LATER

Lest you assume it's only women who have a hard time coping with loss or committing to change when it comes to hearth and home, heed the story of Jennifer and Tim Clark.

Jennifer, sixty-one, a former software saleswoman, lives with her husband of twenty-two years in a 4,700-square-foot house on the North Shore of Boston that looks as if it belongs in the English countryside. She has legitimate reasons to believe the house doesn't suit their needs as well as it once did, but she says she wouldn't dream of insisting that her husband, seventy-one, sell their five-bedroom home, situated on a hundred acres of land.

"I couldn't budge Tim from this house when I married him, even though he'd lived here with his first wife and raised his kids in this house," she confides, "and I couldn't do it now. He's been in this house forty years."

Jennifer met Tim when she was thirty-eight. He'd been recently divorced, and she advised him to call her in six months, when "he could talk about something besides his former wife." Six months to the day, he rang her, and when they married two years later, Jennifer moved into the house to join her new husband and his three sons, eleven, fifteen, and seventeen.

Jennifer recalls, "There was a stuffed deer head and antlers hung over the mantel; dead, stuffed ducks and geese everywhere. I told him, 'It's not a hunting lodge! Choose one room and put all those things there,' so he took most of the dead animals to the basement, where there's now a pool table, a TV. It's a very guy-type hangout, and it's his kingdom."

Then, as the years rolled by, Jennifer proceeded to put her personal stamp on the interior rooms on the floors above.

"The house was never a shrine to his first wife," she says. "He knows that I'm a nester, and he's expressed his appreciation to me about the house's multiple transformations. A lot of it is tied up with [feelings about] his dad." Tim's father had gifted him with the original sixty acres, and nearly every day, weather permitting, despite knees that are candidates for corrective surgery, Tim hikes around his property. "To him, I think this house represents his family's past. He cuts brush and loves hunting on it," explains Jennifer. "He's a big, woodsy guy who loves to observe the birds and hunts ducks . . . a real New Englander."

While Jennifer, too, loves their home, she's come to feel that the house they own free and clear "is too big for the two of us now. It needs constant decorating, painting, insuring, but Tim will not even consider moving, and I just decided to accept that's how he feels. Fortunately we have a master bedroom on the first floor, and we shut off the upstairs to save on the heat and don't go up there until the kids come back to visit." The couple has many sets of friends who have migrated from Massachusetts to warmer climes in the winter, "so we're certainly not hostages here. We visit people all over the place."

The Clarks have purchased long-term health insurance, so the plan is eventually to have caregivers come to the house if they are needed. "I think we've got it reasonably well organized. Sure, I see what could be improved and how my life would be easier if I didn't have to spend so much time in the car, if we didn't need a new furnace and new windows, or if we didn't lose the electricity so often out here."

"I've made peace with it," Jennifer says of her husband's determination to stay put. "I expect that if I'm really beleaguered one day, I think Tim would be respectful of the need for a move, but we aren't there yet. We've achieved equilibrium. I don't feel put upon or resentful, but if circumstances change, we may be forced to do something different."

As couples and individuals think about rightsizing for the next phase of their lives, decisions need to be thoroughly and fairly discussed among anyone else impacted by such a move. A timetable for change that makes sense for you may not sit well with someone else in the mix, and before you drop a bomb on a family member, check out if everybody's on the same page, or even close to it.

In the case of the Clarks, Jennifer felt the time was ripe for a change, and Tim didn't agree. They reached a compromise that both can live with for now because they sought to understand each other's point of view. Tim supported the changes she'd made within the house to make it more livable for them *now;* she accepted his emotional attachment to staying in the house and didn't whine about it. They were diplomatic and showed consideration for each other's needs and desires. Most significantly, neither one demanded to have things go entirely his or her way.

Through this process Jennifer and Tim checked with each other in a deferential manner about their likes and dislikes and *listened* to each other's responses. Each has made some concessions and accommodations. For the time being their 4,700-square-foot house on one hundred acres of land, which probably sounds pretty substantial to most people, is "rightsized" for them.

The Clarks and the other people you'll meet in this book exemplify the key principle of rightsizing your life: it's more about what's *right* for all concerned at a particular age and stage than simply applying some formula about square footage or what you "ought" to be doing compared to other people your age. There *is* no age-determined formula.

IDENTIFYING THE DIFFERENCES

But what if you're having difficulty achieving Jennifer Clark's version of "equilibrium" within your own family circle when the subject of the family's future housing is brought up?

One suggestion for pinpointing where interests overlap or diverge is to make a list of family members and close friends who would be directly impacted by a change in living arrangements. Put yourself in their shoes. Before you bring up the subject, and knowing them as you do, jot down what you assume their reaction would be to the kinds of changes you could envision making. Yes, I'm urging you to walk a mile in somebody else's moccasins!

Take some time to look at a proposed living scenario and attempt to see it through their eyes or, as they say in the movie business, from their POV (point of view). Later you can evaluate how close you were to seeing things from their vantage point and not merely from your own.

Make a second list of those who would be peripherally affected, including adult children, if you have them; grandchildren; nieces and nephews; second-tier relatives; close friends; your medical professionals; your lawyer; tax accountant; the PTA Board; your garden club — whoever would find their lives altered in one way or another if *your* circumstances changed.

Combine the two lists and review them carefully, making sure you've imagined both the positive *and* negative reactions you could reasonably expect to receive from these groups. Just as I was startled to learn my son wouldn't have objected to the idea of selling our family

CLOSE FAMILY MEMBERS			
Name	*Relationship*	*Rightsizing Proposal*	*Possible POV*
Mary			
John			
The kids (21 and under)			
Mary's parents			
John's parents			
Best friend Joe or Jane			

home while he was in high school, you, too, could be surprised how far off the mark you may be — positively or negatively — when you actually talk over your proposed plans with your inner circle. At least if you take the trouble to investigate how others feel, you might avoid being blindsided by an eruption from someone when you least expect it.

These two exercises are also a good way to search for common ground and to begin to think about whether you have similar goals and where your goals and those of your "significant others" might seriously diverge.

THE ART OF LISTENING — AS WELL AS TALKING

According to professionals with experience moving the elderly into downsized quarters, *being heard* helps people let go of those pieces of their life that still have meaning but are part of the past. One assumes the same is true for the under-eighty set.

Beth Warren, the owner of Welcome Home Relocation, a senior-move management firm based in Tampa Bay, Florida, observes, "We *have* to hear the client's stories. Regardless of your age, moving and sorting means saying good-bye to a big chunk of your life." She believes that you can release an object — or an entire household — by telling the story about it, provided someone does you the honor of *listening*.

One way to align the people involved in any rightsizing move is to grant them the courtesy of *hearing them out* when it comes to any reservations about plans that may be on the table. Jennifer Clark of Massachusetts was willing to *listen* carefully and be sensitive to husband Tim's *reasons* for feeling so attached to their rambling house and wooded grounds. Laurie Rotella Mathers *heard* her mother's grief over the loss of her husband and her reluctance to make such a radical move so soon after his death, and so didn't force the timetable. If from the outset the Chicago heart surgeon had empathized with his wife about the loss she'd feel abandoning the beautiful home she had created for her family, if he had recognized the sense of mourning she felt that her role as mother and matriarch of her family was coming to an end or acknowledged her loneliness in the face of his all-consuming career — in other words if he had *listened actively* to her side of the equation — chances are their transition would have been less problematic.

By the same token, if the good doctor's approach hadn't been so high-handed, his resentful spouse could probably have paid more attention to his logic that the hard Chicago winters and the burden of caring for a big house with stairs and grounds had become too much for both of them and that it was time for a change.

Fortunately, his wife's innate resourcefulness and independence paid off. She found a way to honor herself by producing the DVD that chronicled in living color the extent of her accomplishments. She told her own story in a way her friends and family could hear. She grieved over her loss and could move on, keeping intact a marriage of long duration. Once she'd gotten the personal validation for the way in which she'd spent her time (which she managed to give to *herself!*), she was able to listen more actively to the "sensible" proposals her husband offered.

FEELINGS FIRST, FACTS SECOND

John Kotter is a Harvard Business School professor who has studied people and organizations in the midst of turmoil. He's discovered that the key to motivating people in extremis is to consider their emotions *before* bombarding them with the facts that lie behind life-changing proposals.

"Changes in behavior happen mostly by speaking to people's feelings," says Kotter. "In highly successful change efforts, people find ways to help others see the problems or solutions in ways that influence emotions, not just thought."

Don't assume that you know what somebody in your family feels about your ideas without checking with them. Don't feel their feelings for them. *Find out* what they're feeling by asking!

Dr. Dean Ornish, founder of the Preventive Medicine Research Institute, offers another take on the same idea. "*Joy* is a more powerful motivator than *fear*" (my italics).

It's pretty clear that trying to scare or browbeat someone into agreeing with you rarely works. Likewise, threatening that you'll all be in the poorhouse if you don't make a move is probably not going to be an effective strategy.

In addition to promoting the practical sides of making a particular change in lifestyle ("we'll have a lot more discretionary income" or "you won't have to haul laundry to the Laundromat anymore"), defining the goal of rightsizing in terms of *emotional* benefits to each family member may be your most effective tool. Ask yourself, where's the "joy" for so-and-so to be found in making these changes?

Some will find pleasure in simply being relieved of annual chores like shoveling snow. Others will feel their spirits lift when their new surroundings allow for a computer room, or a hobby nook, or a perfect spot to sip tea and read a book. Still others will find emotional sustenance in waking up each morning by a lake, volunteering at a hospital, or working for the local Habitat for Humanity.

Think hard about what delivers contentment to those involved in the decision and find ways to feed that aspect of their life. Happy campers make any transition a lot easier.

BE A REPORTER AND GET THE FACTS

Feelings are facts, so be sure to gather some.

You've lived with these people, so much of your information and observations about their reactions should be reasonably accurate, *if* you resist filtering what you know about them through the distorted lens of your own judgment.

Instead let their emotional responses tell you where they are in the process of considering a big change of scene — and simply accept that's the situation at the moment, without putting in your two cents' worth.

You say that's hard?

Few of us have ever been taught the skill of paying close attention to clues and cues about other people's feelings, but as you go over your list of family members and study the reactions you might anticipate, try not to ignore the psychological, emotional, or even the spiritual dimension of their responses.

Once you've identified the key players and their views about a potential course of action, and you've thought about the situations and activities that bring them pleasure, be sure to take a close look at the practical details of any major change you're proposing.

These include, of course, financial data regarding the way in which key decisions would affect your family's budget. Additionally, don't ignore the way a change in living arrangements would impact the everyday well-being of your intimates. Will one party have to give up a job he or she loves? Will that person miss out on the weekly V.F.W. meeting or book club? Will he or she regret not being able to hit the neighborhood coffee shop at eight-thirty every morning to shoot the breeze with the usual suspects?

Think about the things — big and small — that are important to *them* (even if it might not be important to *you*). Consider what makes them happiest; name the friends they treasure; list the activities integral to their lives. If someone *has* to give up weekly lunches at Rotary, find out if the new location you're proposing has a Rotary organization. If leaving the members of the garden club would be a wrench, you can gently suggest that being nearer your kids and grandkids might, in part, compensate for such a loss.

But don't just fixate on the minus column. Spend some time making a list of the *benefits,* as you see them, to each person in your immediate circle, so you can emphasize these during family discussions.

On the other hand, don't expect each person to view the "good things" exactly as you do. After all, they have their own POV, right? What you think they find important might be weighted differently from their perspective or not register on their radar screen at all.

People embrace change, say behaviorists, when they can see the *personal rewards* of such a move, so arm yourself with as much knowledge about the positive aspects of choosing a new home (or simplifying an existing one) as you think would result in a yes. Talk up how rewarding it could be to build your own place designed for your age and stage from the foundation up. Or be positive about the pluses of living in a better climate or what a relief it would be to have fewer steps to climb or fewer weekly chores to perform.

Bottom line? *Be the bearer of good tidings.* Learn everything you possibly can about the area you're proposing moving *to*, so you can allay anxieties with the facts, not vague platitudes.

Be warned, however! If the changes you're suggesting involve a major shift in your current environment, don't just offer a "snow job." Be scrupulously accurate in what you say. Temper your enthusiasm with truth, and don't be heavy-handed with assurances of how great you think such changes will be unless you know the benefits will be of real value to your partners in this effort — including rewards they resonate to and can accept and not just the ones *you* think would be good for them.

Behaviorists have proven that people can't merely be manipulated into embracing change. There needs to be genuine respect for the ways in which your companions in transition do not see things eye to eye with you.

In time, with goodwill and the facts on your side, opposing viewpoints can shift.

NEGOTIATING AS A MEMBER OF THE "ME" GENERATION

It can be difficult to get to "yes" or solve a problem if you can't agree on how that problem is defined or if the other side refuses even to attempt to see things from your perspective. If this is your situation, you may run smack into what at least one psychologist dubs "boomer self-absorption." Are the generations born during and after World War II overly self-involved? It's probably a bit dangerous to categorize all of us so easily. But we all have had some exposure to extremely self-absorbed people and the negative fallout of the Me Generation. The clinical term for this is *narcissism* — as in the Greek god Narcissus, who was in love with his reflection.

As boomers and war babies enter the latter stages of their lives, psychologists report seeing inadequate mediating and negotiating skills among these clients when they're faced with major quality-of-life decisions. And of course these are the very life skills that help make relationships work. This, in turn, makes it difficult to agree on a problem's definition, let alone come to a consensus about what action to take to solve it.

The joke "it's all about *me*" can take on ominous overtones when it comes to working through conflicts between people for whom it's *always* been about getting what they want. Notes one shrink with undisguised exasperation, "Some of these folks spent so much time 'self-actualizing' in the seventies and eighties, they never learned to empathize with the other guy."

A huge number of people — millions, in fact — "did their own thing" during the second half of the twentieth century as flower children and protagonists of the Me Decade. The job of being a "family" was basically outsourced to the schools; institutions and advisers; full-time day-care centers; summer camps; surrogates like coaches, nannies, and housekeepers; and "virtual" babysitters like TV and video games — anything and everything that would keep the kids occupied while the group now approaching retirement "did their life."

The result is millions of two-career couples who didn't actively parent their own children. They and their kids didn't have enough modeling as they grew up to understand how to work through conflicts. From the vantage point of the mental-health professionals who are now dealing with this group, many war babies and boomers never learned traditional manners or any other way of behaving than to be angry or leave if they didn't get their way.

And what is the impact on society if large numbers of people haven't had much experience in working through differences with some patience and tolerance?

"They never passed these qualities or skills on to their children," says therapist John Grenner. "They can't teach what they never learned, and they haven't even learned to cut the other person some slack if things don't go their way."

This can certainly prove a serious handicap when it comes to discussing and debating any differences about a joint decision like selling a house, perhaps moving to a new location, and especially about late-life adventures like joining the Peace Corps or chucking it all to hit the road in an RV.

On the positive side, more and more people at fifty and above have recognized the terrible emotional and financial cost of latter-stage marriages ending in the garbage heap. They've witnessed the wreckage that followed in the wake of their friends' soured unions over these types of allegedly irreconcilable differences. This sadder-but-wiser group yearns to establish a format for decision making that will allow relationships among spouses, lovers, siblings, or close relatives and friends to endure, despite having to undergo the sometimes painful process of figuring out what comes next.

"I'm starting to notice these boomers wanting to see their rocky relationships endure, but they're going to have to develop patience, tolerance, the ability to suspend judgment and curb their cynicism and disdain," advises Grenner. "What I want to hear this group say is, 'We know we made mistakes, but we'd like to do it differently in the time we have left. We want to find a new way to be together in harmony so we can enjoy this last act.'"

This will no doubt require everyone involved taking personal responsibility for their feelings and behavior. For some it will mean learning a completely new skill — having empathy for others — and perhaps gaining genuine maturity as late as sixty-five or seventy years old.

DEBATING DIFFERENCES FAIRLY

Let's assume for argument's sake we're dealing with reasonable grown-ups who cannot be classified as selfish or full-blown narcissists but may be having difficulty mapping out the next chapters in their lives.

Experts in negotiation say that communication skills and developing trust are the two most important aspects of finding solutions to a situation where significant differences exist between the key players. The trust you require is simple: you want to know that the other guy wishes you well.

With the Hammonds, who spend part of each year floating down the canals of France on their barge *Phaedra,* a unique solution was achieved — eventually — because they showed respect and tolerance for each other's views in the potentially rocky period before they reached consensus about selling their house overlooking San Francisco Bay and moving into their former rental cottage in the same town.

Naturally they had points of disagreement, but because their communication and negotiating skills had developed over the course of their marriage and in raising two daughters, they were willing to disclose to each other (without getting enmeshed in a blame game) *how they felt* about the outstanding issues that stood in the way of full agreement about any rightsizing plan.

In the course of this, each went through a process of redefining themselves, which helped them both move in a new direction. Cris Hammond returned to a previous incarnation as a marine-landscape painter. Linda took on the challenge of learning to be a travel writer. Both committed to embracing French culture: its language, food, and society. Cris staked out his private passion: tinkering with an unpredictable diesel engine on their barge; Linda had her own area of expertise: helping her friend launch a new food business. Each supported the other's separate identity, while allowing time together and time apart.

If you don't communicate well and you haven't developed trust among the parties who are participating in making major life decisions, you can always write a letter stating how you view the situation and your differences and outline what you'd like to see happen.

THE FIFTY-PLUS FEAR FACTOR

After age fifty many people report feeling less effective and purposeful. Clearly a lot is going on psychologically when someone hits the

GETTING DIFFICULT CONVERSATIONS STARTED

- Start with something like, "I want to solve these differences we have and want to do something about what hasn't been working between us. From my vantage point, I'd like to see _____happen, and the reason I feel this way is because of _____."
- Own your opinions. Be concrete, but avoid blame or judgment.
- Speak only about *your* views regarding a particular subject or plan of action. Avoid veiled threats, personal digs, and the need to be "right."
- Don't describe what you think the other person's behavior means or what you think he or she should be saying, thinking, or doing. "Just stick to your own knitting" and describe what you could see the future being like from your POV.
- If you compose an angry riposte or blast-o-gram about what's led up to your disagreement, you may get momentary satisfaction, but the other side won't hear you at all, and you'll be in a worse situation than before you put pen to paper. As the classic Twelve-Step recovery program suggests, "keep your own side of the street clean" during the letter-writing and discussion stage.
- Express your willingness to hear the views and opinions of significant others. Offer the idea that you have every expectation you'll be able to work out your differences — something like, "We have a great future . . . let's do something about it before it slowly fades away."

midcentury mark. As one jokester put it, "You turn fifty, so fasten your seatbelt. It's going to be a *bumpy* ride!"

Typical fears that create roadblocks around late-life decision making are usually the ones hardest to voice. Does any of this sound familiar?

- What if I/we run out of money?
- Without a job/kids what am I?
- Without a job/kids, what am I going to do all day?
- What if I find something I want and it freaks out my partner?
- I'm worried what it's going to be like being with him/her all the time.
- I'm worried what it's going to be like being alone.

- What if my partner abandons me?
- My partner is feeling nuts, and so am I. How can we possibly have a decent life together?

How to get past all these fears? For some the prescription may be hard to swallow. As one friend put it, "We need to move from the Me Decade to the Me-and-Thee Decade, as in 'Me-and-Thee Till Death Do Us Part.' Let's hear it for mature adults with sensitivities for something and someone *other* than themselves."

And yet this season of second adolescence, the push-pull period between middle age and old age, is a dynamic time of life. This group is often winding down or disengaging from primary careers, winding up parenthood, forging new careers and relationships, new identities and new ways of being constructively engaged. It's *reinvention* time, big time — but with equal parts of "Let's go for it!" and "Oh, my God, everything's changing!"

There's no ignoring that there can be even more serious problems that are part of this midlife mix. If your job, or aspects of your life that have defined you as a person, is called into question, you and your intimates may be struggling with that scariest of all questions: what value am I? Some third agers are beset by serious depression in this regard and have difficulty even summoning enthusiasm or "a reason to go on."

If this is true for someone in your circle who is part of the decision-making process at hand, these issues can compound the difficulties of getting all parties concerned on board the rightsizing process.

Mental-health experts say that everyone needs something that inspires them to get up in the morning. Even after retirement there's a basic human need to search within for something that gives meaning to daily life — that core passion we talked about earlier. When some people ask themselves what that *is* and they come up with zero, *that's* a problem only the individual can solve, and often it requires outside help.

HEY, WAIT A MINUTE! WHO AM I?

Another underlying issue for people who have been living with, and adapting to, their intimates so routinely is that they don't really have a sense of self, of who *they* really are. They may never have given themselves permission to discover their actual likes and dislikes. For some the distractions of work, marriage, and raising children have resulted in an impaired ability to determine how they *really feel* about subjects that may generate conflict. When asked directly what they want, they go numb and have no answer.

When the specter of change or illness appears on the horizon for these people, they may be thrown for a loop by the unavoidable confrontations such situations create and lack effective coping mechanisms or skills to deal with this kind of turmoil.

If both parties to a decision about rightsizing are going through this type of emotional upheaval, the double whammy can make the goal of getting everyone on the same page about rightsizing especially tricky. To be able to move forward, each must find something that defines or reinvents the self and then discover ways to feel powerful and comfortable with the way life is now. Once this has been accomplished, then perhaps an individual can summon the energy to deal with a life mate who may also be floundering in choppy waters.

Most mental-health professionals would agree that this group usually needs someone trained to mediate and help the process along. The hope is that if people can move through this bumpy patch and redefine themselves, discovering "how I want to be . . . what I want to be doing" for act three, then both parties can simultaneously begin to figure out what the future might look like together, in terms of both hearth and home.

THE ANGST OF DECISION MAKING

Sometimes the task of getting an entire family group on board about rightsizing has little or nothing to do with heavy emotional issues, the chronological age of those involved, or the generation they were born into, but rather with a lifelong, built-in (and rather ordinary) resistance to committing to a decision for fear of making the wrong one.

Welcome to "analysis paralysis" and other mini roadblocks standing in the way of deciding what path is right for you and yours. There are no magic answers when it comes to people who are more or less "change resistant." All you can do is work on your side of things.

A wise former newspaper editor and consummate journalist, Jim Bellows, who is a friend and former boss of my husband's, often said to his angst-ridden reporters and editors, "Here's how to get things done: begin at once and do the best you can."

In later chapters we'll put this advice to use with practical tips about dealing with a jammed attic or rooms littered with everything from pre–World War II road maps to broken vacuum cleaners. In the meantime begin at once to make a list of the things that you and your circle will benefit most from by starting the rightsizing process, and then get going on that list!

Do the best you can by taking the steps open to you right now to get the process under way. Ask yourself, "What part of my life can *I* begin to simplify?" Clean and organize your home office? Sort through and get rid of *your* stuff that you can't use?

"Clean your own sock drawer first, before advising someone else to do likewise," my late mother always said.

In other words, get your own physical and psychological house in order and be clear about what you'd like the next phase of your life to look and be like *before* putting demands on how others should change. This practice can go a long way toward advancing the cause of rightsizing and getting other family members on board.

It's beyond the scope of this book to advise folks who are suffering from immobilizing depression or to offer advice on coping with paralyzing fears that prevent sensible decision making. However, the common, garden-variety worries that beset people attempting to make decisions as they figure out what to do with their "leftover lives" are easily categorized and perfectly normal:

- health — not having it
- money — not having enough
- relationships — not being comfortable in them

The "angst" of decision making about issues within these categories can be soothed by granting those involved in the process the same respect and personal validation you'd like them to show you. Adopting an attitude that "together, we're going to row this boat in the same direction" will do wonders, the experts say.

And how long, you ask, will it take to pilot your craft to the other shore?

There's a good answer for that. Several, in fact, coming right up.

Chapter 4

How Long Will It Take to Rightsize My Life?

Creating a realistic timetable

ARE YOU MOVING NEXT WEEK OR NEXT YEAR?

You probably expect to be told that there are a lot of variables when it comes to estimating how long it will take to rightsize your life and your surroundings. You're right. Your personal timetable will depend on whether you're in the planning stages or you already have a drop-dead date in the very near future. Can you proceed at a leisurely pace or are you under the gun? Don't worry; there's help for you either way.

Looking back on my own rightsizing saga, I would have saved myself untold hours of work if I had begun the process of preparing to leave our family home of twenty-two years much earlier. In retrospect I should have systematically tackled our storage closets and jam-packed garage as soon as my husband and I began to have inklings we were going to make a major move. As a result of my "gun-at-the-head" approach, I lurched through the process of jettisoning household possessions accumulated through two decades of marriage — selling some things, giving away others, *begging* friends and strangers at the eleventh hour to take the rest of the stuff out of my sight!

But isn't that often the way? For so many rightsizing veterans, it's a case of "if only I knew *then* what I know now . . ."

Fortunately, you can learn from those who have walked this road before you. If you are in the earliest stages of making a major shift in your surroundings, the rightsizing principles and prescriptions listed here can make your transition a lot easier on your mind, body, and emotional well-being.

Regardless which stage of the process you may be in, however, or how much or how little time you have to make a physical transition (or transformation — should you be electing to reconfigure the home in which you currently reside), some basic rightsizing guidelines and action points apply to all situations and can definitely help smooth the way while providing a quick estimate of the length of time the process can be expected to take.

Later in this chapter we'll get down to cases and outline the differences in timetables and approaches to rightsizing, depending on your situation. Basically most people fall into one of three categories. Which one are you?

- There's a gun at your head — your move is imminent
- Your lead time is under a year
- Your lead time is three to five years

Regardless of the pressure you feel, or which scenario fits your situation, the worst mistake you can make is to go into what my son calls "commando mode" and start pulling rooms apart, tossing possessions mindlessly into packing boxes or the trash because you just can't face the tedium of decision making or you think you don't have the time to approach the process a bit more systematically.

Remember, even investing a small amount of time in devising a game plan will pay off big rewards. In the corporate world, executives who receive the poorest marks in management reviews are ones who, out of anxiety to succeed or sheer disorganization, adopt a "ready, *fire*, aim" approach to getting the work of the company accomplished.

Most of us wouldn't bake an elegant wedding cake without following a basic recipe or pilot a plane across the country without a flight plan. So, despite the hassle factor, keep the following three simple tenets foremost in mind as you begin to evolve a rightsizing game plan. In fact, jot these down in your rightsizing notebook or on a sticky note and paste it on your refrigerator. These tenets will go far in keeping you focused on the job ahead:

- Evaluate the landscape where you are and — if possible — where you're going
- Create your rightsizing game plan and timetable — details to follow
- Tackle and complete the job

The core of the rightsizing process means taking the steps above in the stated *order!* But as we all know so well, even the best-laid plans go awry, and sometimes you gotta do what you gotta do . . .

RIGHTSIZING LESSONS FROM A HURRICANE

If potential rightsizers ever needed a cautionary tale about the difficulties that ensue if a few, simple steps aren't — or can't be — followed prior to a major move, there is the example of Mary Lou England, who perhaps epitomizes the ultimate "there's a gun at your head" scenario. She had no choice but to go into commando mode when the unexpected happened. Her story encapsulates what it's like having to make a change in living arrangements without even a modicum of planning and preparation and illustrates the difficult fallout that can ensue.

"Katrina swept into New Orleans on Sunday, August twenty-ninth, two thousand five," relates Mary Lou with a shudder, "and by Monday, the levees had ruptured and the city was flooding. My momma lived in Metairie, in Jefferson Parish, in a condo complex on the first floor."

England, the manager of the Goodwill Bookstore in Bradenton, Florida, soon discovered that her eighty-one-year-old mother had evacuated to Alexandria, Louisiana, with friends. She was alive, but she had nothing with her but a few essentials and the clothes she was wearing.

"At the same moment my mother was forced by Mother Nature to leave her three-bedroom, three-bath place, my poor brother was moving out of his thirty-five-hundred-square-foot house in neighboring

Houston, Texas, just ahead of Hurricane Rita, and heading for a twelve-hundred-square-foot place in North Carolina!"

The timing couldn't have been worse for everyone involved, nor the situation more dire. "For a couple of days, we were sure everything was gone, and a kind of grief came over all of us, mourning the loss of our possessions, but also relieved we all were safe."

Miracle of miracles, the sale of her brother's house in Houston went through, and it turned out her mother's condo hadn't flooded, though her neighborhood was a mess. "When we could finally get into New Orleans, we saw at once that Momma could never live here alone [anymore], so we quickly put the place on the market — and it sold in twelve *hours* to a seventy-one-year-old woman who had eleven feet of water in her house over in Lakeview and possessed nothing but a suitcase! She needed to move in immediately, and we were totally under the gun because of my brother's move as well, so we just *did it!*"

In less than a week's time.

Mary Lou and her family's Herculean efforts to clear out her mother's home became living proof that it's physically *possible* to make such a mighty move, "but it nearly killed us all," she says, only half joking.

"Here was my mother, forced to divest herself of her family possessions in a real hurry. It's kinda tragic, but my brother Don and his wife and I [all now living in less than 1,200 square feet] had absolutely no use for hardly any of Momma's beautiful things — nor room for any of it."

The three-bedroom condo in New Orleans where Mary Lou's mother had moved a few years earlier from their family home after her husband had died was full of cut crystal, silver, and family china handed down through the generations. Plus there were a million curios. There was virtually no time to evaluate what to keep or what to toss, and Mary Lou acknowledges that the result was somewhat flawed.

"My momma was a great New Orleans cook, and she was forced to take one frying pan and two pots for her kitchenette in the assisted-living place we rushed to get her that's near me in Florida. I didn't want to offend her, but there was no other way to deal with all her possessions than to give them away or sell them after we left Louisiana. She wanted me to save so much stuff for my daughter, but she's in the

Peace Corps in Africa right now and told me on the phone, 'Actually, Mom, chinaware's not that important to me over here.' "

Not having enough lead time is difficult enough, without the burden of all the decisions that need to be made under terrible pressure and with no real plan of attack. "It was tense at times," admits Mary Lou, "because my brother Don had to be very firm. All the things Momma wanted to take simply wouldn't *fit* in the limited space where she was going."

"We're just not telling her where everything ended up," she confides. "We accepted what she gave us [during that tumultuous week clearing out her condo], and we're trying to dispose of it quietly. My standard reply when she asks where her cut-crystal pitcher is, is, 'I've loaned it to a friend having a party,' and then she kinda forgets. I'm trying my best not to hurt her feelings."

Mary Lou and her brother and sister-in-law had little choice but to jump directly into the deep end of the pool and do the best they could to power through a heartbreaking situation in order to install their mother in a safe, protected environment. Mary Lou breathes a wistful sigh. "There are some wonderful things of our family's out there in circulation, thanks to Katrina."

This story, however, should convince anyone who *isn't* in such dire straits that it's worth the effort (and will make life a lot easier for everyone involved) if you simply assume it always takes more time than you think to thoroughly cull through a lifetime of household possessions and formulate a reasonable timetable based on the particular circumstances of your move.

The process will be a lot more enjoyable and the rewards more gratifying and less traumatic if you gird yourself with a considered game plan from the start.

And when you simply cannot?

Mary Lou says, "Thank heavens my brother and his wife were there to help Momma and me get through it all."

The Lesson When time is short, don't be shy to ask for help, and quickly cut to the chase: sort to the size of the place you're going and let that be your guide about the possessions you move and the ones you find new homes for. It's tough, but the place you're headed is your "new reality" . . . the reality you and your movers will face when your goods arrive at their final destination.

SO OKAY, HOW LONG WILL MY RIGHTSIZING TAKE?

Let's assume for the moment that no hurricane or tornado is bearing down on your dwelling. Perhaps the best way to estimate how long the rightsizing process might require under normal circumstances is to start by taking an abbreviated survey of the surrounding landscape. In other words, the first thing to do is to have a look at the things you already *own.*

Long before the estimator from the moving company comes to survey how much it's going to cost to transport your goods to a new home, designate a section of the notebook I urged you to purchase in an earlier chapter and label it Rightsizing Project. Then, take pen in hand. Make a list of all the rooms in your current residence, including attics, basements, garages, and even the toolshed or potting shed out back, if you have one.

On a separate page make a similar list of rooms (and their dimensions) where you're headed, if you know.

Now, before you become totally overwhelmed — and perhaps even depressed by a preliminary, cold-eyed inspection of all your possessions stashed in every nook and cranny of your current home — keep this in mind: unlike moving an entire household from point A to point B, to rightsize you're going to select only the possessions *you love and use.* These are the things you'll be taking with you. What's left will be dealt with later.

That's right. What a concept! You will be calculating this first phase of your rightsizing timetable based only on the "good stuff," with the ultimate promise of eventually freeing yourself from some of the albatrosses that have hung around for too long. Instead of feeling depressed you will likely engender a sense of liberation from the evaluation exercise.

"Free, at last!" you'll say.

But I'm getting ahead of myself.

UP CLOSE AND PERSONAL

Look again at your list of rooms in your current dwelling. Pick a single room to evaluate, which you will do in a very speedy fashion. In this exercise we are looking only at items you *use* in your daily life. Later we will do a second survey in the chosen room and evaluate those same items for their beauty, value, or sentimental meaning, but for now, we're inspecting simply the *items you use.*

Buy a package of self-adhesive multicolored dots and *write your first initial in the middle of each one,* jotting down the color key in your rightsizing notebook. Then dole out the dots as follows:

- **Green dots** pasted on every item in that room that you have used or handled in the **past week**
- **Yellow** on every item you've handled or used in the **last month**
- **Red** on items you've used within the **last year**
- **Blue** on items you use fairly regularly, but that **don't really suit your needs;** these are things you depend upon occasionally, but you can't afford, or aren't ready, to substitute them for something else that would work better

Even if you use up every colored dot in the package on this first survey of a single room in your home, remember we're going through this exercise *in only one room* to gain a preliminary handle on your timetable for rightsizing your surroundings — not to make any final selections as to what to keep and what to toss.

Unless you've picked your kitchen or a jam-packed basement to evaluate, "dotting" one room should take less than a half hour. When you've completed your dot fest, you should have a better idea of the household items you actually find essential or semi-essential to your daily life and will mentally have started the winnowing process.

As you make these preliminary judgment calls — green, yellow, red, and blue — you'll gain a sense of which things you own that might turn out to be "keepers" — those possessions that serve a useful purpose in your daily life.

Don't worry at this early stage if you've already got the feeling you put too many dots on things or not enough. As we've said, rightsizing is a *process*, not an event, and has its own organic way of self-correcting as you go along, especially when you compare the list of the belongings you use with an accurate rendering of the space and configuration of the new place you plan to live.

Now take a break. Have a cup of tea. Go to a movie. And while you're out, get yourself a package of *white* dots. Write your first initial on each one.

EVALUATING THE THINGS YOU LOVE

Now comes the really enjoyable part of the evaluation process. Initialed white dots in hand, survey the room freckled with all the colorful dots and seek out the possessions — utilitarian or not — that speak to you in terms of their beauty, sentimental significance, or value and put a white dot on them. If they already have a colored dot, so much the better.

These are often the pieces of art or photography you own that you can't imagine not having in your life: the amethyst necklace that came from your grandmother, the cast-iron pancake griddle your dad committed to your care after decades of Sunday family breakfasts.

As you conduct this two-part "evaluate the landscape" exercise in the room you've chosen to survey, try not to second-guess yourself. Don't spend time wondering if you *should* have or *could* have loved or used an item, just focus on whether you *did*, in fact, cherish, touch, use, or rely upon a particular possession within the last year or so.

During this mini-evaluation phase of the room you've selected, console yourself with the knowledge that you don't have to do anything about the dots — or lack thereof. You're merely beginning to take stock of the possessions you own and, most important, how *you* feel about the things you own.

Do these two exercises by yourself. Then, if others are involved in the decision-making process, let them survey the same room and place colored dots with *their* first initials indicated, without you in the room advising them! If multiple dots with everyone's initials end up on the same items, their value to the household is obviously high.

Carefully consider the things you've marked as to their genuine utility, beauty, monetary, or sentimental value in *your* life, not anyone else's (like your mother or spouse or best friend). In this phase of evaluating what you own, it's just about *you*. Then ask the others involved to go through the same process.

It's probably helpful not to "discuss" the choices you've made with anyone else but to just keep your side of the evaluation process going.

At this point you may shift around some of *your* dots or remove a few of them altogether. Look for duplicate items, or items you can live without, and remove any "misplaced" dots with your initial on them. No fair fiddling with other people's dots!

Now that you've had a little time to ponder the subject, move or replace your dots to reflect the way in which you truly make use of and appreciate your possessions.

So what happens, you ask, if you can't decide what color dot an item deserves? Easy: simply don't give it any designation for a while and stick only the green, yellow, and white dots on the possessions you've actually used and enjoyed in the last few months. For the moment leave the rest dot free and see if any further thoughts about the item bubble up.

CUSTOMIZING YOUR RIGHTSIZING GAME PLAN AND TIMETABLE

If you did an Internet search on books about personal organizing, you would find scores of titles. One of the best, in my opinion, is Julie Morgenstern's *Organizing from the Inside Out*. I especially like the way she examines the obstacles that hold people back from either making decisions, from being organized, or from following through on their "good intentions." Best of all Morgenstern suggests plenty of ways to identify those roadblocks and remove them once and for all. In her experience sorting, purging, and deciding what to keep and what to toss is a quantifiable process.

When it comes to making final decisions about what you keep and what you provide a new home for, "the truth is," she says, "most rooms in the home take an average of *one to one-and-a-half days* [my italics] to complete . . . Some spaces like bathrooms and small closets may take only a few hours, while others, such as extremely packed garages or offices may take an extra day or two."

So, what room did you choose for this initial evaluation? Note in the box on page 68 how much time — on average — such a room generally takes to sort and "edit."

These calculations will be far more realistic *after* you've made a conscious "dotted" inventory of the possessions you both love and use that currently reside in a particular room listed in the box. If you think you need to, adjust the ballpark figures given for your sample room. Some rooms — like a basement densely populated with luggage; dead vacuum cleaners; serviceable but outdated computers; tins of nails, screws, and other hardware; five pairs of old skis; your college kid's possessions from early childhood; your Aunt Fanny's quilt collection; and so forth — may definitely take more than a day and a half to sort and purge.

Now that you've "dotted" one room in your home, eyeball the rest of the rooms in your house and their contents and, using the room reference below, make a preliminary *estimate* in your rightsizing notebook of how long you think it will take you to work through the evaluation-and-editing process in each room of your current household. Add up the estimated days required to sort and edit the contents of your various rooms, and you'll have the beginnings of a viable rightsizing timetable by back timing to a drop-dead date for departing from your current home, assuming such a date is already in your future.

If all you know is that at some point down the road you'll be making some significant changes in your living arrangements, don't do what *I* did and conveniently push that fact into the background. What I and my fellow rightsizers have learned is that facing the editing process head-on and taking it one room at a time, *over time*, can actually be an enjoyable exercise. The more time you have, obviously the more satisfying the result is likely to be.

With a calendar and your estimated timetable in front of you, assign specific dates throughout the next few days, months, or year to devote to tackling a room at a time, scheduling the hours it will realistically take you to winnow and edit your things. This is a workable plan whether you've already scheduled your move, estimate you may be moving sometime in the future, or simply want to rightsize the house you plan to live in for the rest of your days.

There's a really cheesy saying that about sums up this early rightsizing phase: "Inch by inch, life is a cinch . . . yard by yard it's hard."

It's a lot easier — and more satisfying — to sort through one kitchen drawer for an hour on a Saturday than to be faced with sorting through in a single day an entire row of cabinets chock-full of Tupperware, pots and pans, instruction booklets for defunct appliances, and piles of menus from restaurants that have gone out of business ages ago.

Anyone blessed with enough lead time can consider themselves fortunate, indeed. If you value and use this precious commodity, the rightsizing process will go much more smoothly.

THE BIG PICTURE — TO BE DEALT WITH LATER

When we advance into the full-bore rightsizing process (chapters 6–9), you'll eventually go through each space and evaluate which things you own are the unquestioned keepers and then make a second judgment as to whether they're suitable or going to physically fit in the space where you're eventually headed. However, for purposes of getting your arms around the job ahead, the "single dotted room" approach can be very helpful in launching you into the reality of what you own and how you feel about what you own — and how much time it might take to deal with what you own!

In my view, every project, irrespective of the time available, is manageable if you do your homework at the start and figure out how long the job will actually take.

For instance, if you store very few things in your garage, you can shave some time from the ballpark figures that it usually takes to sort through such a space. However, if you possess the attic from hell, then you'll know you'll probably need to add a couple of extra days and perhaps even line up additional people to help, especially if time is drastically limited.

Once you have these facts in hand, you also have the choice of either setting aside additional hours in your schedule to ensure that you'll get the job done without extra help, or if time is limited and you have some particularly gnarly areas in your house, you'll have given yourself a "heads-up" that you'd best round up some helpers, either paid or volunteer.

Clearly it's all about grounding yourself in reality. Ask yourself these questions:

- What time frame are you dealing with?
- How many rooms must you sort through?
- Are the rooms sparsely furnished or chockablock with possessions?
- What, among all the things you own, do you use, like, or love?

From that basic assessment, we can come up with a simple rightsizing formula:

Time × Amount of Possessions × Amount of Future Space =
Your Personal Rightsizing Timetable and Game Plan

RIGHTSIZING TIMETABLES MEAN NEVER HAVING TO SAY YOU'RE SORRY

The biggest mistake, say professional organizers, is that many people *skip* the vital step of figuring out pragmatically how long it will take to do each room. Their next error is not setting aside the necessary time and *scheduling* that amount of time in their calendars, along with the necessary help needed to assure it gets done.

Waiting until the last minute, or wishfully thinking you'll rightsize your life in your "spare time," can lead to disaster — or as the hapless victims of Katrina discovered, a free-for-all piled on a disaster.

Be advised that our example is a modest two-bedroom house. If your home has four bedrooms or a rumpus room with a pool table, shelves of board games, and lots of sports equipment in the closets, adjust accordingly. Should you have possessions stored off-site, don't forget to add *that* to the total days it will take you to get out of Dodge!

SO HOW LONG IS IT REALLY GOING TO TAKE ME TO RIGHTSIZE?

Boxing, disposing of, or selling unwanted household items and physically getting everything off your property can add another week or

CALCULATING YOUR RIGHTSIZING TIMETABLE

Here, ladies and gentlemen, is where the rubber meets the road.

Compare the rooms you'll be dealing with in your current home to the ones in this box and see how much time you can expect it will take to edit your possessions without losing your mind.

The following is an example of a two-bedroom, two-bathroom home and a formula to create a realistic timetable for rightsizing that starts with the process of sorting and purging.

Room	*Average Number of Days to Sort/Purge*
Living room	1.5
Dining room	1.5
Den/office	2
Master bedroom and closets	2
Second bedroom and closets	1.5
Bathroom 1 and linen closet	.5
Bathroom 2 and hall closet	.5
Kitchen	1.5
Back pantry	1.0
Garage and/or shop	2.5
Basement and/or attic	2.5
TOTAL DAYS	17.0

(2.5 to 5 days more, if you have an attic *and* a basement)

two, which means that a realistic rightsizing timetable for the dwelling described above is close to a month of solid work. If you don't have the luxury of a month, or you can't commit the time it will take to edit everything you own, you'll need to beg or pay for extra help in order to get through the process in haste and still end up with a good result.

Paula Skinner discovered this truth only too well when her spectacular 7,000-square-foot 1886 Victorian in the heart of Charleston, South Carolina's, historic district sold after a year on the market to a family from New England.

There was a very big catch, however. The sale depended upon the Skinners agreeing to vacate within two weeks so the new owner could throw her husband a fiftieth birthday party in their just-acquired fancy digs!

"I called everybody I knew, and we did a blitz pack," recalls Paula. "I had to decide what could fit into our furnished beach house (not much) and what to put in storage and what I never wanted to see again. I got rid of very little because I wasn't even sure of where we were going, long term." Into temporary storage went marble-top tables, a pool table, four-poster beds, massive chests of drawers, twenty Persian carpets, a dining room for twelve, a grandfather clock, portraits, and everything else that characterized their old house. It all went into climate-controlled storage and stayed there at about a thousand dollars a month for three years.

You do the math.

Paula hadn't begun a serious winnowing process during the previous year to jettison the things she knew she probably wouldn't want, regardless of where their next residence would be. Like so many of us, she put off facing the music until the moving van was virtually at her door.

Due to the insane two-week time crunch, it would be a couple of years before she could carefully go through each item and make decisions based on the dimensions of the new house they eventually built. And she's the first to admit that such procrastination resulted in some very expensive solutions to her unanticipated moving dilemma.

It should be clear by now that no matter how big or small your living quarters are currently, the more you can invest in time and preplanning, the bigger payback you'll experience at the end of the process in terms of your sanity and your bank account.

However, bad things happen to good people, and so we all cope as best we can. In Paula Skinner's case, she did a very intelligent thing: she called every one of her Charleston pals and pleaded for help. She got through it all, with ultimately an excellent result (see chapter 5). You can, too, but as the Wise Woman says, "There's gotta be a better way."

THERE WILL BE A SHORT QUIZ

Let's pause and recap here. How much time do *you* anticipate having to allow for the rightsizing process, based on the size of your house, condo, or apartment, the number of possessions you own, and the other factors at work in your particular situation?

Whether you have a week — or five years — to accomplish a shift in your household environment, here are the keys to getting the job done:

- *First* evaluate the things you own.
- If possible, accurately assess the amount of space into which those possessions will go.
- Make the basic choices as to what will move with you and what won't.
- Based on the above, realistically estimate the time it will take to deal with everything.

With this information in hand, you can then create a rightsizing game plan and timetable. In your notebook make the following entries with space to fill in information as you go along.

It's probably fairly obvious by now that optimum rightsizing is not a "spare-time" project, unless you're one of the lucky ones who has the luxury of laying plans well ahead of time and you are willing to commit a day or two a month to systematically tackle your place, one room, one closet at a time.

PLOTTING YOUR RIGHTSIZING GAME PLAN AND TIMETABLE

- The time needed for the room-by-room decision-making and editing process (sort and purge) is the following by room (list) _____ and will total _____ days.
- The specific days or weeks that my rightsizing events need to be scheduled for are as follows _____, in the order listed.
- The personnel I need to execute the plan (friends or professionals to estimate, sort, purge, and pack, hire movers, research storage options, prepare the new space, etc.) will be (listed by category)_____.
- The list of supplies needed to do the job (boxes, tape, labels, etc.) are _____ to be purchased or assembled by (date)_____.
- The final plan and calculations of the time it will take to execute it — give or take a jammed attic or packed toolshed — are as follows _____.

That, in fact, is probably the best method of all, and believe it or not, there are people who have done this. Let's stay, however, with the normal course of events and see how you can anticipate various real-world time constraints that are bound to surface and affect the best executed rightsizing timetables. See if any of the following scenarios come close to your own situation.

UNDER A YEAR TO RIGHTSIZE

Carol and Harold Forshey of Oxford, Ohio, had some advance warning of their need to rightsize their life, but given the burgeoning tasks that eventually confronted them, they soon discovered that the amount of time they had scheduled turned out to be a tight squeeze as a series of unexpected events began to unfold during their preparation.

The couple, who'd lived in their house nearly three decades, had been thinking about their ultimate retirement plans for several years but had taken few concrete steps to begin the actual winnowing process in anticipation of a change they figured would come after age sixty-five.

Then, suddenly, Carol's bosses told her — she was then fifty-nine — that her project at work was being shelved, effective immediately. She didn't want to be reassigned somewhere else in the company, so she abruptly "retired."

Her husband was scheduled to retire from his academic job a few months later. Tenured faculty at his university were allowed to teach one term for each of the next three years, which provided this comparative-religion university professor a smooth transition from full-time work to full-time retirement.

Once these major life changes were in the works, the couple decided to spend part of the winter academic term in Tucson, Arizona, to see if they might like to live permanently in the area where Harold had resided when he was a child. He'd fallen in love with the desert landscape, but Carol wasn't so sure it was the place for her.

In the end, says Carol, "Harold loved Arizona, and I love Harold."

Meanwhile, back in Oxford, a looming zoning change that would affect the value of their home prompted them to accelerate their timetable for relocation by a full year. In less than five months, they elected to convert their 1915, two-story, 3,100-square-foot Craftsman bungalow into a duplex — a substantial construction job, affected by the weather.

Then came selling that property and buying a house in Arizona. This was accompanied by an arduous process of "purging and packing up our stuff collected during thirty-seven years of marriage," Carol recalls.

The Forsheys held a hurried yard sale of furniture and bric-a-brac, but a fair amount went to Goodwill or was given to cleaning or repair people, admits Carol. The couple's worldly goods were then shipped to their new, one-story stucco home (with one third less space), which they'd purchased in a subdivision north of Tucson.

Carol says they managed to accomplish it all with a fair amount of backbreaking work, adding, with characteristic understatement, that it had been "a year of many changes for us."

What was their biggest rightsizing challenge on such an arduous timetable? Two things: "old papers and photographs," groans Carol. Harold was faced with sorting through a career's worth of academic and student papers. In only six weeks he wore out a new shredder. "When we ran out of time at the end," Carol says sheepishly, "we threw the remainder [of his papers] in garbage bags along with the used kitty litter for at least some protection against identity theft!"

What could the Forsheys have done to make their lives easier, or at least reduced some of the angst? "Early on, prepare prioritized lists of what needs to be done, by when," Carol says emphatically. "That way, high-value things will get done; the things that didn't get done were lower priority anyway. I don't think self-imposed deadlines are as compelling as, for example, [knowing that] 'the packers are coming January second and the moving truck is coming on the fifth.' "

In other words, once a change of venue is definitely on the calendar, *realistically* back time to crucial events in the moving process in such a way that you build in enough workdays to get the job done without completely exhausting yourself.

In retrospect, five months to accomplish what was needed to rightsize their lives — including editing their possessions, buying and selling houses, and pulling off the move itself — was simply not long enough for such a huge undertaking. Carol realizes, looking back, that she and Harold had years during which they could have been culling and purging their piles of paperwork on a yearly basis.

Why, you ask, is it so common, so typically human for even very smart people like the Forsheys not to do what we all know is in our best interest?

Psychologists will tell you that for many of us possessions constitute part of our identity. For Harold and Carol, the paperwork filed away all those years represented an important aspect of their professional lives and perhaps stood for a lifetime of hard work and dogged determination. For Harold, nostalgia may have played a part in his holding on to so much of his students' work. Generations of college kids had passed through his classes, and their files were living proof he had been their teacher and mentor. Shredding the files meant the end of the important role he'd played for so many years.

But in the end, some of those "important" papers ended up in the kitty litter. What does that say about the need to purge papers as the years roll by?

"The moral of this story?" Carol Forshey asks rhetorically. "Don't keep papers!"

What, I inquired, would this couple recommend to others about getting the rightsizing process under way in a more timely fashion?

"I think early daydreaming and brainstorming would be a good way to start, though it's not what we did," Carol admits ruefully. "I would allow a couple of years, at least, for exploring options [when it comes to such a major relocation]. Then commit six months to a year for selling an old house. Build in enough time for having any necessary work on the new place done *before* you schedule the move."

Rehabbing a house *and* making a major move before enough advance sorting and purging had been accomplished definitely added to the pressure, Carol believes. Conflicts, she says philosophically, were bound to surface.

The Forsheys held it together during the big push to remodel their old house and sort and dispose of years of acquired household possessions and paper files. They even managed the move out of their Ohio house in reasonably good order, Carol recalls, but then the to be expected happened. Once they got to Tucson, they faced up to the fact that their new home was, indeed, 30 percent smaller than their place in Ohio. They thought they'd planned for this, but with this and that thrown into boxes as the pressure mounted to vacate the Oxford house, they simply moved more than they had room for.

"I was surprised that we had more conflicts while we were unpacking and settling in than we did while preparing for the move."

Perhaps they had brought too much stuff and were exhausted, I wondered?

"Yes, and you definitely should allow some time for R and R," Carol advised diplomatically, "to prevent burnout."

During the course of their rightsizing saga, Carol and Harold developed individual guidelines for figuring out what to keep and what to toss when truly under the gun.

"My rule of thumb [was] to keep it if it's beautiful or useful, or you love it. Harold leans more to keeping things with sentimental value or family history."

Carol admits she became very *un*sentimental about the masses of photographs they'd collected and had to dispose of in record time. She unframed many pictures on the walls and stashed them in three shoe boxes to be sorted when they got to Arizona. "Throw away the negatives," she urges. Given the whirlwind of leaving one place and moving to another, her attitude about the pictures became, "If you want another copy of something, you can always have it scanned."

The Lesson Be as realistic as you can about how much time things take, so you can plan your move as if you were moving an army. At the same time, as Carol Forshey says, "Don't be afraid to forge a new way of living, whatever the bumps in the road turn out to be. This is a terrific opportunity to reshape your life the way you would like. One of our friends described the whole ball of wax as an adventure. So, who wouldn't like to have an adventure?"

THREE TO FIVE YEARS TO PLAN

Very few people will ever rightsize their lives without a single hitch, and there's always opportunity on the other end to make some adjustments and corrections. As some wag put it, "Sure, you can plot everything down to the last paper clip, but where are you going to get the angels to execute that plan?"

Remember Paula and David Skinner of Charleston, who had two weeks to move out of their large family home of seventeen years? They are in the unique position to chronicle *two* types of rightsizing experiences: the gun-at-your-head transition, as we have already heard; and later, the luxury of having more than *three years* to plan and execute a move into their "dream house" on Sullivan's Island, six miles from Charleston "but a world away," says Paula, with a satisfied gleam in her eye.

But first they had to decide on how much space their ideal new life required, and therein lies the tale of the next part of the rightsizing process.

PART II

The Time Is Right

RIGHTSIZING IN SEVEN SIMPLE STEPS

Chapter 5

Step 1 — Decide on Your Space

Examine your life through the rightsizing looking glass

THE SPACE YOU KNOW VERSUS THE SPACE YOU DON'T

When you start to look at your world and begin asking yourself how you're going to rightsize your life, there's one big question that looms above all others: *will I need to move?* The answer, of course, is *maybe*. Some of us will be able to modify our living spaces to fit our needs and desires in later life; others will end up moving to another place entirely. In this chapter we'll discuss the first step in your rightsizing process and help you make your initial (and arguably most important) decision — should you relocate to a new home or should you stay put?

Paula and David Skinner's rightsizing saga took more than three years to unfold, and in the end they experimented with both rightsizing options until they found the fit that was right for them. Their story underscores the importance of carefully calculating the space you'll require in order to decide if you should move to a place that better suits your current needs or if your current home can be modified to make it work for you now (and in the future). The Skinners' tale underscores the lesson that intelligent preplanning really pays off.

Their rightsizing journey began the day that David, a radiologist at Roper/St. Francis Hospital in Charleston, South Carolina, drove into the driveway of their jewel box historic house after "one of those very tough days at work," recalls Paula. As he parked his car, David scanned the lineup of numerous vehicles outside his home . . . none of which belonged to his family. Relates Paula, "There were the trucks belonging to the pool guy, the plumber (we were always having pipe problems), the cleaning service people, plus our handyman's car" — all the various (and expensive!) workers the Skinners needed to keep their 1886 Victorian functioning properly.

On that fateful day, the doctor walked through the door and declared, "I am working my ass off for all these people! I don't want to do this anymore." Paula said that as soon as these words were uttered, it hit her that "I didn't want all these people in my house either!"

Only a month elapsed from that "ah-ha" moment to actually putting the place on the market. The selling phase took a year. Thanks to their buyers, who wanted to throw an impromptu fiftieth birthday party, they vacated the premises in two grueling weeks as mentioned in the previous chapter.

Fortunately, the Skinners' timing in other realms began to work to their advantage. Both Paula and David were in their early fifties with no immediate plans to retire, and their two teenage sons were away at school. The couple moved into a furnished beach cottage that they'd owned for many years on Sullivan's Island, a two-and-half-mile-long spit of land only six miles across two bridges from downtown Charleston.

The Skinners decided to live at the beach for an entire year to see what full-time residency in their vacation spot would feel like. Paula had renovated and fixed up several houses over the course of their two decades of marriage and wanted to get a sense of what it would take to remodel the place for year-round habitation, including hurricane season. "We mutually decided that the house [on Sullivan's Island] was my project. David has a very demanding job, and I'm the one with the tool chest and can fix most anything."

The Skinners left all their possessions in storage as they wrestled with plans for retrofitting the 1980s-era beach house that was desperately in need of renovation. "We went through two or three architects trying to figure out how to make the old house work for the next phase of our lives. It was against our Yankee inclinations to tear down a perfectly good house, but it didn't meet the new hurricane regulations [and we knew it wasn't built] high enough off the ground."

Another problem: as configured, the floor plan wouldn't suit them very well year-round or meet their needs as they grew older. The Skinners took the time necessary to consider exactly how the square footage they had to work with could be best arranged, what their dream house should look like inside and out, and most important, how it should function in their new phase of life. They both still wanted office space (they were only in their fifties, after all, and still intended to work for many years to come). And they wanted their home to still have room for their sons and their future grandchildren, too.

The Skinners' floor plan was also dictated by the new rules regarding hurricane provisions and strict building requirements on Sullivan's Island. Paula supervised the job of sinking pilings seventy-six feet into the ground, designed to support the main two-bedroom, two-bath, two-office home, plus guest quarters connected to the house by a covered porch. "Every single window has big, old, louvered hurricane shutters, a metal roof, and shakes and shingles that look like wood. We're up off the ground eighteen feet, with a breakaway lattice around the pilings. If we get a notice to evacuate, we can button up the house in two hours and be safely on higher ground."

Three years after they'd left Charleston, Paula had all their goods from storage delivered to the large, protected area under the newly built house. Fortunately, despite the mad whirl to vacate the place in downtown Charleston, she'd made inventories of all their possessions from their previous family home. She pored over the list and her new floor plan before the movers arrived, comparing measurements and the styles of their furniture with the amount of space and its configuration in the new home. Ultimately Paula's planning allowed her to keep only the pieces from the old house that worked — and fit — in the new square footage.

The first move had been rushed, but Paula's organization allowed their *second* move to be much saner and their rightsizing efforts to be successful. They employed what is known in the building trades as universal design, an approach that is appealing to look at but also provides for accessibility — or to put it specifically, room for wheelchairs and walkers. After all the Skinners are a medical family and have no illusions about people growing old. The doorways in the new house are extra wide, and their shower has no steps and is double sized.

The guesthouse has a bedroom for each visiting son (and potentially for future wives, with room for grandchildren) and could even, eventually, accommodate on-site caregivers.

Says Paula, "I want to live here forever . . . and I plan to leave the place feet first, in a box." So after a rocky start, the Skinners managed to plan and build their rightsized dream house, and it suits them perfectly.

What was the key to their success? They paid close attention to the kinds of *space* they would actually use in the next chapters of their lives.

The Lesson Even if you don't have the resources to build or buy your perfect, rightsized dream house, the more you invest in carefully sizing up the space you'll need in the foreseeable future, the happier the result, wherever you choose to be.

OPTION #1: RIGHTSIZING JUST WHERE YOU ARE

So, which will it be? Will you rightsize your existing home, build a new house, or make a move? See how many of the reasons in the box below for staying put match up with your current living situation.

If you put a check mark next to the first eight of these ten reasons to remain living where you are, you are hardly alone in preferring what's familiar. As a matter of fact, a majority of Americans age forty-five or

TOP TEN REASONS TO STAY WHERE YOU ARE

1. Current house physically suits most needs with bedroom and bath on the ground floor
2. Love the neighborhood and surrounding area
3. Family members live nearby
4. Own or rent a suitable home that doesn't require major maintenance and that retirement savings can continue to support
5. Medical facilities nearby
6. Network of friends and activities nearby
7. Climate is acceptable
8. Recreational services available nearby
9. Excellent public transportation
10. Religious community and/or social network at hand

older told researchers at the American Association of Retired Persons (AARP) that they would ideally choose to remain indefinitely in their present home irrespective of their age or level of physical mobility.

It's also important to note, however, that the concept of "aging in place" means different things to different people. Jane M. Rohde, an architect and interior designer with offices in Ellicott City, Maryland, says that it's vital to pinpoint what *type* of "staying put" you want. Do you picture yourself:

- remaining in the family home and, if required, making changes to accommodate your shifting needs as you age?
- remaining in the same neighborhood in a smaller dwelling?
- eventually moving into a "continuing-care" retirement community near your current home where you can choose either independent living, assisted living, or skilled nursing?

All of those designations are commonly regarded as "aging in place." Anyone considering rightsizing the home they've lived in for years must first perform a detailed physical survey to see if their house is suitable for elder living and calculate whether enough money is available to make any required changes. Is there a bedroom on the first floor? Can ramps overcome the problem of stairs? Can doors be widened? A case study conducted by Illinois State University in 2005 discovered that the cost of remodeling a house for these purposes was between $50,000 and $65,000. The same features could be *included in new* construction for an additional cost of $3,700!

And these are just the practical issues. There's another problem that's a lot subtler.

"Boomers, especially, refuse to think about getting older," observes Cynthia Leibrock, an interior designer based in Livermore, Colorado, with a passion for "visually integrating design ideas so you don't segregate by age." An instructor at the Harvard Graduate School of Design, Leibrock believes that a design works if it works for *everyone*, regardless of age or contingent disability.

"It's the kiss of death to talk about 'aging in place,'" asserts Leibrock. "The subject [of space planning for one's later years] needs to be couched in terms of quality of life, not stigmatizing certain design features or space layouts by calling it 'senior' . . . or 'for the disabled,' or even 'barrier free.' Boomers have rebelled against the way we think about older people and the way America has treated them. It's got to be put in more positive terms. Universal design," she continues, "is [space planning] for *all* people, it's not a special design for a special population, but rather one that's so adaptable and so well designed it can change to suit the needs of anyone that uses it."

When you think about universal design, she says, "you're not thinking necessarily about smaller, you're thinking about *better* . . . you're thinking about suitability . . . lifestyle . . . accessibility for all."

For the living space in her own life, Cynthia Leibrock and her husband, Frank, are rightsizing their lives by *adding on* to their house in Colorado, not by leaving it and scaling down. "The remodel will include an additional thousand-square-foot 'laboratory' for my interior-design work to demonstrate hundreds of ideas promoting health, safety, and longevity. The house will include a spa, which makes exercise [and even hygiene] fun. I'm even planning a bath that includes an inconspicuous ceiling lift that looks like track lighting and another bathroom that is gurney accessible. All these features are visually integrated so the house will never billboard age or disability."

On the drawing boards are Zen-like rooms with clean, uncluttered lines. The new kitchen will be equipped with a magnetic induction cooktop that prepares food faster than gas, and thanks to its advanced technology, the surface never gets hot. "It's a great safety feature for people of all ages and abilities," emphasizes the designer.

For Cynthia Leibrock, rightsizing means "cleaner, simpler things. I want space to entertain. I don't want clutter or bric-a-brac. I'm replacing things [in my own house] with simpler, better-designed objects, and I'm getting rid of the things that are high maintenance. I want well-designed possessions that are also beautiful. My life's mission is to design so we can go through these passages with relative ease. You have to think about taking care of yourself in your own house and ask yourself, what do you need? It's a different kind of thinking than stigmatizing an entire group. We want a better lifestyle that suits our circumstances *as we age*."

As both the Skinners and the Leibrocks can vouch, designing a house from the ground up has many advantages, but it's certainly not within every rightsizer's budget. To explore the cost and benefit of remodeling an existing house so that you end up with the space you require, configured in the way that suits your individual needs, Leslie Marks, executive director of the National Association of Home Builders' 50+ Housing Council, suggests asking yourself these questions before deciding to stay put:

- Is physically maintaining your home something you enjoy?
- Is the equity you've accumulated in your home going to be needed for *other* financial purposes later on?
- Will property taxes likely become a burden if your annual income declines after retirement?
- Is the home larger than you really need or costly to heat, cool, and maintain?
- Does the layout of the house conform to the way you live *now*?

Getting Specific about Space Needs

Property developer Dick Willhoit, whose homes for "almost seniors" and retirees in California tend to be smaller in size than the "average" American home today of 2,349 square feet, recommends getting very specific about what needs to be changed inside a particular house. He suggests you do a walk throughout your home (or even a home you may be considering for purchase) and answer the questions in the box on the next page.

These are just a few of the architectural questions whose answers will help determine whether to rightsize your existing house to suit your changing needs or to sell it and find a home that better fits the bill.

Retrofitting an Existing Home

If after close scrutiny it makes sense to adapt an existing home into one with universal-design features, the next step is to get an opinion from a space planner, interior designer, and/or retrofit expert and get him or her to create drawings of any modifications that need to be made. Together you can work through plans for an architectural retrofit and create storage solutions to facilitate your long-term residency (see the Resource Directory at back of book).

A LASER LOOK AT MY HOME

- Can I create a ground-level, barrier-free bedroom?
- Is it practical and economically feasible to make ground-level showers and bathtubs accessible for someone who is disabled, with grab bars and other safety features?
- Could the doorways be widened enough to accommodate wheelchairs or walkers?
- Are the kitchen and home office countertops accessible to someone confined to a wheelchair?
- How feasible is it to build ramps over stairways — where necessary — for easy, one-level access and maneuverability inside and outside the house and garage?
- Is it economical or practical to reconfigure excess space so part of the residence can be leased out to generate income or house a caregiver?

West Coast interior designer and "rearranger" Linda Banks is one of a burgeoning roster of housing professionals who consult with homeowners on how to adapt their physical space to their changing requirements, as well as how to pare down and make better use of what they have. Banks helps her clients determine if it's possible to adapt their present house to better meet current needs. Her first step is to hand them a detailed questionnaire that she says "serves as a fact-finding mission for me and a voyage of discovery for them."

The interior designer not only probes how the clients use the house currently but tries to draw out of them what features they *wish* it had. She'll suggest the names of architects if the changes needed to make the house workable involve structural modifications beyond the scope of interior design.

"I also remind them to think out of the box. A formal dining room may be much more useful as a study or dedicated home office," she notes, especially if the homeowner plans to retire from his or her job and intends to keep working from home as a consultant or entrepreneur. A laundry room for empty nesters or a single adult can accommodate a smaller, stackable washer-dryer, freeing up space for a winter potting shed, mini wood shop, wine "cellar," or sewing room.

When thinking about creating a new floor plan and calculating the use of existing space, Banks likes to ask these questions: "What was your favorite hotel room you ever stayed in? Describe how it felt. What elements would you like to incorporate when you reconfigure your current square footage?"

An Army of Home Retrofitters

There is an entire army of home builders and other shelter-related professionals eager to help the aging population figure out the modifications needed to remain in their homes. For instance, the National Association of Home Builders has established a program called CAPS — Certified Aging-in-Place Specialists — designed to school its members in assisting clients who want to retrofit their houses. The three-day course trains building professionals in the specific skills required to guide maturing adults through the process of tweaking their homes for safety and accessibility.

Be advised, however, that contractors, architects, interior designers, professional organizers, and senior-move managers nationwide are climbing onto the retrofitting bandwagon in this, the fastest growing segment of the residential remodeling industry. It behooves homeowners to ask all potential builders about the past projects they've done and to *verify* that they have the appropriate state and local licenses. Insist that you visit finished sites, view photos of completed projects, and most important, speak to previous clients. If such information is not forthcoming, employ somebody else.

OPTION #2: MAKING A MOVE TO RIGHTSIZE YOUR LIFE

Perhaps upon close examination the family home, apartment, or condo of many years doesn't lend itself to alteration or otherwise fit with your rightsizing plan. Unfortunately, many people who initially intend to remain in their homes eventually discover it simply isn't possible due to prohibitive remodeling expenses or because their present abode cannot be physically reconfigured for simplified, "easy living." Stairs, inaccessible bathtubs and showers, or various other physical impediments can complicate any attempt to modify a home for improved accessibility. Even if the house is a suitable place in which to grow older, perhaps the lack of nearby medical or recreational facilities disqualifies it as an ideal shelter for the years to come.

In some instances a family home may indeed be modified cost-effectively, but the owners simply have the urge to make a change. All told there are many reasons why a new living environment may be in order.

Take a look at the box with the top ten reasons to move and see if many sound right to you.

John and Lynne Mangan can truly qualify as veteran "serial" rightsizers in search of an adequate amount of space to suit their changing needs. Lynne, a self-described "Aussie" in her fifties, has a wicked sense of humor and infectious laugh. She met John, a national amateur tennis champion, investment professional, and divorced father of six grown children, twenty years ago in an elevator in New York. They married and eventually she moved with him in 1989 to Woodside,

TOP TEN REASONS TO MOVE

1. You desire a change of scenery, climate, and/or adventure.
2. You want to be nearer family members.
3. You desire to reduce the physical and/or mental stress of the current environment.
4. You need to be closer to medical facilities over the long haul.
5. You or a family member has had a change in medical status, and your house has become a hazard to health and safety.
6. You need to make a financial midcourse correction.
7. You've been struck by disaster (fire, flood, earthquake, or rental house sold out from under you).
8. You desire to relocate to better-configured living space near social and church facilities that meet current and future needs and desires (downsizing or upsizing).
9. You've suffered the death of a close family member or divorce that prompts personal and financial changes.
10. Your remarriage inspires blending households.

California, south of San Francisco, where they lived in a sprawling home for several years.

"After spending enough time in the burbs," Lynne says, "we began to want the bright lights of the city and some culture." At that point, most of John's children were married and leading lives of their own.

The couple rented a 1,600-square-foot, third-floor apartment in a building designed by famed California architect Julia Morgan that had been constructed immediately following the devastating 1906 San Francisco earthquake and fire. It was loaded with charm and had a spectacular view of Telegraph Hill and San Francisco Bay. The couple plunged into the pleasures of urban dwelling: theater, films, and entertaining on their beautiful terrace with its colorful container garden, as well as charity work.

Then their best-laid plans went slightly awry.

Battling arthritis since childhood, Lynne had both her hips replaced, and John had knee surgery shortly thereafter. They soon realized that a third-floor apartment (with no elevator) in hilly San Francisco was not a good idea. Fortunately, the two also owned a second home a few hours away in Lake Tahoe, so they temporarily moved there full time. Both Mangans came through their surgeries in excellent shape, but Lynne had endured enough of the snowy Tahoe weather. "In 2005 I gave the old boy an ultimatum. If he wanted to stay in the mountains, he could, but I was heading for the sunshine."

John, in his late sixties, didn't need much persuading. With his new knees, Lynne says, "he was desperate to play tennis, but there'd been so much snow on our side of the lake and in Carson Valley, he was housebound, which was driving him crazy. Also the Tahoe house, at more than 3,000 square feet, was far too large for us, considering the grown children and grandchildren visited us, at the most, twice a year."

The Mangans moved to the Palm Springs area, but before they bought, they carefully considered the space they needed, the kind of floor plan and its configuration that suited them, and ease of mobility approaching the house and within its rooms.

In the course of their several moves, the Mangans became experts at jettisoning possessions that no longer suited them — Lynne and John disposed of it all with moving sales and kept only the household items they love and that suit their less-encumbered lifestyle. When

John's adult children and grandchildren visit, they rent their own housing close by. "It means a lot fewer bedsheets to change after they leave," Lynne says with a wink.

The Lesson Make sure your dream spot — and the type of space you choose — fits your *current needs*, as well as your desires.

The Art and Science of Advanced Space Planning

As the Mangans discovered, once you've decided that your best move is to a *new* space, there are many ways to live.

What shall it be? A condo or apartment? The city or the suburbs? A cabin on a lake? A cottage by the sea? A houseboat? A modular home? A flat in London or a town house in Las Vegas? Perhaps even a home on wheels? For many active, reasonably healthy boomers and older compatriots, the choices can be overwhelming.

Whatever you decide, the amount of square footage you've chosen and the way in which the space is configured will determine many of the furniture-placement and design decisions that flow from your choice. What's needed next is an understanding of the most basic element of interior design: space planning.

But how much space are we talking about?

As we proceed through the twenty-first century, the median size of a single-family American home has grown to 2,349 square feet. That's increased by 654 square feet in thirty years, even as the size of the average family dropped from 3.1 people to 2.6. The newer the home, the larger it is likely to be, with McMansions proliferating in the new exurban subdivisions, homes that run 6,500 square feet and more, and trophy houses like television producer Aaron Spelling's modest 56,000-square-foot bungalow in Beverly Hills.

At the same time, architecture writer Michelle Kodis in *Blueprint Small* maintains that "a parallel trend is steadily emerging, shaped by the premise that scaling back, choosing a smaller home and, by default, a smaller footprint . . . can be the more desirable alternative."

A related trend, as exemplified by the Mangans' move from the suburbs south of San Francisco to atop Nob Hill, is that boomers and war babies are abandoning their suburban nests and transforming the downtowns of cities from Seattle to Miami.

According to *Realty Times,* a trade publication for real-estate agents, people born in the 1940s, 1950s, and early 1960s will ultimately want "smaller square footage homes. After years of sprawl, new construction buyers want less space with better finishes . . . and one level homes."

Architecture writer Kodis agrees. "Many people feel an undeniable attraction to well-planned and thoughtfully arranged small spaces . . . which remind us of the emotional appeal of cozy, intelligently conceived rooms, creative ways to store belongings, and structures that encourage a strong connection to community and the environment. The singular rule underlying this philosophy is simple: All the space is used."

The irony is that many Americans have built their new outsized homes only to find they live in just a few rooms. Like our feathered friends, humans like to nest.

But perhaps the recognized guru of scaled-down living Sarah Susanka, architect and author of the *Not So Big House* series of books that have become a cottage industry all their own, expresses this yearning for coziness the best.

To those poised on the brink of making important housing decisions for their futures, she says, "It's time to rethink our houses and to let them become expressions of the way we really live. Instead of thinking of a house as a series of rooms, think of it as a sequence of places . . . In a Not So Big House, each space is defined by the activities that take place there."

In deciding upon and planning out the use of space, Susanka asks her clients to first examine their existing home through the lens of how they actually *use* the space they currently live in.

She suggests making a list of the rooms you have, along with the approximate square footage of each. "Under each room name, list what happens there. Under each activity, list the frequency of the activity and who does it. Finally, reorganize the list of rooms in order of most used to least used."

You may be in for a shock, she says. The room with the largest square footage may be the room you use *least.* If the formal living room is used twice a year, such a space could probably be put to far better use in your next home. Certainly having this information in hand *before* you choose your next abode could help you decide whether your current house — or any home you may be considering — really, truly accommodates the way you'll be living *now*.

I did this exercise in my own 1,200-square-foot home and quickly saw why my husband and I are so content in our new surroundings. *All* the space is used by one or the other of us on a daily basis. Try such an exercise, both for where you live currently and where you may be planning to move. The results for my house, to get you thinking along these lines, are in the box "How I Use My Living Space."

How Much Space Do You Need?

So, how do *you* use your living space these days? Do you also have a "wish list"? List the activities for which you wish you had a place — or a *better* place.

Space experts generally agree that in planning interior living

HOW I USE MY LIVING SPACE

Living/dining room 14.5 × 31 = 449.5 sq. ft.

Eating breakfast, lunch, and dinner daily

Reading books and newspaper daily

Listening to music twice weekly

Watching television morning shows daily

Working at dining room table when guests staying twenty-five times a year

Entertaining twenty-five times a year

Talking on the telephone daily

Galley kitchen 5 × 6.5 = 32.5 sq. ft.

Cooking three meals at least four times a week

Making tea and coffee daily

Washing dishes daily

Feeding cat and dog daily

Foyer 25 × 3.25 = 81.25 sq. ft.

Entering and exiting home daily

Hanging up coats daily

Suiting up dog for walks daily

Greeting guests several times a week

Master bedroom 13.5 × 13 = 175.5 sq. ft.

Sleeping nightly

Watching television nightly

Reading in evening at least three times a week

Storing winter clothes

Storage of wife's clothes used daily

Guest bedroom/office 11 × 13.5 = 148.5 sq. ft.

Writing room used daily

Storage of books on library shelves

Storage of husband's clothes used daily

Storage of gift-wrapping supplies used several times a month

Guests sleeping twenty-five times a year

Watching early evening news daily

Bathroom #1 6 × 4.5 = 27 sq. ft.

Husband uses bathroom daily

Guests use bathroom when visiting

Kitty litter box used daily

Bathroom #2 4 × 5 = 20 sq. ft.

Wife uses daily

Husband shares bathroom when guests stay

Bay-facing deck 5 × 40 = 200 sq. ft.

Six months a year in use daily to dine al fresco and admire the fabulous view spaces, function dictates form. In other words, once you identify how you live and the activities you perform within specific spaces, then you can determine how much room you'll need and how best to tailor the space available to accommodate those needs.

What my husband and I discovered is that we're basically using the same amount of space to perform the same activities in our 1,200-square-foot apartment in the San Francisco Bay Area as we did in our 2,700-square-foot house in West Los Angeles or our subsequent 3,200-square-foot house and 700-square-foot guesthouse in Santa Barbara.

These days, in our smaller home, we use our space more efficiently. The room with the largest square footage actually gets the most use, unlike our dramatic 540-square-foot sunken living room in LA that we entered and sat down in perhaps twice a year!

When it comes to deciding on the amount of square footage you'll need to accommodate a new chapter of your life, the question becomes not the number of rooms you have — or even their size — or the names given those rooms, but whether you have the space you *need,* configured in such a way to accommodate your present-day activities.

Space planners also urge their clients to think about living quarters in terms of public and private spaces and the activities that take place in each.

"To make any floor plan work," says architect Susanka, "there has to be a balance between open spaces and closed; between public and private . . . [Living quarters] should offer a hierarchy of spaces, each appropriate to its function and to our mood."

Once you've found a place that suits you and fits the way *you* prefer to live, given all the elements currently at play in your life, your next best move is to get your arms around the idea of *pre*planning. With your list of the functions that are performed within the walls of your living quarters, you can map out exactly *where* those functions will best take place. It's a simple matter of sketching the dimensions of the rooms on graph paper and thinking through what activities could take place within which rooms. For example, you may have several choices for where you put your bed or your computer desk.

Armed with the dimensions and configuration of the floor plan *and* accurate measurements of the furniture you're considering taking (or new pieces you might purchase down the road), try to think "outside the box" as you noodle about their possible placement.

This exercise is easier for some than for others.

Jill Culver, originally from Michigan, left her job as a facilities director in the corporate world at midlife to become a portrait painter. She moved from a three-bedroom apartment into a two-bedroom, two-bath place in order to be on the water. Surveying her new environment, her artist's sensibilities made her acutely aware of the malleability of space.

Her guideposts for laying out her furniture were determined principally by the way in which she *uses* her space rather than merely being influenced by traditional designations for each room.

She selected the smaller of the two bedrooms to sleep in and watch TV during the evening, since it's the room in which she spends the fewest waking hours.

The largest bedroom became her painting studio; the light was better for her work, and she spends the majority of her day there. She designated a forty-two-inch space on one wall of the studio for her electronic keyboard, which substitutes for the full-size piano she had in her youth. Both bathrooms can be used by guests, although the bathtub off her studio often contains drying clothing or a place to store the kitty litter box behind the sliding glass doors when clients come to call.

Jill does daily e-mail and bookkeeping for her business on her computer, so she put her "office" in a corner of the combined living/dining room behind a tall, decorative screen, yet still within sight of the spectacular, 180 degree view — one of the principal reasons she chose this particular apartment. The arrangement still left plenty of space for entertaining guests or reading at night — two activities that were important to her.

Her artist's eye told her that her heavy, wooden dining-room table and chairs from her previous apartment would indeed fit in the dining room, but their volume and mass wouldn't suit the light and airy environment of glass walls that faced the water. She sold the entire set and bought a used, but pristine, rectangular glass table that features white wrought-iron legs, along with six armless Parsons chairs sporting ivory damask slipcovers.

The long hallway from her front door to the living room has track lighting that illuminates her framed artwork, creating an arresting gallery effect for both customers and friends as they enter her home.

Jill has designed her new space to be both functional and elegant. She's found the perfect place to ply her craft and has also created a warm, wonderful home to relax and entertain her friends in after she's cleaned her brushes for the day. The way in which she arranged her space was dictated by her taste, her style, her professional and private needs, and most important, by the way in which she uses every inch of available space.

The Lesson Survey your needs; ignore the nomenclature of the new house, condo, or apartment; and utilize the space in ways that serve *you* best.

THE ART OF PROPER MEASUREMENT

Nothing is more embarrassing than to have a pair of burly movers tell you that your eight-foot couch will fit through the front door but *won't* turn the corner into the hallway.

It happened to us, and the only "fix" was to have four additional beefy guys literally heave our couch up and over the railing of the second-floor deck where our long-suffering movers "caught" it and miraculously managed to carry it along the outside deck and through the sliding glass doors into the living room.

Rightsizers learn to measure *accurately*.

In your rightsizing notebook, list every piece of furniture you own and measure its height, width, and depth *exactly*. It helps if you group like with like: upholstered furniture on one page, tables on another, lamps on another, and so forth.

When it comes to room dimensions, graph paper and a ruler will go far in helping you recreate the spaces where your furniture and household possessions will ultimately reside. If a wall bumps out four inches under a window, be sure to note that in your floor plan. If baseboards stick out an inch or two, note that as well. Jot down window placements, the width and height of a fireplace, the configuration of molding, and other architectural details that can affect the placement of furniture.

Once you have determined the dimensions and configuration of your rooms, study the likely traffic patterns, based on how each area is to be used. All this information will be invaluable as you begin to plot the best use of the space you will soon call home.

Know Thy Space

Knowing precisely how much space you are moving *into* (or rearranging for better utilization) and the exact dimensions of the furniture you think you will be using allows you to map out a floor plan that reflects the functions that each room serves. This, in turn, helps determine what possessions you will be able to use from your current home and helps you eliminate those you will not be able to adapt to the new place.

With accurate measurements in hand, use a pencil so you can erase ideas that don't work well and sketch in your activities on the "blueprint," trying various combinations of furnishings to accommodate your daily needs. Again, think out of the box. A cabinet in your old living room that you used to store CDs might also work as a place to keep supplies out of sight in your new home office. A coffee table and a wooden blanket trunk can be swapped out for a single upholstered storage ottoman with a large tray on top that can do triple duty as a coffee table *and* a place to prop up your feet *and* a spot to store linens.

It also pays to study every inch of your floor plan's dimensions to see what new pieces of furniture (or built-ins) will be required to make optimum use of the space you've got.

The wonderful thing about space is its flexibility and adaptability. So take some time to think hard about the way you like to *use* space. Have fun with trying various solutions for furniture placement in each room. And for the moment, as noted earlier, forget about the number of rooms you'll have or the names usually associated with those rooms. Instead, like artist Jill Culver, simply focus on the activities that take place within the four walls of your home and let the ideas flow.

Visualize Your Space

When it comes to figuring out how much storage space you'll ultimately have, measure the closets, cupboards, and kitchen cabinets of your new home and jot those dimensions down on a separate page of your rightsizing notebook. Sometimes it's hard to know what those measurements really mean in practical terms. Try the following little rightsizing trick to help you visualize your space.

At the hardware store buy a fat roll of blue painter's tape. Then, in front of your *existing* closet, for example, outline the exact dimensions of the new closet you'll be moving *to*, using the painter's tape on the floor. That's a visual representation of how much space you'll actually have for your clothes.

If the blue tape represents a larger area than your existing area, whaah-hoo! If the area is smaller, you'll know quickly how much clothing you can take with you and how much you'll have to send on its way. For many, this time of truth is the moment when they decide to put in a call to a professional closet-organizing company!

Do this same exercise with your kitchen cabinets. If you have *six* cabinets in your present home, put down blue painter's tape on the floor in the precise configuration of the *four* kitchen cabinets you may have in the new place. This can be a sobering experience, but it tends to focus the mind on reality.

If thinking spatially like this is something that utterly confounds you, plenty of space-savvy professionals can come to your rescue (see the Resource Directory). Or you can ask a friend whose home you admire if he or she will help you plot out your floor plan to make the best use of the space you have, filling it only with the things you love. What could be more fun than figuring out what your dream space looks like, room by room?

Okay, you've got your vision of what you kinda, sorta want your simpler life to look like, with spaces that are warm and welcoming and with functional places to nest, ideally close to services and people that will offer enrichment and support for your new way of life.

You may even have already purchased a new house, condo, or co-op or signed the lease for a place that makes your heart sing. Before the packing starts, however, *pre*planning the move itself can provide a passport to a happier outcome, regardless of the destination.

Most important, this is a chance to start unloading the clutter you definitely do *not* want to haul to your next home.

You knew this decorating "diet" was coming, right? Trust me, this is when the true liberation begins!

Chapter 6

Step 2 — Identify Your Favorite Things

Analyze how you use (and why you love) what you have

WHAT DO YOU NEED IN YOUR LIFE TO BE HAPPY?

Have you ever experienced one of those "Uh-oh, this *can't* be happening to me" moments?

A few months after the horrifying images of the tsunami in Southeast Asia flooded our airwaves in December of 2004, an earthquake occurred one early evening off the coast of northern California. It set off the state's emergency warning system, but for some reason San Francisco's emergency network didn't get the word. Apparently the news media *did,* because our phone began ringing off the hook with friends calling, alarmed that our waterfront property was about to get inundated by its own tsunami.

"It's on Channel Four!" my friend Wendy exclaimed. "As of right now, you've got exactly thirty-nine minutes to clear out. Just grab the important stuff and come up to us on the hill."

My husband had just taken the dog out for a walk along the waterfront, where a cellular black hole made him impossible to reach; he was a dead-on target for any wall of water that came through Golden Gate Straits and bounced back at our maritime village from Angel and Alcatraz islands. Panicked, I looked around my 1,200-square-foot apartment, praying he'd come home in his usual ten minutes, while I wondered what I should take with us as we headed for high ground.

Questions bubbled up. What would I need the most? What were my favorite *portable* possessions that I could throw in the back of my car?

Then my mind went utterly blank.

Finally some functioning part of my brain registered a thought: I.D.

We would need identification! Documents to establish who we were, what we owned, and how to get reimbursed for what we lost.

But where were our passports, the registration for the two cars, our marriage license, our insurance policies, proof of my membership in my performer's union so I might one day get my pension? The art on the walls was too cumbersome to carry; my good jewelry was in a hopeless jumble; and how could I begin to choose a photo album among so many? And while we're on the subject, where was my *actual* Social Security card, for God's sake?

At least I had recently downloaded all my published books and ongoing projects from my computer onto a mini flash drive hanging from my key chain. Then I remembered that the last few chapters of my book-in-progress hadn't been updated.

Oh, boy.

Did I give one thought to my two winter coats, the vacuum cleaner, my seven wire whisks, the eight sets of bed sheets, my crystal, silverware, my mother's gold-rim dishes I never use, or the piles of unread paperbacks on top of my desk?

No.

I really, *really* wanted to locate my husband; my Cavalier King Charles spaniel, Ensign Aubrey; and my no-account alley cat, Dandy, who could be relied upon to take a powder whenever the going got rough.

I proceeded to yank open file drawers and frantically burrow through them like a mole in a trench that was fast filling with water. I was desperate to find the documents that would prevent my becoming a hapless homeless victim like some of my friends from New Orleans. Next I grabbed my purse — and my laptop as an afterthought — as I lunged for my mother's diploma and my own hanging on the wall of my home office, along with a picture of myself at age eighteen, dancing in a college production of *Bye Bye Birdie*.

I know, I know, my choices were pretty cuckoo, but ask anybody. People grab the damndest things when a natural disaster is headed their way.

My husband and Aubrey were just walking through the front door when the phone rang again.

"Are you watching TV?" a voice said.

"No. I'm too busy trying to decide what I can't live without. What's going on?"

"Not to worry!" my friend Wendy reported cheerfully. "It was a side-to-side slippage kind of earthquake out on the ocean floor, not the up-and-down sort that pushes a wall of water toward the shore. The tsunami warning's just been called off."

I inhaled deeply and leaned against the nearby wall, my heavy canvas tote bag in hand, and thanked Wendy for caring enough to warn us of the unthinkable. I hung up the phone, gazing at the small mound of earthly possessions piled on the floor. My husband and well-walked dog stood looking at me in puzzlement.

"You won't believe what just happened," I murmured.

It was obvious from this little exercise that even an *aborted* tsunami warning provided me with a very clear understanding that, at least for me, what mattered most weren't my "things."

It got me to thinking . . .

What are your *priorities* when it comes to identifying your most precious earthly possessions? And how do you decide what they are? This is the important Step 2 in your rightsizing journey . . . and I hope it won't take a tsunami scare to jolt you into taking action to figure this out. I'll give you a few pointers to show you how.

WHAT ARE *YOUR* CHERISHED POSSESSIONS?

The act of asking yourself what you would take if you had to evacuate your home in less than an hour has a marvelous power to focus the mind. It also speaks to the question of what really, truly matters *most* in your life. Such an exercise can serve to jump-start the process of identifying your favorite things as well as pinpointing the *reasons* you've come to feel so attached to them. It's a short cut to prioritizing and that helps us make our best decisions.

In other words, what of all the things you own do you love the best? What aspects of a particular possession are vital, in your view? The object's beauty? Its functionality? Value? The sentiment attached to it?

Just for the heck of it, get out a couple of tote bags or open a suitcase on the bed and then look around your home. Imagine a natural disaster is threatening within the hour. Walk around your rooms with your rightsizing notebook in hand and jot down the most important items you own that you could haul out in a couple of duffle bags, ignoring the issue of whether you could get your hands on them quickly. (I finally found my original Social Security card, by the way, and now have it in my steel grab-and-go box in a safe place.)

Now let's move on to the big stuff. Imagine you had a mere three hours to select furniture that movers were coming to pick up at the end of the day. The objects you choose can be of any size or weight, but the one criterion is that you have to *love* and/or need them to make your life work. Jot down these choices in your notebook as well or paste sticky notes or adhesive dots on them.

These items, plus the ones you'd stuff in the tote bags, we can call your nonnegotiables.

If you already have a timetable for moving, do this exercise "for real" and organize your choices by moving methodically from room to room, selecting the things you'd choose if it were a matter of life or death.

It's difficult, of course, to make all of your selections if you don't know where you're going *to*, but let's assume that the items you need or can't live without will magically fit into your next space.

Continuing our fantasy, keep in mind that if you don't like your couch, for instance, and thus don't feel like choosing it, you will be allowed to buy one later with funds from an unexpected bequest. This additional "rule" is to keep you on the path of choosing what you truly *like*, not what you think you *ought* to put on the moving truck.

A much-abbreviated sample of what the two lists could look like appears in the boxes on the following pages.

GRAB-AND-GO LIST	
Portable Item Chosen	*Why I Love/Need It*
Bedroom	
Gold bead necklace	Given me by my father for college graduation
Carol Little black slacks	Mainstay of my wardrobe; fit perfectly; I feel great wearing them
Petit-point pillow	My mother made it during the last six months of her life
Bathroom	
Makeup bag	Wouldn't leave home without it
Extra contact lenses	My backup lenses, plus prescription on box for future needs
Prescription medicines	Will keep me healthy
Home office	
Insurance policies	Will facilitate claims for any losses
Passports	The foundation block for proving identity
Work-in-progress	Will create income eventually
Small framed picture	My husband, son, and I on the porch of a house we loved
Living room	
Framed wedding picture from the mantel	Captures a wonderful day; no negative available
Small ceramic statue	Replica of the statue of the Sausalito seal mounted in the shoals of Richardson Bay; bought it our first year in SF

THE BIG-STUFF LIST	
Item Chosen	*Why I Love/Need It*
Bedroom	
Four-poster bed	Love the bed; leave the lumpy box spring and mattress
Bathroom	
Seashell shower curtain	Love being enclosed in an "underwater world" as I bathe; curtain keeps the floor dry and is of unique design
Home office	
Desktop computer and printer	State-of-the-art equipment; need it for work and pleasure
Living room:	
Mahogany armoire	A valuable antique in beautiful condition; useful for storage and belonged to favorite aunt

YOUR EMOTIONS INFLUENCE YOUR "FAVORITE THINGS"

When it comes to choosing your favorite things, one person's "need-and-love" item can be another person's "can't we get rid of this thing?" This happens a lot when couples launch into rightsizing, so it's important for all parties involved in the process to participate on their own in the exercises outlined in the "Grab-and-Go" and "The Big Stuff" boxes.

Keep in mind that it's not merely the household object itself that's important so much as the *reason* a person loves it and needs it to be happy.

Take, for example, a pair in their early sixties about to move into a dreamy home nestled beneath the Santa Ynez mountain range in Montecito, California, an enclave adjacent to Santa Barbara. The wife is thrilled about the move but concerned about the reduced amount of living space.

"The property is really gorgeous," says my anonymous friend, "but it's essentially a one-bedroom guesthouse with a 'study' and a two-car garage that's nicely finished. The big question — other than the lack of closets — is what do we do with all our furniture and the stuff stored *in* it?"

A typical problem, but nothing that can't be handled with careful preplanning, accurate measuring, and the discipline to take only the things you love. Right?

Not necessarily.

Things became gnarly when the husband adamantly refused to divest himself of his cherished collection of *WoodenBoat* magazine. He had every single issue of the magazine ever published.

Boxes and boxes of them.

"Mind you, these are copies he never even looks at!" reported the wife.

The suggestion was made to donate them in their entirety to the local library in their new town. That way, the husband could visit them whenever he wished and perhaps gain a sense of satisfaction that he'd enhanced the lives of the many other sailors who lived in the area.

"I suggested this, too," laments the wife, whose move had to be accomplished in only a month, "and I got a big fat sneer! I've spent the day throwing away all manner of stuff in bags, and he's been 'taking stock' of his boxes. I fear I am about to become a gigantic nag. What do you do when one spouse or partner is eager and feels liberated about scaling down and the other *clings* to things?"

The party who is eager to get rid of somebody else's "treasures" can stop and consider for a moment if there is perhaps some reason behind the sanctity of a particular item. It helps to understand *why* certain objects have more importance attached to them for some of us and not others. Truth is, most of us are prisoners of our possessions (see the box for ten reasons why) in some form or other, so see if you or your fellow rightsizer resonates to the list of rationales for holding tight to household items that don't really make sense to move to your next address. This can provide the basis for discussion concerning certain roadblocks to rightsizing — and hopefully a resolution can be negotiated without starting World War III.

TEN REASONS WE'RE PRISONERS OF OUR POSSESSIONS

See if you or someone you're rightsizing with can identify with any of these statements, which complete the following: I don't want to give up this item because _____:

1. I might need it someday.
2. I feel guilty getting rid of it since (it's a gift; belonged to a relative; it's brand new; hand made; might be valuable someday; I'll hurt someone's feelings if I trash it).
3. I paid a lot of money for it.
4. I just need to fix it.
5. I don't know where to take it to get rid of it.
6. I promised to take care of it forever.
7. I just need a few more pieces to make it a set.
8. I can use it for parts.
9. I am identified by everyone for collecting it.
10. I'll lose a part of myself if I get rid of it.

For some people, holding on to possessions that won't work in the next chapter of life has to do with maintaining control within the relationship. "She wants me to get rid of it; I'll refuse. So there!"

It's a tricky process, for sure.

ACKNOWLEDGING THE EMOTIONAL SIDE OF RIGHTSIZING

For so many of us, what we own defines who we are, or think we are, or wish we *were*. And the stuff in our drawers and closets and garages, even if we never use it or look at it, can evoke every conceivable emotion. Our possessions can make us happy, miserable, proud, ashamed, in control, out of control, satisfied, or filled with longing.

As you saw from the "Grab-and-Go" and "Prisoners of Our Possessions" lists, the key here is probably to devote some time to figuring out the reasons we feel the way we do about the things we own and to give some careful consideration to the material items that are on the rightsizing chopping block. That means not only your own possessions, but those belonging to any partner going through this with you.

Take, as an example, all those copies of *WoodenBoat* magazine.

The husband had owned boats years earlier and had even lived aboard one during a prolonged cruise in the Caribbean as a happy-go-lucky bachelor. He is a proficient sailor, despite battling a chronic disease that periodically lands him in the hospital. The dream he'd refused to give up, despite his medical condition, was to one day own the "perfect" wooden boat and perhaps even make a major voyage before his sailing days were over. Part of the impetus for their move was so he could do day sailing out of Santa Barbara harbor when he felt well enough to cast off.

He *loves* wooden boats. He loves what they represented in his life: freedom, wanderlust, adventure, and *health.* Even if he never, ever read the various editions stashed in a mountain of cartons, those colorful publications chronicling ocean voyages and boat-building projects by his *psychological* compatriots may have represented his dream.

Everyone is entitled to a dream, however unlikely it is to come true. Denigrating a person's "deep wish" can feel like the equivalent of denigrating *them,* even if a partner doesn't intend that at all. After all, this couple was moving from a spacious apartment into a cute little guesthouse with a severely limited amount of room. There were simply a lot of practical considerations about selecting what to take with them. Boxes of unread magazines, to her, seemed like a luxury they couldn't afford.

During a heart-to-heart chat, the husband acknowledged that the magazines were indeed associated with his hope to return to some serious sailing and "part of" the reason he didn't want to give them to the local library.

"What's the other part?" pressed the wife.

"I don't know," came the answer.

They'd reached an impasse until they remembered they had a "well-furnished garage." Fortunately, it was big and roomy, with enough space for cars, and then some.

The "then some" was first precisely measured side to side, concrete floor to ceiling. Then each spouse agreed to claim exactly half the square footage to store whatever possessions couldn't fit in the house. It was up to the individual to choose what items were worth giving up his or her precious, strictly allotted storage space. Their new reality was that limited space was . . . well . . . *limited.* It had a defined amount of square footage and nothing more, nothing less. If the husband wanted to fill his area with multiple boxes of magazines he rarely looked at, that was his right, for it represented a dream he was not yet willing to give up.

The operative word was "yet." So often in my experience with rightsizers I have observed that living with the new reality sometimes has the effect of eventually reordering a few of their original priorities. The trick here is to grant any partner the dignity to come to his or her own conclusions as to the wisest use of space. If rightsizers can learn to *accept* things as they are at the moment and assume that reason will ultimately outweigh nostalgia or angst or a need to "run the show," the person can still save face if later he says, "You know, I think I'm ready to donate *some* of those magazines to the library" and isn't made to feel like he's eating crow.

The ultimate test will be if both spouses are able to divest themselves of many of their *other* possessions that aren't as highly charged. Can they accept the basic premise that psychotherapist and professional organizer Cindy Glovinsky proclaims in her book *Making Peace with the Things in Your Life:* "None of us owns a single, solitary [thing] permanently"?

In other words, our possessions flow through our lives on a *temporary* basis, on their way to somewhere else after we fall off the perch — or in the sailor's case, fall off the quarterdeck. Either now — or "later" — we give up the things that don't suit us, don't work for us anymore, don't make sense to keep anymore, or take up too much room. Eventually everything we own will land elsewhere or in the hands of someone else when we go to our final reward.

After all, what's the alternative? If we cling to possessions after their usefulness is done, or when we don't have room to store them efficiently, we often choose to *pay* to store them somewhere else.

This may ultimately be the pricey solution for all the other household items our Southern California couple owns that don't fit into their new, significantly smaller house and well-appointed garage.

Perhaps it's merely a matter of one or both members of this rightsizing team not being ready — yet — to divest themselves of their surplus so quickly.

Hey, that's life in a mass-consumer society, right? We Americans, especially, have a powerful need to keep our stuff close to our hearts and minds, even if we can't quite think why.

Cindy Glovinsky postulates that some of us are actually at war with our THINGS, as she says in capital letters in her treatise about taming our need to possess material goods. "Every one of us has the ability to develop healthy Thing-management skills. This means learning to say no to yourself about excess . . . to let go of those [items] you can no longer use or enjoy, and to effectively organize and maintain those you keep, so that instead of taxing your energy, they serve your needs and beautify your life."

Rest assured that order is always possible, even if it's lurking in the midst of chaos. No human will ever achieve perfect order in one's home or life or a perfectly organized guest cottage or garage. But a balance between order and chaos is certainly an achievable goal, once you get the hang of honoring other people's dreams and taking to heart some simple organizing principles.

There's a beautiful passage in Anne Morrow Lindbergh's classic little book on simplifying one's life, *Gift from the Sea*, where she writes: "Perhaps middle age is, or should be, a period of shedding shells; the shell of ambition, the shell of material accumulations and possessions, the shell of the ego. Perhaps one can shed at this stage in life as one sheds in beach-living: one's pride, one's false ambitions, one's

BASIC ORGANIZING PRINCIPLES

Here are some simple principles to keep in mind as you consider what to keep and what to pass on to the "Universe" during the process of identifying your favorite things.

- Gather like with like as you make your assessments
- Select *only* what you love and need
- Identify *why* it's important to you
- Keep only the best of what you own
- Grant yourself permission to change your mind later

mask, one's armor . . . Perhaps one can at last in middle age, if not earlier, be completely oneself. And what a liberation that would be!"

EMOTIONAL HURDLES TO DECISION MAKING

Humans in general appear to have a deep-seated aversion to change, so overcoming that antipathy when it comes to choosing your favorite things is job one. As you read this book, you've probably already had an inkling that change is a-comin'. So how can you rev yourself up about selecting the possessions that are going to make your new home the best one you've ever had?

If you want to feel "lucky me" instead of "poor me" when it comes time to sort and purge your possessions, go for quality over quantity.

You won't be alone.

Lowe's vice president of trends and design for their stores has identified some interesting "macro trends" for 2007 and beyond. The company's research shows that customers report they have "too much of everything." What they want now is to be more selective and obtain goods of higher quality. They don't just want less, they want better. "Simplicity and affordable luxury" are the new watchwords.

Let these be your watchwords when you're making choices about what to keep and what to release. This means you choose the fluffiest of your towels, pick the bed linens that are in the best condition, pack the six wine glasses with no nicks in favor of eight pieces of mismatched cut-crystal stemware you got as wedding gifts that now have a few chips on the rims.

Pass up any of your possessions that have flaws that will keep you from utilizing them fully and with complete enjoyment in your new environment, regardless of how much you've loved them in the past.

You know what I'm talking about: the cushy bath mat with the faint stain, the silk flowers that are faded and coated with dust, the wastebasket with the dents in the side.

Keep telling yourself, "I'm *worth* owning the best of the best!" when it comes to having the choicest of your current possessions surrounding you, even if you wind up with far fewer things than before.

Pack-Rat Syndrome

Serious psychological problems involving one's material possessions may require the help of counselors and professional organizers (see chapter 10).

I didn't realize when I was a very young child that my great-grandmother fit the profile of a genuine pack rat. I remember going along with my beleaguered mother, who had been given the task by the elders in her family to clean out her grandmother's home after she died. Nobody gave it a name back then, but a ninety-four-year-old woman who hoarded *five hundred* pristine-but-empty tuna-fish cans on her back porch because "you never know when you'll need an ash-tray" probably had some serious mental-health issues.

A great beauty in her day, Elfie McCullough was famous in family lore for ditching her hard-drinking husband, Ben Bolt, and running away from Harris, Missouri, to New York with a violinist around 1890. A couple of liaisons and many years later, she ended life in a California bungalow living with a Chinese houseboy she paid weekly in cigarettes and an entire home filled with enough newsprint to put the legendary Collyer brothers to shame.

This woman saved string. She saved rubber bands. We even found a pink-and-white-striped peppermint candy bag filled with five diamond engagement rings she'd "saved." Elfie may have been a bit dotty, but she knew her jewels. Not only was she a serial fiancée, she was also Scottish and held on to her gems each time she broke it off with a beau!

Nowadays we'd call my ancestor an "obsessive compulsive" or just plain looney tunes. For pack rats, choosing favorite possessions among many household items becomes a painful, almost impossible task.

Short of having a defined psychological disorder, however, many of us fall into a gray area that can be equally frustrating to those without this problem; I call it the "holding-on syndrome."

Sandra Keighley of Essex, Massachusetts, would be the first to admit she falls into this category. "I'm not so much a pack rat, but all my life I've loved to pick over stuff at the swap shop in my town. I see things that are too nice to throw away . . . I walk in with three items to donate and come out with four. Every square inch of the walls in my house has a knickknack shelf, a wreath, a clock, a picture. If there's any empty spot, I put a plant."

Despite her humongous number of possessions, Sandra's house is not slovenly. "I'm neat and tidy. Everything has a place . . . there's just a lot of it."

Sandra, fifty-five, is still working full time. Like people in the Lowe's survey, she admits she's growing weary of having so many things to take care of. "I want to simplify my life. I'm tired of having so much. I don't want my son to have to deal with it."

People change. What pleased us or fired our imagination ten years ago may leave us cold today. Circumstances evolve. The possessions we couldn't live without don't seem so important to us now or have become downright burdensome.

Take all this into consideration as you engage in the process of deciding what to keep and what to toss. It may result in some *re*-editing after you've made what you thought were your final selections. That's fine. That's *great*, in fact. Rightsizers always have the right to change their minds.

IDENTIFYING WHAT YOU NEED *NOW* TO BE HAPPY

During the selection phase, keep envisioning your simplified surroundings as you'd ideally like them to be. Don't be shy about speaking up to your fellow rightsizers, if you have any, about specific elements you need in your environment to feel happy.

Marlene Farrell has both personal and professional experience in this realm of winnowing possessions to furnish the next phase of life.

Marlene is not only the program director in Interior Design and Interior Architecture at the University of California Berkeley Extension, she is also a recent widow whose husband of forty-eight years died suddenly in 2005. In May of that same year, her mother-in-law, who had been living with them, also passed away.

"I needed to be healed . . . to learn who I was as a widow," she said softly when we spoke less than a year after her two losses struck a terrible blow.

She also realized she needed to leave the 2,800-square-foot home that had housed her family and to find something that suited her new life as a suddenly single woman. Both her children were grown and had young ones of their own.

After several false starts she ultimately found the "perfect place," a 1,475-square-foot Mediterranean-style town home near one son's household that now includes twin grandsons. She began the process of throwing out "fifty to sixty years of stuff from my life with my husband, along with many possessions that had belonged to my late mother-in-law."

So, how does a design professional in deep mourning gather the will to select her "favorite things" to begin a new life?

"The most wonderful thing happened to me. An old friend and colleague, designer John Wheatman, had also been recently widowed, and he gave me the best advice a person could offer. 'Marlene,' he said bluntly, 'I'm going to tell you how to be happy alone. Clear out your house! Get rid of Ron's things. Make a place that's perfect for you as a woman alone.' It was tough medicine, but he was totally correct."

Marlene proceeded to evolve a personal litmus test about whether she would keep or discard a possession. "I had been feeling so cornered by all the household goods that had accumulated, and I realized clearly that I wanted less in my life, but *better*." So if the item didn't fall into the "better" category, out it went.

"Between July, when I bought my place, and October, when I moved in, I edited and edited. Now if a piece doesn't pass muster [in the new place], it's gone. I have to *love* it, and it also has to be totally functional. I have to need it, as well. I'm not completely finished, but this place is going to be a jewel box!"

Didn't she feel terribly sad giving away so many household items that had important associations with her former life? Of course. "I gave away my entire life, in a sense. I kept one, wonderful photo of Ron, which I keep near my armoire. We were lovers and best friends all those years. I kept my wedding ring, and after [the winnowing process] was all over, for the first time I felt in control. What I have in the new place is comfortable, the right scale, and in my view, ultra-elegant."

Marlene leaned across her desk in her office at UC Berkeley's School of Interior Design and said conspiratorially, "What people don't really understand is that you don't own a big house and all the things in it; the things own *you*."

The way to escape the tyranny of possessions owning *you* is to summon the courage — as Marlene Farrell did under the toughest of circumstances — to face whatever new reality confronts you. Then choose the things that both fit with this reality and "make you smile."

In other words, show your things who's boss!

EMOTIONAL "BEST PRACTICES" WHILE YOU RIGHTSIZE YOUR LIFE

As you've heard from other "veterans," change is hard; so don't ever discount the emotional side of editing your possessions. As Marlene Farrell discovered, making choices among several nice-to-have household items can sometimes also be experienced as "loss."

Take your emotional pulse and that of others involved while you go through your household items. Like the couple dealing with their piles of *WoodenBoat* magazines, it can be helpful to keep asking yourself as you go through the steps of weighing your favorites, "What does this particular object signify in my life?" Is there any meaning beneath the obvious: "I like boats? I like quilts. I like old tools." Is there also a ghost lurking there as well?

Then continue to ask yourself whether a particular object will be useful or beautiful or fit in your new home. Search for any additional meaning that you've attached to a possession that can perhaps explain your reluctance to part with it when that little voice is saying, "Now, where am I going to put that?"

We attach deeper significance than we may realize to certain things, and until we figure out what that significance is, deciding on what we love and can't live without and what is just weighing us down can be problematic.

"Sorting through a lifetime of possessions, reminiscing, feeling sad, and saying goodbye . . . is a necessary part of the grieving process" for some, says Barbara Kane, a licensed clinical social worker in Bethesda, Maryland. In her view moving to smaller quarters, especially for some people, can be "about the loss of our role as householder, the one thing we have control of . . ."

The upside of all of this is that you definitely know when you love something and cannot get through a day without it near at hand.

For example, I *love* my graduated tea canisters: caffeine for me, decaf for my husband, herbal teas for all my New Age pals who think black tea is poison.

Why do I love these old things? Because they're still good-looking, fit perfectly on my kitchen countertop, and most important, connect me to my adored father, with whom I always had tea at four o'clock when I was growing up. And another reason I love my canisters: I married the only other man I ever knew who, in the words of the Duchess of Devonshire, "gets that sinking feeling" in the late afternoon unless a cup of tea is brewing in the pot.

You see, tea is a very big thing in our lives. It represents family coziness, a time to take a break from work, a moment for reflection, a chance for my husband and me to reconnect at the end of the day. Therefore, I would be very put out if someone recommended I trash my tea canisters, even though they take up room on the counter of my rather small galley kitchen.

Just remember, the meaning of an object can serve as a guide for determining whether or not it's truly a "favorite" thing and deserves a spot in your new surroundings.

YOUR "I LOVE IT, I USE IT, I CAN'T LIVE WITHOUT IT" GUIDE

Continue to survey your possessions with these guidelines in mind:

- Can you use it in your new home?
- Is it the right shape, size, style, or type of object you prefer?
- Does it have meaning for you on an emotional level?
- Is it valuable while *also* meeting the other criteria above?
- Can a treasured household possession be creatively repurposed to meet a need in the new home, e.g., a fireplace log bin converted to hold plastic recycling buckets in the kitchen?

As you reflect on the above criteria, you may note that many of the things you own have value but are no longer suitable in your life as you move forward. These are the objects you can consider selling, either by yourself at a tag sale, on eBay or craigslist, through newspaper ads, by hiring professionals to hold a large sale on your premises, or by placing your goods in a consignment shop or auction house.

SIGNS OF SERIOUS SEPARATION ANXIETY

So, let's say you're fine about divesting yourself of possessions you no longer need or want. But what do you do if someone close to you is morbidly unwilling to part with possessions — to the point where he or she can't even *begin* to decide what his or her favorite things are?

Beth Warren, a respected senior-move manager from Tampa, Florida, routinely speaks at active-adult community centers, offering her "How to Move a Lifetime" presentation to people in their fifties, sixties, seventies, and even late eighties. "Moving and sorting can be very, very stressful," she says. "It's more like grieving. The difficult moves are with the people who let their possessions own them. They never become ready to release their material things. They want to keep five sets of china even though they never even cook anymore."

I mentioned to Beth Warren what a friend of mine had said about the "widow decor" he'd observed in the place where his elderly mother resided. In his words it was "that horrible look of a small apartment crammed to the gills with huge wooden hutches, sideboards, armoires, overstuffed couches, easy chairs, and tons of bric-a-brac that once lived in a large family home. *Horrible!*" he'd said and shuddered.

"Oh, yes," Beth replied, nodding. "I know it well."

A certain amount of wistful "holding on" tends to be a part of any major transition and is perfectly normal. I felt it, certainly, as did most of the rightsizers interviewed for this book, when they described what they'd gone through while making a radical shift in their surroundings.

But full-blown depression can get a grip on someone at any age. So if you or a person close to you is showing signs of being unable to cope with the mere act of choosing the possessions they love, and they appear overwhelmed by the act of letting go of things they clearly no longer need, it may be time to seek professional intervention. Help can be located through therapists and social workers specializing in life transitions (see the Resource Directory).

A KINDER, GENTLER ALTERNATIVE TO BEING EXASPERATED

Just to recap, garden-variety difficulties in identifying what household items will make the journey with you to your new home can be ameliorated by following a few simple guidelines.

- Show tolerance and respect to anyone else involved in the process of singling out "favorite" possessions — including yourself! Just keep repeating your mantra: "Change is hard, but worth it."
- Always remember: SORT TO THE SPACE YOU'RE MOVING INTO . . . then deal with what's left.
- With every household item considered, ask yourself *why* you like it and *envision* it in your new surroundings. Ask the same of any rightsizing partner.
- Creatively repurpose possessions you love. A dresser from a bedroom can become a sideboard in the dining room. A CD cupboard from the living room can become a storage cabinet for supplies in the home office.

A FINAL THOUGHT ABOUT IDENTIFYING YOUR FAVORITE THINGS

As you go through the various stages of identifying your favorite things, remember the "beach wisdom" of Anne Morrow Lindbergh: "Certain environments, certain modes of life, certain rules of conduct are more conducive to inner and outer harmony than others. There are, in fact, certain roads that one may follow. Simplification of life is one of them."

Simplification means doing the final editing of what is no longer suitable for your rightsized life and deciding — object by object — what makes the cut.

Which brings us to Rightsizing Step 3: taking the plunge to edit your possessions room by room, item by item.

The ultimate prize? Finding the gold that's under your nose.

Chapter 7

Step 3 — Edit Your Possessions Room by Room

Sort and purge to find the gems

WHERE TO BEGIN?

One of the most daunting moments of the entire rightsizing process comes when reality dawns and you come to grips with the fact that you own a lot of *things*. But take heart. This is the beginning of the liberation promised in this book: a sense of freedom that will evolve as you simplify your surroundings while keeping what matters most.

We will tackle various categories of possessions, starting with the biggest items and ending with the smallest. We'll begin with furniture and household appliances and work our way eventually to sorting through clothing, personal papers — even your paper clips!

The sheer number of possessions lurking inside your cupboards, at the back of your closets, in all your drawers, stashed in the garage, basement, or attic can, of course, make your eyes glaze over. How in the world do you even *start* sorting what to keep and what to toss?

Not to worry . . . there are plenty of answers to that question. The trick is getting the process jump-started.

MERGE AND PURGE

Following their wedding, Tom and Tina Green didn't know what to bring into their new home. Each formerly married and parents of grown children, they were confronted with selling two houses, merging their possessions into one location, and then choosing the household items that mattered most to both of them so they could start a new life together. And what an inventory to choose from: duplicate couches, a variety of beds, pots and pans, chinaware, and more than ten thousand family photos.

Tom's house, where he'd lived with his first wife of thirty years, was 3,650 square feet. Tina's home was 1,600 square feet, "a tweaked tract house, snug and cozy."

At first Tina moved into Tom's place. She soon discovered that "there was nothing of mine that fit into his house. His rooms were set, so we left everything as it was." Then she adds mischievously, "We did buy a new bed, though."

But a few years of this was more than enough for Tina. "Tom had so much history in the old house. I wanted to have a beginning that was new to us both." When I spoke to them, they had been in their joint abode six months. Says Tom, "I have my memories [of my former life], Tina has hers, and it was time to create memories we could share."

Agrees Tina, "You've got to let go of the stuff that doesn't fit anywhere, remove the excess, and choose what you *both* like. We still have boxes from our two former houses and here we are, dealing with them seven years after we said 'I do.' You open the stuff and just stare at it all. The next few months it will be interesting. Those boxes and extra furniture need to be dealt with."

That's the stark reality about owning possessions. You get to deal with them now, or you deal with them later. Unless, of course, you punt and let somebody else deal with them after you die. While you're still around, however, the longer you *don't* deal with the things you own, the more bogged down you may eventually feel.

SETTING UP THE RIGHTSIZING SYSTEM

An important aspect of editing your possessions for the next phase of your life is establishing a *system* before you go into high gear to tackle the job ahead. This involves assembling the tools you'll need to make your tasks easier.

The first thing to keep by your side at all times is your rightsizing notebook, with all the information you'll be gathering or have already jotted down: measurements of your furniture; your thoughts about what possessions are important to you (and why); vital phone numbers, like the television cable company, the power company, the movers, and so forth. These, plus all the notes and scribbles you've made, are now consolidated in *one place*, where you can retrieve them as needed.

ASSEMBLE THE RIGHT(SIZING) TOOLS

The next step is to put together your "tool chest," which will become a virtual appendage as you advance into the winnowing process. Find a "staging area" within or adjacent to the place you intend to tackle first — a little-used bedroom, an enclosed porch, the corner of a living room — and designate that spot as your *processing center*, where you can keep the "tools" you're going to assemble to help you with your task. The truth is it doesn't really matter *where* you start paring down your household goods, provided that once you start, you keep going. If you begin the rightsizing process in a room where you can see the quickest progress, chances are excellent you'll be inspired to keep at it.

In your designated staging area, set up the following:

- At least nine sturdy cartons or large bags labeled KEEP, REPAIR, TRASH, GIFT, DONATE, RECYCLE, SELL, TRANSFER, and DON'T HAVE A CLUE
- An ample supply of large, *clear* plastic disposal bags — for use when it's important to *see* what's stashed inside; that way, good things don't mistakenly get discarded as trash
- Several boxes of large, *opaque* plastic disposal bags — used for items that will be disposed of in the trash.

Next, get a plastic home-products carry canister, a multipocket apron, or a moveable canvas shoe bag that attaches over a door. Label each shoe pocket with a black marking pen as to contents so you can find the item you need with no hassle. Assemble the following "tools" in the canister, apron, or shoe bag to make the job of sorting, editing, purging, and packing much more efficient:

- retractable measuring tape
- felt-tip pens
- small scissors
- Phillips and standard screwdrivers
- a small hammer
- a box cutter with a safety catch
- sticky notes
- a packet of plain, white 3″ × 5″ self-adhesive labels
- small notepad and pen
- self-stick color-coded dots
- packing tape and dispenser
- a list of useful telephone numbers you're likely to call
- a cell phone, if you have one
- a small container of bottled water
- an energy bar or two

To preserve your sanity return these tools to the same place after every use.

READY, SET, GO!

If you have taken the steps recommended earlier in the book, you've started to target the things you own that are your favorites, household goods you love and use and want to be part of the next home environment you create. Remember the colored-dot system we discussed in chapter 4? If you haven't yet made those choices or want to revisit the ones you've made earlier, do that *first,* while you're also surveying the big items you know you want to get rid of. Here's where you can use your green adhesive dots for "this is a keeper" and your red dots for "this goes." This step is the most fun and can be accomplished fairly quickly.

If dots aren't your "thing," you could use adhesive labels or sticky notes to mark your choices as you circulate, room to room. It's up to you. The point of this exercise is to begin making choices about the larger items in each and every room that you want to KEEP or RELEASE, things like sofas, beds, bookshelves, and lamps. (Later we'll deal with groups of items, such as books, clothing, photographs, and collections.)

Make a second pass through the rooms of your house and mark the smaller household goods you *want to hold on to* — things like your aunt's silver vase, a set of golf clubs, a laptop computer, and so on. You'll deal with even smaller possessions you want to keep or jettison when we get to the serious editing process, so don't worry about these at this point.

Obviously, you'll constantly be re-editing as you go along, especially if you learn more about the place you're sorting into (such as there's no storage available to rent in the complex, the shed at the back of the property leaks, you've found a sleeper sofa that will work much better in the den, and so forth).

If you are merely sorting and purging as a kind of super-duper spring-cleaning exercise, you can still feel wonderful having made decisions about the things you love and want to keep with you for now — and in getting rid of the stuff that really doesn't work for you anymore.

This first foray into "stuff sacrifice" should only take a couple of hours.

BEGIN AT ONCE AND DO THE BEST YOU CAN

Remember those words "begin at once and do the best you can," spoken by my husband's former boss? Everyone who has ever had to sort through possessions says the hardest part is *getting started.* You need to adopt the old Nike commercial slogan and "just *do* it!" Even taming a single kitchen drawer will give you a tremendous lift when you see the result. Once you've conquered the drawer, tackle half a cupboard.

Now you're ready for the rightsizing Big Time! A wonderful payoff awaits you because the simple act of clearing your clutter and passing on the possessions that don't have use or meaning to you anymore can transform your life.

Purge the Big Items

One way to see some fast improvement is to begin by tagging and removing from the house the large and/or obvious household furniture and appliances you are already certain you're not going to want or need in your next phase of life. The kinds of things I'm talking about include the rusted refrigerator taking up space in the garage or on the back porch; the scarred chest of drawers in the attic; pieces of luggage with broken wheels and handles; the hulking computer monitor that's been replaced by a cool, new flat-screen model.

It really advances your rightsizing cause to start getting rid of "big clutter" first and work your way down to the smaller stuff, which will include kitchenware and your personal collections of photographs, books, heirlooms, etc. (see chapter 8). By focusing first on the larger items, you'll find it feels wonderful to eject outworn furniture, outdated home appliances, and nonfunctional home-office equipment from your immediate surroundings. The overall rightsizing game plan is: START BIG and work down to the smallest items you want to get rid of. You'll start to enjoy pasting "NO!" markers on various items you're definitely not taking with you to your next abode as you make your decisions.

If you let yourself get mired in the small stuff first, chances are good you'll feel frustrated and overwhelmed, and that's not the "rightsizing way." I guarantee that you'll feel a great weight begin to lift when that old dresser or ratty couch or dead air purifier is carted out of your house and onto the Goodwill truck.

However, for some people, getting rid of a large item that has hung about in your life for a long time feels too taxing. Or maybe, after you've made a few big decisions, you just don't have the stomach for more drastic cuts. If you fall into this group, jump-start your rightsizing efforts by first decluttering your kitchen junk drawer or the entranceway to your home. Just identifying a single task and checking it off the to-do list can be an enormous lift. It'll give you a feeling of instant gratification and accomplishment . . . and send you back into the garage or the basement with a renewed sense of purpose.

Try to get as many of the large items off the premises as expeditiously as possible. But even if the items physically remain in your home until a later date, you'll still feel your spirits rise just noticing how many red dots or "NO!" stickers you've put on unwanted possessions.

"By allowing yourself to create space for the things you want," says Karen Kingston, author of an inspiring book, *Clear Your Clutter with Feng Shui*, you also "clean up your life" as well as the physical world you inhabit.

Kingston defines clutter — big and small — as:

- things you do not use or love
- things that are untidy or disorganized
- too many things in too small a space
- anything that is unfinished

I would certainly add to this things that are broken and can't easily be fixed. This is the clutter you're going to clear out of your life!

CREATING A CLUTTER-FREE ISLAND

The unvarnished truth is you can also feel bogged down when you *do* start dealing with the things you own! So as you begin to tackle the nitty-gritty editing process, you need to create what I call an "island of sanity." That's a space somewhere in your home environment that's free of clutter, boxes, and the paraphernalia that goes along with the sorting, culling, and purging of your possessions.

Pick a corner in your kitchen, a section of a porch, or an area in your bedroom in which you can create your own reflection space — where you can sit down and rest, have some refreshment, and maybe watch five minutes of television or read the paper for a bit. This can be a great antidote to the chaos that will temporarily ensue.

RIGHTSIZING ROOM BY ROOM

Keeping Kingston's definitions of clutter in mind while stashing your tool kit within reach, select a room in your home where your efforts will have the greatest immediate impact on your daily life. Let's assume you've disposed of the big items you're eliminating from your life or have at least designated which ones will go.

Now we'll deal with what's left in a particular space. This could be the living room or family room where you spend most of your waking hours at home or a guest bedroom that's become a dumping ground for things you don't know what to do with or don't have room to store anywhere else.

In or near the chosen room, place the boxes (or clear and opaque plastic bags) labeled KEEP, TRASH, DONATE, SELL, GIFT, REPAIR, RECYCLE, TRANSFER (to another spot in your home) — plus the all-important carton with the DON'T HAVE A CLUE label.

Face a corner, *any* corner. A number of clutter experts suggest that you position your open palms on either side of your eyes and observe the space that falls within your field of vision. *That* is the amount of space you need to tackle in the next ten or fifteen minutes, if it even takes you that long.

Pick up each object in that 3-foot space *once* and decide where it belongs, i.e., either right where it is (because it's a definite keeper), in a better spot somewhere else in your house (it goes in the TRANSFER box), or in the TRASH carton, the REPAIR carton (are you *sure?*), the DONATE or RECYCLE cartons, or the SELL carton for disposal at a tag sale, consignment shop, or in a "live" or online auction. Item by item, put the individual possessions in the appropriate boxes.

Like with Like

While you're working on a particular area, you want to stay focused on cleaning up that specific spot. But there's one exception to this single-minded rule: rightsize like with like. In other words if you're dealing with a corner of your garage where you store your luggage in an overhead rack, be sure you gather not only the suitcases from that area but also the ones you keep under your bed or in a back closet so you can do a like-with-like survey of all the luggage you own. That allows you to select the best pieces among everything you have in that category. This, in turn, results in your having a set of suitcases and carry-ons that may be fewer in number but are bags you will actually use.

In the next two chapters we'll emphasize this like-with-like philosophy for evaluating other groups of possessions — especially things like dishes, glassware, flatware, kitchen items, linens, children's possessions, artwork, photos, clothing, office equipment, books — as well as taming the awful of awfuls: piles of paper.

Let's get back to that initial 2- to 3-square-foot area. Sort through every item in that limited space, remembering to ask yourself each time you lay a hand on something, "Is it useful, is it beautiful, is it valuable, is it sentimental?" So much the better if the items are useful *and* beautiful or valuable *and* sentimental. These are probably your keepers.

Just continue to tell yourself the object of the exercise is to *get rid of as much clutter and as many dust catchers as you can!*

Stick with one room per session and don't allow yourself to wander around the house. Your rightsizing tool kit, with all its supplies within handy reach, will help prevent such aimless drifting about midpurge.

When you finish your first 2- to 3-square-foot patch, move to the space adjacent and repeat the process — surface by surface, drawer by drawer, closet by closet — "filing" the possessions in the appropriate boxes or bags as you work yourself around this first room until you arrive back where you started.

Congratulations! Pat yourself on the back. You've "edited" your first important area. If you are tempted to quit midway through a drawer, resist! *Finish* that particular chore, then call a halt for a while and head for the island-of-sanity spot you've created. Just make a note of where you stopped so you'll have a marker to remind you exactly where you'll want to continue after a short rest.

If you only succeed in decluttering, sorting, editing, and purging *one* fourth of *one* room at a session, that's fine! Such decision making can be physically, mentally, and emotionally taxing, and most people tire after an hour or two. If feasible, finish one room before starting another, as this method allows you to register your progress.

I HAVE TO BE OUTTA HERE IN A WEEK!

Of course, if you have the proverbial gun at your head, all bets are off. Don't be shy about asking friends for whom you've dog sat, collected mail, or fed fish to lend a hand, or call in the professionals (see chapter 10) to see you through the crunch. It's up to you, of course, to make the ultimate decisions about what to keep and what to pass on to someone else who can make use of it, but it helps enormously to have some sidekicks while you make the big push to vacate the premises.

Teach your helpers the rightsizing system for sorting and purging and instruct them about using the "tag-and-bag" system and the tool kit. That way things will go a lot more smoothly for all of you.

Once you've got the first room you've tackled pretty much the way you like it, Margit Novack of Moving Solutions, in Philadelphia, Pennsylvania, suggests a second step.

"Take snapshots of picture arrangements, curio cabinets, and bureau tops so things can go in the same spots in your next home," she says. And remember, she advises, people who are trading a house for a condo won't need five garden hoses.

Beth Warren of Welcome Home Relocation in Tampa Bay, Florida, has another word of advice for those moving to a place in the city. "Don't pack the contents of the garage if you won't even need a toolbox."

Bottom line: you might even discover that you have entire *categories* of possessions that go directly into the appropriate boxes for their removal without your having to spend much time mulling over their fate.

The tough moments usually come when you consider a once-valued possession that won't fit into your new life. For some rightsizers it helps to embrace the concept of returning these former treasures "to the Universe" by means of gifting friends or charities with the things we love but have no room or use for in the next phase.

END EACH DAY ON A HIGH NOTE

During the decluttering and editing process, the last job of the day requires you to put the discards from the box labeled TRASH into the opaque garbage bags. Immediately take them outside to the refuse receptacles (or into a vehicle for removal to the town dump). If you have an inordinate amount of trash, you may have to call your refuse company and book a date for a large pickup.

If you've been using sorting boxes for your nontrash items, transfer what's in them into the *clear* plastic bags marked with 3″ × 5″ labels that remind you where the bag is headed: the nearest charity outlet of your choice (some will even pick up from your home) or to the repair shop, the consignment shop, the public library, the tag sale, and so on.

Promptly stash these bags of items destined to *leave your house immediately* into the back of your car so you can drop them off at the appropriate destination on your *next* trip to the grocery store, the post office, or work.

Like some Clutter Cassandra, I sorrowfully predict that a cloud of gloom will descend on you if you merely move the stuff you're getting rid of to the back porch or the trunk of your car and then just leave it there for a couple of weeks. Don't let this happen! You're making terrific progress, so for the sake of your mental health properly dispose of the things you've edited out of your life as promptly as you can. The sooner you get the excess stuff *off* the premises, the better you'll feel and the more rewarding your rightsizing process will seem. Why? Because you'll notice the significant feel-good changes in your surroundings in very short order.

IF AT FIRST YOU DON'T SUCCEED —
KEEP GOING

Keep up the momentum. For the sake of efficiency, not only should you take the piles of winnowed possessions from the house promptly, you should bestow the windfalls on your lucky GIFT recipients as soon as you can.

As for the DON'T HAVE A CLUE items, chances are a solution will come to you after a day or two, once you've made it clear to yourself that you might be willing to part with these possessions.

Soon after we moved to our little maritime village, we were unpacking a large apparel box that had been in storage for several years. Out popped my husband's dress naval officer's uniform from the Vietnam era that didn't quite fit him anymore. At all.

Sorting conscientiously, he put it in the DON'T HAVE A CLUE pile. It sat there a few days until I tentatively made the suggestion that perhaps he could give away the tight trousers to a local thrift shop, keep the jacket for costume parties, and confer the ceremonial dress sword upon our son for his twenty-fifth birthday. To my amazement he agreed. It almost seemed as if we'd found a kind of spiritual solution for a practical problem. Wearing the jacket to various nautical events seemed just the right touch of respectful irreverence this piece of his personal history required.

The point is, it takes a little time and a little creativity to figure out solutions to these kinds of issues, but there's always an answer if you sort through the feelings attached to "special category" possessions like these. Placing the items about which you're uncertain into a kind of "way station" keeps you from getting distracted from the main goal: continuing the process of editing until you've dealt with every single thing you own. This will help prevent that horrible, bogged-down sensation where you are stymied by a decision you have to — but aren't ready to — make and get so aggravated you chuck it all out in frustration.

TAKE IT EASY — EVEN IF YOU'RE UNDER THE GUN

Heavy-duty sorting, editing, and purging can be exhausting. As was recommended in an earlier chapter, estimate the amount of time a task might take and then assume it will probably take a few additional hours to complete.

Unless you have no choice in the matter, work in one- to two-hour increments, eat regularly, and reward yourself with a brief walk or at least a five-minute stretch period. Remember to visit your island of sanity whenever you need to. Keep that one small area of your home open and clear of clutter with a table and chair where you can sit down and take a breather, have a cup of tea or coffee, or call a pal to have a little yak fest. These short respites allow you to pace yourself and still keep going. At the end of the day, reward yourself with dinner out or a movie or arrange for a friend to bring over a salad and a pizza. Then fall into bed at eight p.m.!

SELLING, DONATING, AND OTHER DISPOSAL TRICKS

Once the earthly goods you possess are culled, sorted, and edited, the items that didn't make the cut need to be disposed of one way or another.

But *where*, you ask?

The good news is there is a systematic method for unloading possessions you no longer want, need, or have room for now or in your next abode.

Selling your surplus goods is always an appealing option if you have the time to devote to such a project. Consult the Resource Directory at the end of this book for additional guidance about staging a tag sale or professionally conducted home sale or selling goods on eBay or craigslist. When it comes to online commerce, there are even in-the-flesh or online "trading assistants" you can engage for help. They'll write zippy ad copy, digitally photograph your Barbie dolls in their original boxes, and manage the virtual sale, as well as ship your goods to their new owners, for a 20 to 40 percent cut of the action.

Another option is to take items of value to a local auction house or consignment store, but be sure to ask for a written explanation of terms and fees and get an invoice before you leave your goods. Typically commissions for this service run around 40 percent.

Donating to a good cause is always a rewarding solution for passing on functional items you no longer have any use for. Check online (see the Resource Directory) or by phone with one of the nationally recognized come-to you charities like Goodwill, Salvation Army, Jewish Family Services, St. Vincent de Paul Society, etc. for a list of items they'll accept — usually with an offer of documentation to facilitate tax write offs. Ask each one of the outfits above for a list of things they *won't* take, as well, so you don't waste your time or theirs.

Neighborhood thrift shops benefiting local charities are usually happy to accept dropped-off donations of clothing, accessories, objets d'art, and small appliances. One manager urged me to remind donors to pass on only clean, intact goods that you would offer to a friend or family member. Ask for a written record for tax purposes.

Local or regional libraries, nonprofit book sales, day-care centers and schools, senior assisted-living centers, and some charitable groups are generally delighted to take books, sets of magazines, records, CDs, and DVDs off your hands and will also provide a record of your donation to back up your charitable tax write-offs. However, not every item in this category is worth saving or donating. Feel free to toss into the recycling boxes paperbacks that are falling apart, *Reader's*

Digest condensed books, and volumes with dated information, including old travel guides and photography and computer manuals, along with CDs and DVDs that don't play.

For stuff nobody wants or is willing to take, there is always the local garbage pickup (call your local sanitation company for rules and regulations) or the city dump (known officially as the municipal sanitary landfill), where there is usually a hazardous-materials section. Furthermore, in many cities and towns there is a "tradition" of putting the odd piece of furniture on the sidewalk with a sign that says, "I'm free! Take me!" The results can be absolutely amazing. We put an old, but still serviceable, valet stand on the curb in our small town, and it disappeared within minutes!

Recycling difficult-to-dispose-of items like big appliances, old computers, printers, cell phones, mattresses, etc. requires a little research on your part. Here is where online search engines can be your friend. Try surfing google.com, ask.com, yahoo.com, msn.com, a9.com, dogpile.com — or your local Yellow Pages — to locate the nearest electronic or hazardous-waste recycling facility. You can also call your local city hall or waste-management company for assistance in locating recycling centers and hazardous-waste disposal facilities in your area (see the "Recycling Almanac" box).

Gifting friends and relatives can be fun and will make a person feel like Lord or Lady Bountiful. Sometimes, though, it makes sense to offer large items of furniture and appliances as gifts "on permanent loan," as is done at museums. If you think there could come a time when your seven-foot leather sofa would work in a house you might live in at some later date, you can offer it with the understanding that you might eventually ask for the sofa back.

I once accepted custody of a grand piano from someone on this basis. Sure enough, she eventually wanted it returned, and that was fine with me as that had been our clear understanding. In the interim we enjoyed the sight of a gorgeous instrument in our living room and had several wonderful evenings singing songs with family and friends. We had gotten — in writing, of course — an agreement from the owner that we'd be held harmless in the event of fire, flood, earthquake, or errant wine spilled by a tipsy guest.

Another tip when giving items to friends and family is to require the recipient to provide transportation to the new destination. You've got enough to worry about, and besides, if you're giving it away, they're getting something very nice for free!

YOUR RIGHTSIZING RECYCLING ALMANAC

Just for reference, here's a basic primer for disposing of the more confounding items you may need to eliminate as you rightsize your life.

Appliances — especially big ones like refrigerators, washers, and stoves — can no longer find their final resting places in many of the nation's landfills (they're full). Check with city hall or your garbage or waste-management company for local recycling information. If you're willing to pay, contact such outfits as www.1800gotjunk.com, www.callandhaul.com, or www.1800ecohaul.com. Also, local scrap-metal companies will sometimes take steel-made appliances. The Steel Recycling Institute offers 800-YES-I-CAN to locate the nearest facility that will take an appliance off your hands. The best solution if you are buying a new appliance is to get the store to agree to haul away your old one.

Arts and crafts, school, and office supplies are in demand by local educational and arts organizations that are in the market for complimentary clay, crayons, finger paints, pencils, brushes, and reams of computer paper.

Dead batteries can be dropped off at Radio Shack and Walgreens or to a hazardous-waste facility. The same is true of car batteries, or you can recycle them for free at some vendors, such as Kragen Auto Parts.

Cell phones can often be reconditioned and given to someone who could use them. A program run by www.wirelessfoundation.org refurbishes cell phones for victims of domestic violence. Electronics stores such as Radio Shack will often accept defunct cell phones and landline phones for recycling.

Computer parts, TVs, and monitors should be disposed of in a fashion that is EPA approved, usually through official recycling centers and governmental hazardous-waste facilities. Your local city hall can usually provide a list of approved places. Dell Computers, for instance, operates www.dell.com/assetrecovery. They will issue a detailed settlement report and certificate of disposal that verifies that your hard drives were overwritten, inoperable disks were shredded, and recycling was done in accordance with EPA guidelines. Some experts are of the opinion that the one sure way to destroy your hard-disk data is to remove the device itself from the computer yourself and smash it with a hammer!

Cosmetics may contain toxic substances, including formaldehyde, which is a carcinogen. Don't throw them into the trash! If the products are still good, local homeless shelters or providers for low-income families may be your best bet for unopened bottles of hair dye, nail polish, makeup, and those travel-size personal products you collected on your trips but didn't use. For the "dead stuff," it's off to the local hazardous-waste facility.

Eyeglasses and **hearing aids** are welcomed by Lions Club International for donations to the needy in other countries. LensCrafters also accepts such items for charitable redistribution. Check with www.uniteforsight.org for additional donation opportunities.

Garden tools still in good shape and not destined for sale can be gifted to neighbors or donated to local community garden projects. Barring that, ask your local plant nursery for advice.

Lightbulbs, especially mercury-contaminated fluorescents, are considered hazardous waste, so head for the recycling center.

Linens, especially worn bath towels, may find a welcome home at pet shelters or your local vet's.

Lumber, Sheetrock, tiles, paints, varnishes, tools, and other *usable* remodeling items may be welcomed by your local Habitat for Humanity organization. If they are not usable, take these items (except lumber) to hazardous-waste facilities or local recycling centers.

Luggage that doesn't suit your current purposes might be welcomed by local social-service agencies that deal with foster care.

Magazines can always be recycled with your other mixed paper or passed on to other enthusiastic readers. Hospitals, the local hospice, assisted-living facilities, and other public-service providers who have waiting rooms might take them. Local libraries sometimes accept them to fill in gaps in their collections.

Mattresses are not accepted by most charities due to strict sanitation laws. However, locally based charities serving the homeless and poor will sometimes take them to give to the needy. When buying a new mattress, inquire whether the purchase includes removal of your old one. If not, call your local garbage or waste-disposal company for disposal instructions.

Medicines flushed down the toilet are reportedly getting into the drinking water of some municipalities. Take outdated drugs to a hazardous-waste facility.

Medical supplies such as used crutches, neck braces, walkers, blood-pressure cuffs, etc. — if still good enough for your mother to use — would be welcomed by charities that specialize in aiding the ill and indigent. Enter "donate medical supplies" into an online search engine to see if there is a local facility. Clear Path (206-780-5964) sends certain kinds of medical supplies to land-mine victims.

Musical instruments are precious commodities to many school districts, or you can offer them to your local theater group as stage props. Arts councils in your area can also provide guidance.

Trophies from your Little League or ice-skating days that won't blend with your new decor can be offered to local boys' and girls' clubs or community organizations dedicated to helping needy children. These groups often recycle them with new plaques and present them to at-risk children, supplying a much-needed boost in self-esteem. The same destination might be suitable for unwanted **bicycles** and **sporting equipment.**

Wigs and **hairpieces** can be cleaned and are often accepted by some charities supporting medical facilities — or the hospitals themselves — whose patients suffer hair loss due to medical treatments.

Once again, when all else fails and time is of the essence, look under "hauling" or "waste disposal" in your local Yellow Pages or through an online search engine or contact www.1800gotjunk.com, www.1800ecohaul.com, or www.callandhaul.com. These for-profit firms with many local outlets will generally take the items no one else will — for a fee. On a positive note, you don't have to sort the stuff.

DEALING WITH "SERIOUS" COLLECTIONS

For several years I collected anything that had a French fleur-de-lis on it: candles, boxes, stationery, jewelry, napkin rings. You name it, I owned it if it had that distinctive, three-pronged insignia emblazoned on the item. Eventually my household became so seriously overrun with this symbol of French civilization and the American city of New Orleans that my husband begged for a moratorium. Even *I* was starting to tire of the look, so I ultimately complied with his request and informed my friends of the "freeze."

That brings us to the question of what to do with this and similar collections: framed family photographs, ceramic frogs, Lalique figurines, classic cars, Civil War weaponry, silver mustard pots, antique linens, men's cuff links, women's beaded purses . . . and, lest we forget, nifty assortments of Mardi Gras feather boas!

Our legacy as a hunter-gatherer species is all too apparent when one considers the fascinating (and frightening) list of things people are prone to assemble under one roof. This can become a stumbling block, especially when you're seriously committed to simplifying your surroundings. Such accumulations of "dust catchers," as one friend irreverently dubs them, can begin to give a person major heartburn — or heartache — depending on one's point of view.

Since I ultimately gained control over my fleur-de-lis addiction, I feel this gives me the wherewithal to ask what *you* are planning to do with the possessions that you, or someone you live with, have so diligently amassed over the years?

Not sure?

Well, that's a definite reason to move on to the next chapter of our rightsizing saga, wherein we fine-tune our selections, both mundane and treasured.

Chapter 8

Step 4 — Fine-Tune

Cull those collections — big and small

CORRALLING ABUNDANCE

Not only is America the world's largest consumerist economy, we are also the world's foremost collectors, whether of rubber bands and tuna-fish cans (like my late great-grandmother) or antique Santa Claus figurines, Spode dessert plates, frilly lace mantillas, duck decoys, or classic cars. There is just something compelling about owning *a lot* of something that "speaks to us."

Whether you are choosing among multiple examples of vintage dolls, old LP records, or run-of-the-mill multiples of fishing poles, frying pans, or frayed blankets, the winnowing process is the same.

- Do I love it?
- Do I use it?
- Do I have the *proper* place for it in my new environment?

So, before we get to the serious treasures, let's look first at our "collections" of mundane household items. We've already discussed corralling things — bringing together like with like — such as furniture, home furnishings, glassware, china, flatware, kitchenware, luggage, and home appliances, choosing only the best, and properly and appropriately disposing of the rest.

The same approach can be taken with linens, artwork, pantry items, games, sporting equipment, kids' possessions, and that real toughie, family photographs. In the next chapter we will deal with clothing and accessories, papers and files, and the entire range of home-office supplies.

Let's first consider the items that can only be considered humdrum. We'll get to the guilt-producing possessions (unwanted gifts, children's artwork) in due time.

HOW MANY BLANKETS CAN YOU SLEEP UNDER AT ONE TIME?

As mentioned, one of the simplest organizing principles is the well-known rubric gather like with like. When trying to decide what to keep and what to toss, collect *all* your linens, or *all* your can openers, or *all* your board games in one place and survey the group as if it were a collection.

As a first step, cull out the items with tears, nicks, dents, missing pieces (jigsaw puzzles are not exempt!), and imperfections that limit their use. Put them in the boxes or clear plastic bags labeled TRASH or REPAIR, depending.

Then consider the duplicates. If you have three ice-cream scoops, four varieties of curry powder, eight packs of playing cards, pick the one or two you like best, or most, or simply admire. Put the remainders in the containers labeled DONATE, GIFT, SELL, RECYCLE. The objects you love and you're certain will be used will either stay where they are, get relegated to the TRANSFER box to be put in a better spot in your house, or — if you're moving — will be tagged to go onto the moving truck. Bestow the "edited" items on friends and family as soon as you can or send them to a charity, consignment store, auction house, or recycling center. You can also put them in a tag sale or sell them online.

FIRST PASS, SECOND PASS

Think you're through with these household items? Not so fast! Look again. Among the items you kept, which ones do you really use? Once more ask yourself if the object you have in your hand is beautiful. Does it have enough sentimental value, today, to warrant its inclusion in the next phase of your life? Is it valuable enough to be kept for its resale potential or merit as a gift?

Once you've made your *final* final decisions, send the most recently culled items on their way immediately to their proper destinations, just as you did on the first pass.

I can almost hear you say, "But what about sending some stuff to storage?"

That subject deserves a discussion all its own (see chapter 12), so we won't deal with it here. The object is to eliminate, once and for all, the possessions in your life that don't serve a genuine purpose anymore. And don't forget, there's always 1-800-Got-Junk or its local equivalent, the town dump.

So those are the general rightsizing principles for things like sheets and towels, puzzles and games, jars of nails and screws. If it comes in multiples, think seriously about when you last had the items in your hand and employed them in some useful way.

But what about the really difficult categories? Items such as books and all the little mementos that represent a lifetime of travel and good times? Or the hardest one of all — kindergarten artwork that once belonged to you, your child, grandchild, or grandparents?

Let's get down to specifics.

HONING YOUR TREASURES TO KEEP THE GEMS

Collections are officially defined by *Webster's* as "an accumulation of objects gathered for study, comparison, or exhibition." I would add to this that these objects are also "accumulated" for the pure pleasure of enjoying them within the confines of one's home.

Like many of us, I've never considered myself a serious collector, but I certainly have been know to fall into the "some's good, more's better" camp. A devotee of historical novelists Daphne du Maurier and Alexandre Dumas, I had been buying British, French, and American historical fiction for years. Suddenly I had an entire bookcase full of them, and before long the volumes were spilling onto the floor in alarming piles.

Then, not long after I'd cured my fleur-de-lis addiction, I also began to amass red-and-black-feathered Mardi Gras masks. Within a year I was displaying some thirty-five of them to great effect in our blood red New Orleans–style dining room. Unfortunately it was a look that wasn't going to translate well when we decided to move to our waterfront abode, with its neutral "beachy" color palette and a combined living room/dining room that fronted San Francisco Bay.

Suddenly I had several "collections" for which I needed to find new homes.

Woe is me! I loved those feather masks and swashbuckling novels.

As for the historicals, I was on to new writing projects far removed from eighteenth-century Britain, and we had a limited number of bookshelves in our new environment.

Before I could decide on what to do with all those volumes, the feathered masks, or the things I owned stamped with fleurs-de-lis, I had to ask myself why I was attracted to such objects.

Collections tend to link us to people, places, and periods in our lives that are meaningful to us, so before you can make decisions about the way they fit — or don't fit — into the next chapter of your life, it's helpful to understand what they represent to you on a psychological level. Then you can decide if you absolutely must find a place for the entire collection or for just a representative sample of what you have amassed.

In my own case, my father adored swashbuckling films starring Errol Flynn. We used to share movie dates in Hollywood when I was quite young where he would take me to see the picture, followed by a trip to a local ice-cream parlor. There, my-father-the-published-author would expound on the original novels from which many of the films were made, noting with a wag of his index finger, "Just remember, it all starts with the *writer* and the words he puts on the printed page!"

These were magical times for me, and clearly my collection of historical novels was not merely a tool of my trade but a carryover from childhood, a reminder of paternal affection, just as my Mardi Gras masks and fleur-de-lis candleholders and decorative pillows served as reminders of the wonderful times I had as a frequent visitor to the French Quarter in New Orleans when I was writing a novel set in that city.

The sad fact was that if we were going to rightsize our lives into a little more than 1,200 square feet (which was what we wanted to do so we could travel more and work less), I had some hard decisions to make.

Since I hadn't read any of the historicals in more than five years, I forced myself to cull out my absolute favorites, put them in the new house on a shelf (along with a framed picture of my heroine, du Maurier), and give the rest to my local library, where they happily reside should I ever want to read one. For me, keeping a couple of my favorite novels is enough to maintain the wonderful memories I have of my father.

On the other hand, I once wrote a book with the word "swans" in the title and for years received replicas in porcelain, silver, glass, and even rhinestones of those long-necked birds. I truly appreciated the thoughtfulness of the gift givers, and many of the swans were beautiful and delighted me. As with the fleurs-de-lis, however, there is a limit to how many representations of this particular creature a person can possibly enjoy, especially when it comes to swan salt-and-pepper shakers, metal bookmarks, and clay flowerpots.

On my last move I kept only a swan pin from a good friend and a crystal figurine that my husband had given me. After all, *Island of the Swans* had been published nearly twenty years earlier, and it was truly a case of "been there, done that, got the swan." I simply did not have the emotional investment in the swans anymore, so I made my choices accordingly.

TRUE TREASURES

Ask the same question of yourself: why do you fancy the things you've chosen to assemble as a group? Once you know why you love certain objects enough to collect a lot of them in one place, the next thing you want to know is: are you still emotionally invested in the collections you've assembled?

As we all know, the one constant in life is change, and with change comes the need to divest oneself of some of our possessions that don't have the same meaning they once did, especially when they come in hard-to-manage groups.

So, as you think about the collections in your life — be they big or small, serious or lighthearted, valuable or worthless — ask yourself if there are still reasons to hold on to them.

Perhaps you're still torn, despite some serious soul-searching. Fortunately, there are two other ways to think about groups of items you may own. First ask yourself if you would be tempted to sell your collection if someone offered you a lot of (or even decent) money? Second, if a hurricane or tornado or flood swept away your entire collection, which items would you mourn?

If some of the reasons in the "Top Ten Reasons to Liquidate a Collection" box resonate with you, or you would be even the *tiniest* bit tempted to sell your collection should someone suddenly offer you good money for it, perhaps it's time to consider becoming a "rightsized" type of collector: *hold on to only the pieces of your collection that mean the most to you.*

TOP TEN REASONS TO LIQUIDATE A COLLECTION

1. **The thrill of the chase no longer excites.**
2. **There are nicks or pieces missing, so the set will never be complete.**
3. **The set is complete, it might have value, and the money would be nice.**
4. **Trading is no longer the fun it once was.**
5. **The collection isn't worth the room it takes up.**
6. **Other interests have replaced the passion for collecting.**
7. **No one else in the family is interested in maintaining the collection.**
8. **It's gotten too expensive to keep collecting.**
9. **One or two items would be as satisfying as keeping the entire collection.**
10. **There is simply NO room to house so many similar items.**

A POSTSCRIPT ABOUT FEATHERED MASKS AND OTHER TREASURES

On the top of a tall, wooden cupboard the color of cinnabar stands the pair of feathered Mardi Gras masks I kept from my original collection of thirty-five. One is bright scarlet, and the other is a vibrant hue of azure with gold-painted filigree, designed to be worn with sweeping red-and-turquoise taffeta monks' robes with hoods edged in yards of matching tulle ruffs. These ensembles were worn by my husband and me in the St. Anne's Parade that wound its way through the French Quarter in February 2003.

It was a wild and unforgettable day. In fact, it was one of the most exciting moments of our lives to hear the bands play and the crowds roar their approval as we strutted down Royal Street.

My two remaining masks now flank a gold-framed picture of my husband and me surrounded by our friends, who are also costumed in multihued taffeta robes. We'd dubbed ourselves the Rainbow Inquisition, and the masks now conjure up a cherished memory of that joyous Mardi Gras morning before Hurricane Katrina washed away so much of the true New Orleans.

I realize now that I picked the best of the best when I selected what to keep and what to pass on, and I've never been sorry for the choices I made. I could bear to let the other masks go because the two that I retained represent the perfection of a passing moment. It's all I need of the original collection to make me happy.

This, I think, personifies the rightsizing philosophy: select what you love, what you have room for in your new life, and what gives you a glow of contentment.

If you're *still* not ready to start that process yet, don't fret. Only a fellow collector could understand. However, things may change.

THE "SERIOUS" COLLECTOR

The word *collection* came into the English language in the fourteenth century, when life wasn't quite as hardscrabble as in earlier days and people began to have the luxury of owning more than one of a particular item. Monarchs, aristocrats, and religious orders were the first serious collectors, and as wealth spread to other classes, the race to amass material goods — both artistic and mundane — began.

By the twenty-first century, especially in developed nations, collecting had become a part of daily life. It included everything from Elizabeth Taylor's diamond stash to the Beanie Babies amassed by every neighborhood kid.

Many wonderful collections are valuable to their owners but not to the world at large. Those who eventually must deliberate about collections that could fetch significant money on the open market will have to call on all their powers to prune them.

Here are a few questions the serious collector can ask:

- Do I still enjoy looking at the items I now own?
- Do I continue to care for them scrupulously?
- Do I actually have room to put them on display in my current home?
- Will I have room for them in any future home?
- Even if I do have room, is their display the best use of available space, given my current needs and desires?

If the answers are "maybe not," I want you to meet a friend of mine.

LAURIE GRAD'S COOKBOOKS

Laurie Burrows Grad, in her late fifties (and looking forty-something, if not younger!), is a food writer, author of four cookbooks, and former host of her own television cooking show. Lining every wall throughout her house were bookshelves, and on those bookshelves sat more than seven thousand cookbooks, the tools of her trade.

One day she looked around her home and realized that if there ever were an earthquake in Southern California, where she lives with her husband of thirty-nine years, "the library could be lethal. There was a really good chance we could all be killed by flying cookbooks!"

She was making a joke, although there was a ring of truth because Laurie and Peter recently became the proud grandparents of a little boy and live not far from an offshoot of the San Andreas Fault. They entertain their grandson one day a week, and he often sleeps over in their guestroom, surrounded by floor-to-ceiling cookbooks, of course.

"I wanted to make a room for him when he comes to visit, and *he* certainly doesn't want to read about coq au vin!"

That got her thinking. "I wanted more space throughout the house. The cookbooks were on shelves in the den, our bedroom, the room we'd turned into a gym, and they even lined the hall! They were nice 'decoration' in our house for a long time, but now I use the Internet for research (Laurie is an editor with epicurus.com), and if I need to reference a recipe, it's all online . . . *Gourmet Magazine, Bon Appétit* — everything I need."

And besides, she adds, "I'm moving into a new phase of my life. I had to dust all those seven thousand cookbooks," she points out, and she was getting good and sick of it.

And then she had a brainstorm. She was coming up on her fortieth college reunion at the University of Pennsylvania.

"I decided to see if I could donate the books *now*. Why do it when I'm dead?"

Turns out the library had started a collection of rare books in the culinary arts where historians could learn about recipes, food philosophics, and lifestyle attitudes of the past. Laurie's titles, going back to an 1886 edition of Sarah Tyson Rover's *Mrs. Rover's Cookbook*, were welcomed with open arms as a wonderful addition to the library's existing collection.

"They even sent a huge truck and a bunch of nice men to pack and take away the one hundred eighty-seven boxes!" she said with a grin. She'd had a well-respected appraiser evaluate the haul and as a result will receive a tax deduction for her admirable largesse.

But didn't she keep *any* of her cookbooks, I asked, thinking nostalgically about my own collection of historical novels?

"A few."

But wasn't it hard to let go of her mini collection of fabulous Junior League cookbooks she'd gathered from all over the country?

"Yes," Laurie admits. "They reflect our culture as well as our country's food. I used to get great ideas from them for recipes of my own. But I'm not going to write any more cookbooks, I don't think, and the way I cook now is totally different. I don't look at cookbooks for inspiration anymore. I go to the market to see what's fresh, and *then* I cook."

But what about all the other types of cookbooks? The big, beautiful picture books, and the ones by friends and colleagues. Weren't they equally hard to let go?

Laurie laughs. "I got my clutter buddy, cookbook author Diane Worthington, to come over and help me pick out the few books I was going to keep. We'd look at a book, and I'd say, 'Yes!' and she'd say, 'No, no, NO!' Then she'd relent and say, 'Okay, you can keep that one.' "

In the end, Laurie retained about fifty of the original seven thousand cookbooks. "One good one representing each type of food — Italian, French, Chinese, and so forth — and I kept some classics like *The Joy of Cooking*. I kept all of Diane's books, and a few *Cook's Illustrated* magazines, and my own four, naturally."

As both Grad and Worthington know, cookbooks go out of date, and new culinary philosophies come in. "Nobody *sane* is eating so much butter and cream," notes Laurie, "meaning that butter-and-cream recipes never get looked at much."

How did she feel now that the books live three thousand miles away from her kitchen?

"I felt so *relieved* when I saw that truck pull away. I felt FREE! I can actually see stuff in my house now. I can put picture frames with family photos on some of the bookshelves, and it warms everything up. And now that all those books are gone, our old guestroom is being completely revamped. It will soon have twin beds for my grandson and his little friend so they can have sleepovers and give their parents a break. And not only do I have room for my grandson and framed pictures, we can fit DVDs, and even other books we never displayed: mysteries, novels, biographies. We can see what we have. It's divine, it's open, it's *nice!*"

Laurie also was wise enough to send the notice of her library donation to all her friends, "as a subtle way of putting everyone on alert *not to give me any more cookbooks!*"

WHAT'S ON *YOUR* SHELVES?

Not everyone will have to wrestle with accumulated items that number in the thousands, but even rightsizers with modest collections of original art or lead toy soldiers are likely to confront some of the same issues.

- What do you keep?
- What do you release?
- Where will your former treasures ultimately reside?

For hard-core collections, the part of Laurie Grad's tale that is specially instructive, I think, is to observe that she was able and willing to recognize that her life and her profession had changed. She wanted different things — space in her house used in a different way, fewer things to dust, a place for her new grandson to play and sleep. She also recognized how her own profession had been transformed both by healthier eating trends and by the way the Internet enabled her to gather whatever information she needed to ply her trade as a food expert.

She also paid attention to what she was feeling about those hulking seven thousand volumes on shelves throughout her house. She wasn't enjoying reading the books or even appreciating their usefulness as decoration. They had served a good purpose but no longer gave her the pleasure they once did. She was ready to pass them on to people — students and scholars at a beloved institution she'd attended — who could make excellent use of their contents. She would even receive a tax break!

LESSONS FROM LAURIE

Laurie knew that her decision about the 187 cartons of books she gave away was the right one for her because she felt a sense of liberation once the truck pulled away from her front curb.

The ability to recognize shifts in one's environment and adapt to them is akin to Darwin's observations of the natural world and the subject of his *On the Origin of Species*. We survive and thrive when we adapt to the reality staring us in the face and then find a way to make it work in our favor.

If not we may stagnate, get cranky, and end up feeling stuck.

So, make a survey of your collections with new eyes. Do they still serve you well, please you, intrigue you, teach you about a subject that continues to hold fascination?

If so, that's great! Hold on tight.

Or are they weighing you down? Have you outgrown them? Are you ready to relinquish part of them, keeping a few pieces that still speak to you? Would you consider giving them to someone or some place that would appreciate them or perhaps consider trading some or all of them for something you do want in your home as it is now? How about collecting for a grandchild or a friend? Do you have the time, energy, and motivation to sell your collection through an auction house or piece by piece on eBay?

There are many solutions to the question of keeping or passing on "serious" collections. Pick the one that will result in a feeling of "Yes! This is the way I want it to be."

FINDING GOOD HOMES FOR TREASURES AND MAKING A PROFIT

Most of us are familiar with the sense of relief we feel when a truck from a recognized charity rolls up and loads up items we can no longer use and gives us a tax form for our trouble or the joy when 1-800-Got-Junk arrives and hauls away gnarly things like leftover shingles and flat tires — possessions we can't cope with disposing of "properly" ourselves.

In chapter 10 we will consider in more depth using professionals — such as estate-sale stagers, auction houses, and consignment stores — to help us sell our surplus goods that still have value.

Here we'll deal with simpler situations. For people with the time and inclination, a new world has opened up with online selling on the Internet. However, for those overwhelmed by the pressure of meeting a deadline to move, there is a hassle-free way to sell goods spawned by niche entrepreneurs on the Web. Companies such as Snappy Auctions (www.snappyauctions.com), QuikDrop (www.quikdrop.com), or NuMarkets (www.numarkets.com) are in business to do the hard work for you — for a fee.

Here's how it works. If there is a franchise for one of these outfits in your area, you take the goods you wish to sell to a drop-off location. The company then coordinates the entire process of photographing your goods, uploading digital pictures to eBay, managing the sale online, and shipping the items to the ultimate buyers. When the sale is complete, you'll receive a check, minus a fat commission of 15 to 40 percent, depending on the company and number of services you choose.

The other online sales site is www.craigslist.com, encompassing more than 190 metropolitan Web sites in all fifty states. Both eBay and craigslist also have online "trading assistants" who get paid to help you with the process of coordinating the listing and selling of your stuff on these virtual auction sites. In fact, many people simply hold "virtual" tag sales instead of garage or yard sales with help from an experienced trading assistant.

If you locate a Web-savvy seller in your neighborhood, there are several services they might offer. Some have storefronts where you drop off your goods and they do the rest; others will pick up the goods from their clients and then expose the wares to millions of people, instead of just a few folks from the neighborhood. To find such a person, type "online trading assistants" in a search engine, and many choices will pop up.

Regardless of the method you use for placing your wares for sale online, ask for references from previous customers or check the company's "feedback" feature, which offers customer ratings of their performance. Some of these companies or individual trading assistants will even facilitate your donating items to charities and provide you with a tax receipt in the bargain.

PHOTOS, PHOTOS EVERYWHERE

Nearly every person in the Western world collects snapshots, so there's no avoiding tackling this problem anymore. You have to deal with the mountains of pictures you own and have added to for eons.

There are no quick fixes here. If your picture albums don't have acid-free paper, the images affixed to them will eventually "die." One woman I know had eighteen fat albums poking out on her bottom bookshelf. The plastic slip covers stuck together, the pictures' colors were fading, and each page had scores of school-picture duplicates of her children, nieces and nephews, and grandchildren.

I asked her if she ever looked at the albums.

"Rarely," she admitted. "They're such a mess, they just depress me."

So here was an entire length of a wall taken up by objects that the owner considered a downer!

No, no, no! This is not the rightsizing way!

I warned her that taming this problem would take more than a few days but that she could accomplish this feat a little at a time while watching the nightly news on TV. I suggested that in a series of small work sessions she remove the photos, one by one, from the faded albums and musty shoe boxes. Due to the inhospitable plastic covers and sticky backing, some photos would have to be sacrificed (they were toast anyway). Those that weren't stuck or otherwise damaged could be slipped into paper envelopes (or plastic or waxed sandwich bags, if she was going to complete the process quickly) until they could be reorganized.

As she removed the images from the albums and boxes, however, I urged to her to ask herself these essential questions:

- Do I recognize the person?
- Do I like the person?
- Do I find the photo of the subject(s) flattering?
- Do I have more than one copy of this photo?
- Do I have fond memories of the event?

If a photo didn't make the cut, she always had the option to toss it or give it away (including all those duplicates and negatives) and create a new album with the photos that were keepers, affixing them on acid-free paper when she had time. Meanwhile she could store the "liberated" photos she'd put in the envelopes in two archival boxes available from a photography or art-supply store.

She set up headings such as "family events," "trips," "ancestors," etc. Then she removed the pictures from their temporary envelopes and stood each photo that actually meant something to her on its edge, filed in the proper category. The images would remain safe until she got around to placing them in new albums with the all-important acid-free sheets.

If she ever wants a copy, she can have a particular photo professionally scanned and printed or do it herself on her computer. Another perhaps more radical option for permanent storage is to digitally scan the culled photos onto CDs or store them in cyberspace on such photo sites as kodakgallery.com, smugmug.com, or snapfish.com and then toss out the paper versions (gasp!).

One way to ameliorate the job of taming large photo collections is to tell yourself it's simply going to take some time and do it in stages, preferably while you're doing something else like watching television or listening to music. Tackling the job with a photo buddy can actually be fun as you reminisce about old times, cry a little bit over any lost friends or family members, and cackle when you deep-six some images of yourself that you'd rather not bestow on posterity.

A FOREST OF FRAMED PHOTOS

Remember Tom and Tina Green in chapter 7, the couple that remarried and eventually moved into a new house, merging their belongings, including an estimated *ten thousand* photographs?

"In Tom's old house, he had a large galvanized tin wall to which scores of photos in Lucite picture frames were adhered magnetically," recalls Tina, a former wedding photographer. "I mean, we had *tons* of photos!"

It took them several years, but now most of the ten thousand images are digitized and available on their computers, including the photos that were once framed on the wall they never got around to replicating in their new place.

Look around your home. How many framed photographs do you have? (At one point in my life, I had sixty-four . . .)

A stylish gathering of silver-, brass-, or wood-framed photos clustered on the grand piano might look fabulous in one house but come across as excess clutter in another home, where there's no piano and not enough shelf space for all the picture frames.

The answer? First, give careful consideration to the space you are in or will inhabit. Pick out the appropriate number of your most beautiful frames and, as houseguests come and go or as the mood strikes you, rotate images from among those pictures stored in your archival photo boxes. I have been known to slip a picture of my mother-in-law or friend into a prominent frame before her visit and then substitute another after we bid farewell. That way I don't hurt their feelings but can keep the number of framed pictures to a manageable level when space is at a premium.

WHAT'S ON YOUR WALLS (OR HIDDEN FROM SIGHT)?

Think back to the first piece of art — original or otherwise — you ever hung on the wall of a place you lived. Do you still own it? Is it a part of your decor?

Poster or Picasso, tastes change over time, and chances are good you don't still possess the first image that caught your fancy when you were younger. What we love and want on our walls at midlife and beyond is as subjective a decision as it was when we were twenty. The difficulties begin when you realize you'd just as soon leave behind framed objects you've had for years, even if some of it is artwork you (or friends and relatives) created.

The same holds true for other kinds of art: collages, pottery, quilts, sculpture, weavings, any form of creative expression. Somehow, knowing how hard someone worked to bring the object to life makes it seem criminal just to toss it or even give the piece away.

There are a couple of options open to art mavens when there are too many pieces to hang on a wall or put in a bookshelf. See the box below.

CURATING YOUR ART COLLECTION

- Set aside at least a half a day to go through your art.
- Assemble as much of your art in one area as practical to do your survey.
- Compare your wall space to the size and amount of your hanging art.
- Compare your shelf space to the size and amount of your remaining art.
- Tag the immediate "keepers" with a green dot or sticky note.
- Make a simple "blueprint" of where the keepers will be placed.
- Tag the obvious "rejects."
- Photograph the art objects rendered homeless and store the images digitally or create a special album before finding them new homes.

ORPHANED ART

The method for disposing of your artistic orphans that no longer suit you depends upon the time available.

You can sell them privately or through online or physical auction houses. If the art has established value, it's probably a good idea to have it appraised first.

You can gift friends and relatives, but try not to feel insulted if their tastes don't match yours. You may be surprised, however, that a piece of art a child has grown up with or a friend has enjoyed when visiting your house — even one of little monetary value — might be welcomed with enthusiasm. As long as you keep your expectations in check, this could be an excellent way to find a good home for a treasure you loved.

You can even hold a mini art show of your own and invite people over for coffee and say, "I'm looking for new — and possibly permanent — foster homes for these images." Whether the art is a gift or a loan is up to you, but you can certainly set some ground rules. Tell your guests to negotiate among themselves or pick a number from a hat and select what they'd like in that order in a round-robin.

Another choice is to consider donating valuable art objects to institutions that are qualified to give you a tax deduction. If your possessions have humbler origins, consider offering them to a senior center, community organization, school art department, or charity auction.

GIFT HORSE ART

Not everyone has encountered the problem of owning an object of art that you're ready to pass on except for the fact that you know the artist. When this occurs it's a big problem and one that can be handled a variety of ways.

Offer to give it back. This is not as insulting as it may sound if you explain that you're making a change in your living environment and you want to give the artist the "right of first refusal" before you offer the piece to your children or friends or put it up for sale.

Offer it to a relative or friend. Again, don't be cheesed off if they politely decline. The piece may not be to their taste, or like you, they may not have the room.

Sell or donate. You can find new homes for these pieces the same way you can for your other art objects. Release them and make room for your new life!

BUT LITTLE JOEY MADE IT WHEN HE WAS THREE!

There are certain objects in life you pretty much keep forever. My son's little handprint mashed into clay held paper clips on my desk for years. Now it's wrapped in tissue in a box with a knit suit he wore on his first birthday in case he someday has a child of his own. If that makes me an imperfect rightsizer, so be it!

But the boxes of his artwork from age two to thirteen? Most of it went into the recycle bin in the course of our several moves, and I felt a lump in my throat every time it happened . . . and still do when I think about it.

Some of the same options apply to this kind of emotion-laden art as to the rest of your holdings:

- Offer the "collection" to the artist first.
- Save a few of the "best" and put them in a labeled folder to file.
- Photograph the cutest remaining artwork and file it or create an album for a future gift.
- Have your own little "farewell" ceremony before releasing it.
- If the artist is still a child, dispose of what you must in private. You don't want to demotivate any budding Michelangelos.

WHAT'S LEFT TO RIGHTSIZE?

There may be a scary world lurking inside your cupboards and file drawers, not to mention within boxes stuffed with documents stashed in your home office. Not to worry, though. You'll see in the next chapter that there's a rightsizing answer for those, too.

Chapter 9

Step 5 — Pare Down

Clothing, paper, personal files, and the perfect home office

MORE FINE-TUNING: CLOTHING AND ACCESSORIES

As you may have gathered by now, certain basic principles hold true for paring down the many items you own. In case you need a refresher, the essence is: survey what you have and *pick the best of the best.* The goal is to end up with only the household possessions you need and love, regardless of the category from which you're choosing.

When it comes to the specifics, however, some categories deserve special attention and require a slightly different approach. We saw this in the previous chapter when we dealt with unwieldy amounts of photos and personal collections that sometimes pull on our heartstrings.

In my rightsizing workshops the two other "killer" categories most people consider daunting are clothing and the piles of ubiquitous paper that are the bane of our supposedly "paperless" society. The paper tiger can be tamed, but first let's focus on the issue of surplus wearables.

CLOSET RIGHTSIZERS

Clothing is a category that tends to seriously confound us when we stand in front of our closet wondering how in the world we're going to weed out the best. If you're like most of us, there's so much to choose from.

Fashion expert and veteran retailer Linda Daniels provides professional assistance to people who need what she calls "wardrobe rehab." She has delighted audiences with a lively presentation called "How to Sort Out Your Clothes Closet, Jettison the Bad Stuff, Keep the Right Stuff, and Look Like a Million Bucks!" Linda is a walking advertisement for the notion that wearing only the clothes you love is, in her words, "a gift you give to yourself." Slender, chic, and enthusiastic about all aspects of fashion, her closet is of modest proportions and contains far fewer items than would seem de rigueur for a woman of her keen sartorial interests. Her clothes are grouped by type and color: slacks together, jackets together, and so on. She tends to favor black and gray, with splashes of burgundy or blue, and her accessories fit nicely within this scheme.

So what's her secret?

Daniels believes that the best way for men or women to rightsize their wardrobe is to set aside a specific time to tackle your closets. "Put it on your calendar and make an appointment with yourself" to go through every single item that lives on a hanger, in a drawer, or — heaven forbid — on the floor.

Even better, says Linda, recruit a clutter buddy to help you out. She's found this is often the best way to cut through the "I might wear it someday" syndrome, even though the garment in question hasn't been worn in three years. A good friend is usually more objective and will tend to be honest about whether that blouse is chic or makes you look like a frump or will give you the news that the style of a sports jacket stuffed in the back of your closet went out with the Bee Gees.

She offers a chart in her workshops to illustrate her three-step approach to culling through and purging items that either don't fit properly, are out of style, need mending, or are perfectly good but never get worn "because they simply don't work for *you*." (See the "Send, Mend, or Blend" box.)

Linda, the fashionista, also suggests that before you start tearing apart your closet or drawers, you should first choose one or two clothing items that you both love and wear. "And I'm not talking about our favorite warmup suits, but outfits that make you feel at the top of your game when you've got them on."

Then she recommends asking yourself why they make you feel good when you wear them. "It's *that* zingy feeling that should accom-

SEND, MEND, OR BLEND

Send

Send the clothing that no longer works for you out of your house. That includes items that are not the right size, style, vintage, or type for the life you lead *now.*

Mend

Clean, alter, or repair your new, smaller wardrobe, which consists of only the clothing you love and wear, or *would* wear if it were in good shape.

Blend

Put together outfits and make a written inventory of your creations. Jot down a shopping list for fill-ins that could make your wardrobe even better — purchases you'll make when you have the time and budget.

pany every clothing item you decide to keep in your rehabbed wardrobe," she urges. "These are the *winners.* Anything less is a wardrobe *loser.* If an item of clothing is yellowed, tired, limp, torn, too tight, too loose, minus a button, or out of date, that is exactly how it's going to make *you* look and feel."

Prior to physically purging your closet, decide first on where the rejects are going. Linda suggests you "pre-cycle" by researching the names, addresses, and phone numbers of local charities and consignment shops, along with friends, family, and colleagues who might be eager recipients of your better-quality castoffs.

"After you've decided what you're not going to keep, call and ask if they'd be interested in the sorts of things you're selling or giving away. Have the boxes or hangers or shopping bags *ready* so the items will leave your house as quickly as possible."

The next step is to schedule a couple of hours to edit the "loser" items in your closet. Write the following mantra on a sticky note and paste it to your closet door:

- Do I wear it?
- Do I love it?

- Is it flattering and does it fit well?
- Do I have something to wear with it?

THE DARK SIDES OF THE CLOSET

It's never easy to admit we make mistakes, but every closet has a few doozies. You know what they are! Here's a hint: the tag may still be on them, or you haven't even taken them off the hanger in a year or two. These are not clothes we love, so it's time to send them on their way. You'll make faster progress on your closet clean out if you quickly identify the "loser" items of clothing and set them aside.

The first step is simply to go through everything you own piece by piece. You can do this in short sessions: first tackle your slacks and jackets. Then, if you're a woman, survey your blouses and sweaters; men should go through their dress and polo shirts. Later, assess shoes, socks, underwear, and accessories like belts, briefcases, or purses.

Put the rejects in separate piles, according to type. Once culled, place the segregated items on hangers or neatly folded in shopping bags or boxes. Absolute throwaways nobody would wear go into trash bags destined for the recycling facility.

Apply close scrutiny to the following:

- Outfits not worn in a year or two
- Clothing that's too big or too small (if you lose weight, you'll celebrate by adding some new items that complement your new figure)
- Clothing that's woefully out of style and not likely to cycle back into fashion any time soon
- Clothing that is torn, worn, soiled, or generally something you'd be embarrassed to be seen wearing in public

Employ the same system you did with your housewares: gather like with like, choose the best, and put the rest in appropriate containers labeled: TRASH, GIFT, DONATE, SELL, REPAIR, RECYCLE, or DON'T HAVE A CLUE. Once decisions are made, remove the closet rejects from your house as quickly as you can and drop them at their assigned destinations.

Linda reminds her clients, "You are *sending* all these wardrobe losers on their way to places where they may be winners for someone else. Whatever you do, don't let the rejects hang around your house. Put them in your car and then deliver them promptly to their new homes."

Linda suggests one added step. "Before you banish all the losers, try on the clothing you've chosen to *keep* just one more time. Be sure each piece truly looks good on you. When in doubt, I say let it go and put it with the other 'get 'em outta heres.' "

In Linda's world, closet space is very valuable. "You stand in front of your closet at least once a day and have to make decisions about what to wear. I want the choices to be fun. I want you to walk out of your home feeling like a million bucks."

CLOTHING ON THE MEND

The next step on the path to a rightsized wardrobe is the MEND category, which comes after the SEND phase has been completed.

Sure, it's easy to overlook those little mend or alteration projects, but even though people can't see that double hook that's unraveling, *you* are going to feel better when it's repaired. Either fix those frayed hems and replace missing buttons yourself or send the clothing to a professional. There's nothing worse than when the dry cleaner sends back an item with those little notes that the spot cannot be removed. If you have garments like that, or you aren't willing to get something mended, you must get rid of it!

BUT THIS GARMENT IS PERFECTLY GOOD!

What if an item of clothing is in okay condition and worth a lot of money, but you just can't see yourself wearing it? Truly one of the great recycling stories I came across in my travels was that of a "socially conscious" woman who had a fur coat come into her life through a bequest from a rather tall, elderly acquaintance. The skins, when new, were worth more than her entire wardrobe. The problem was, besides the garment being woefully out of style and way too big for her, she just didn't see herself sporting a mink coat in public.

The winter had been a chilly one, which prompted an inspired solution: she took the large-size garment to a seamstress, along with the appropriate amount of fine tartan fabric. What resulted was a spectacular, wool-lined, mink throw that is now draped over the chaise lounge in her den. Her total cost was around $300, and she'd created something useful, beautiful, valuable, *and* sentimental!

If that answer seems too expensive or self-serving, you can always pass on fur clothing to the nonprofit organization People for the Ethical Treatment of Animals, to be used to line the cages of orphaned creatures that will one day be well enough to be returned to the wild. (For mailing instructions call 757-622-PETA). In the realm of rightsizing, there's always a satisfying answer to virtually every dilemma.

THE PERFECTLY BLENDED WARDROBE

So now you have only the clothes you love and wear hanging in your closet. (Well, let's hope you've nearly reached that state of perfection.) Part of the BLEND phase of wardrobe rehab is to put together "new" outfits from what you've kept and make a shopping list for a few things that could spice up your rehabbed, leaner wardrobe.

To make sure you've ended up with enough of the kind of clothing you need in your current lifestyle, make two lists. One is an inventory of your newly winnowed wardrobe. The second list details the categories of clothing you need, given your current daily routine. (See the "This-Is-Your-Life Clothing Lists" box.) Consulting both lists, ask yourself if you've kept (or even own) the kind of clothing that best suits your lifestyle these days. You may need additional pairs of yoga pants rather than outfits to wear in the office. Perhaps you can replace those high heels with the lightweight hiking boots you've had your eye on.

PIE-CHART SMARTS

Linda Daniels has adopted the "pie-chart" method for further analyzing the wardrobe needs of her clients. With the help of a circle divided into sections, each labeled with a type of clothing and a

THIS-IS-YOUR-LIFE CLOTHING LISTS	
RIGHTSIZER A (works full time outside the home)	*RIGHTSIZER B (retired or works from home)*
Office clothes	Office clothes
Pant suits — 4	Pant suits — 2
Cotton and silk blouses — 8	Blouses — 4
Quality T-shirts and turtlenecks — 10	Quality Ts and turtlenecks — 5
Casual clothes	Casual clothes
Jeans — 2	Jeans — 2
Slacks — 2	Slacks and sweats — 6
Pullover sweaters — 3	Pullover sweaters — 7
Casual shirts — 4	Casual shirts — 6
T-shirts — 6	T-shirts — 10
Warmup suit — 1	Warmup suit — 3
Dressy and black tie	Dressy and black tie
Ball gowns — 2	Ball gowns — 0
Long skirt — 1	Long skirt — 1
Dressy tops — 3	Dressy tops — 2
Cocktail dresses — 3	Cocktail dresses — 1

These lists contemplate the needs of two women and are far from complete but may suggest a way of thinking about the kind of wardrobe that suits your present way of life. Men should also detail every category of clothing they use, including special-purpose clothing. Are you a horse rider, a golfer, or a serious tennis player with the duds to prove it? Put those categories on your lists as well.

percentage number, she is able to see at a glance the types of clothing a client owns and what percentage of her total wardrobe it represents. (See "This-Is-Your-Life Pie Chart" box on the next page.) The trick, then, is to get the percentage of *types* of clothing a client has to match his or her current lifestyle.

A pie chart for someone still working full time outside the home might show "Work clothing" as the largest slice of the pie, while a semiretired person might have "Casual day wear" as the largest portion, with a heavy emphasis on tennis or golf outfits. Two to three times a year, some people will need a black-tie outfit, while others might never dress up like that anymore.

It's like grocery shopping: you need to survey what you have in the fridge so you know what you can cook tonight while still storing what you'll need for that big dinner party in the future!

THIS-IS-YOUR-LIFE PIE CHART

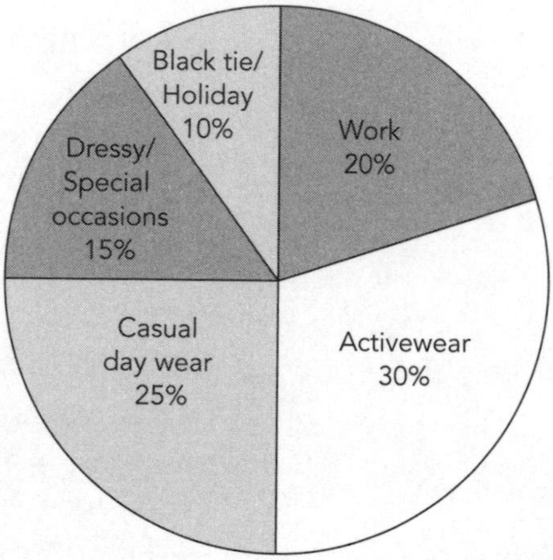

WARDROBE TWEAKING

What are your most needed categories of clothing these days? And the least needed? Assign each category of clothing a rough percentage of the whole on your personal pie chart. If you don't have enough of the kinds of clothes you find yourself actually wearing, you can do a bit more pruning of the garment types that aren't much needed. This way you can better plan future wardrobe purchases.

Both the pie chart and the inventory lists can serve as guides during the process of deciding what to keep, as well as when you're shopping for a "fill-in" purchase after you've culled your closet.

If your inventory reveals you have ten dress suits and you haven't had a nine-to-five job in five years, you can obviously scale back on the office clothes. On the other hand if you've started a new business where you're meeting the public more frequently than in the past, you may need to cut back on your warmup suits and invest in some dressy casual attire for those meet-and-greet cocktail gatherings.

Other categories to inventory for both men and women include shoes, hats, belts, and other accessories. Your basic goals are to know — down to your bedroom slippers — what type of clothing you own, how much you have in each category, and how often you wear what you have.

If you and your wardrobe are "in transition," and you're not really sure what you need or don't need, jot down the following questions in your rightsizing notebook and see if your answers don't clarify things a bit better.

- How do I currently spend my weekdays?
- How do I currently spend my weekends?
- Where do I tend to take vacations?
- What other kinds of travel do I expect to take over the next years?
- If I'm staying close to home, what will I be doing most of the time?
- How has my style changed and to what (classic, trendy, arty, sexy, conservative, etc.)?
- Does my current wardrobe reflect the style I prefer now?
- What colors do I like now?
- Do I prefer prints? Solid colors?

WHAT'S MY STYLE?

Narrowing down your style makes it easier to eliminate those final layers of clothing that just aren't "you." If an item is just okay, maybe you should pass it on.

As for professional wardrobe stylists, their motivation for culling a closet is simple. As Linda Daniels puts it, "Dressing is the art of illusion, and we can enhance the way we feel by wearing only the things we love and [that] make us feel fabulous. A well-chosen wardrobe boosts our confidence, camouflages our real or perceived flaws, and makes us much more comfortable gliding into a room."

A rightsized room, of course.

THE REAL TOUGHIES

But what do you do about the items hanging in your closet that are perfectly serviceable, yet they just don't deliver that "zingy" feeling?

Rightsizers have to toughen up. The rule is that if you don't wear something, regardless of how "good" it is, you need to pass it on. If it's not working for you, just grit your teeth and purge it, the same way you would a tired bag of lettuce in the fridge. Someone else will make use of an item of clothing that's in decent condition, even if you haven't.

According to wardrobe experts I've consulted, the most difficult clothes to get rid of are those purchased for a special occasion: the wedding dress you'll never wear again, the fancy cocktail outfit that's a little tight and everyone in your crowd has seen you wear a million times.

Perhaps the pinstripe suit that cost a bomb has lapels or shoulder pads that date it or your varsity letter sweater has a few moth holes. If you doubt you'll wear it in the next year, and the item is still serviceable, it's probably time to thank the garment for its loyal service and let it go to the "land of Goodwill" or enlist at the Salvation Army. If the piece is a special favorite, lay it on the bed and take a photograph before you send it on its way.

At times people hang on to clothing for which that they have absolutely no use or that doesn't work for them at all. In Linda Daniels's workshop, she has an exercise where clients try to identify both why they still love a certain garment and why it doesn't suit them.

"For some reason, just verbalizing about it to a friend helps you let it go," she says. "This is especially true when the pal gives you that look that says, 'What *are* you thinking?' "

THE BIG PAYOFF

The payoff is looking into your closet at a wardrobe that is both beautiful and efficient. When you reach in to find something perfect to wear, it's there. Like any cleanup project, however, people tend to be very pleased when the task is done. So, how long, you wonder, will it take?

Most wardrobe rehab gurus tell us that the process, if organized properly and done thoroughly, can be completed in about three weeks' time.

The first week usually consists of one- or two-hour sessions spread over six or seven days. You'll go through your closets and drawers, pack up the rejects, and get them out of your house. You'll need a second week to clean and mend the clothing that needs to be repaired. And finally in the third week, you'll try on everything you've kept, do some fine-tuning, and figure out the few things you might want to add to your basic wardrobe.

And if all that seems too much?

Linda Daniels smiles knowingly. "If you continue to procrastinate, consider calling in a professional organizer [see chapter 10 and the Resource Directory] to get you through this process."

In her view, it'll be money well spent.

PAPER, PAPER EVERYWHERE

The same holds true for organizing your piles of paper files and documents, not to mention your cluttered home office. Some rightsizers can conquer these mini mountains with just a little friendly advice. Others need serious help from professionals.

In either case, the mission to rightsize all aspects of your life includes gaining mastery over the paper monster, a three-headed beast that holds many of us in its grasp: documents, paper, and files.

Entire books are devoted to organizing and *re*organizing home offices (see Resource Directory) so I won't presume to tell you how to set up your files and equipment. But before we turn to sorting through the paperwork that's in your files, let's turn our attention to getting *rid of* the things you rarely use, touch, read, or refer to.

Let's start with business-related books. It's time to clear out your outdated almanacs, restaurant guides, telephone, business, and reference books, along with defunct instructional manuals that have no bearing on the equipment you now own or the projects with which you are currently engaged. If you need to look up a bit of data, you can usually locate it online or head for the local library (perhaps to read a book you once owned!).

This is also the moment to eliminate instructional CDs and DVDs you haven't watched or listened to in a few years, not to mention the stray boxes they came in. In most instances newspaper and magazine clippings that never got filed are stale and out-of-date. Don't spend time reading them! Just toss and keep going.

And those binders for projects that wound up DOA or reports that are no longer fresh? Turn on the shredder, my friend. If the binders are still usable, repurpose them for your next venture. There'll be glory days ahead!

Office supplies should be stored out of sight in one place — a closet or cabinet — and the items therein grouped as to type. Put all your pens in one container (the pens that write, that is; pitch the others), pencils in another, and all your binder clips in still another. Boxes of paper clips can be lassoed with rubber bands; reams of paper should be neatly stacked.

You get the idea.

Get rid of what doesn't work or what you never use and organize what's left with comfort and convenience in mind.

WHERE WORK HAPPENS AT HOME

Some people who work at home have found it helpful to pay bills and deal with household matters in a completely separate space from their day-to-day home office. A small desk in a corner of a bedroom can serve the purpose or a built-in desk in the kitchen. I have an "office armoire" in our living room that doubles as a place to hide the TV. It features a fold-down desk, where I keep my checkbook, a pile of stamps, my favorite writing pens, and a stapler. The household files, as opposed to my business files, are in a drawer in the same credenza, which means I have no excuse for failing to file the "paid" receipts as soon as I write the checks.

My son, on the other hand, pays his bills electronically, so he keeps track of his financial obligations in his laptop and has no need for such a dedicated area.

Any office equipment, including the "peripherals," in imperfect working order (cables, modems, power cords, etc.) should be tagged for the haz-mat site (see chapter 7). Keep only the office tools and other office items that are essential to the work you are doing now, or expect to be doing in the future, and clear the decks of unnecessary or outdated paraphernalia. If you've started, or plan to start, a new business or if you've switched from a salaried position to working as an outside consultant, your professional needs have changed. Any home-office space should be recalibrated to reflect new realities.

Organize the equipment and supplies you've kept by type and use. Position your filing cabinets fairly near your desk. Keep your printer near your keyboard. Supplies that involve writing should be grouped together: business stationery, business cards, shipping envelopes and labels, note cards, pads of sticky notes, lined paper pads, reams of paper, and so forth. Once again, it's the familiar like-with-like rightsizing principle.

Group your electronic "aids" in one place: current manuals, peripherals and accessories, diskettes, extra printer cartridges, a label maker, etc.

Anything to do with the telephone should be kept in one place: the phone books you use, your paper or electronic address book, a Rolodex if you still use one, and a telephone headset, which makes typing while taking notes a breeze. Larger equipment that you don't use as often can be boxed in a nearby closet: tape recorders, projectors, screens, cameras, and accessories.

Organizing pros estimate that it should probably take you about half a day to a day to whip your home office into shape, excluding the sorting and purging of paper.

THE "PAPERLESS" SOCIETY — NOT

You knew it would ultimately come down to this, didn't you? I mean stemming the paper glut.

Speaking only for myself as someone who has generated more than her fair share of the stuff, getting the paper and files in one's life to manageable proportions is a pain, pure and simple. Just like conquering those piles of photographs.

So, as apprentice rightsizers, we'll try to focus on keeping it simple, but first we need to understand why we hold on to the stuff!

TOP TEN REASONS WE'RE DROWNING IN PAPER

1. We were taught that if something is in print, it must be important.
2. We're afraid the one thing we toss will be the one thing we need (like a winning lottery ticket or directions to the cheapest parking lot at the airport).
3. The junk mail arrives in such volume we don't have time to process it.
4. Our intentions are good, so we don't ditch pitches for donations.
5. We feel guilty about those pitches when we don't respond, so we hold on to them, thinking we might have some extra cash to give . . . later.
6. We have so many demands on our time, filing gets short shrift.
7. We have so many things we'd like to do, and filing isn't one of them.
8. The more the paper piles up, the more time we know it will take to tame it, so we don't do anything.
9. We're on too many mailing lists and can't stop the flow.
10. We don't have an organized system for dealing with the incoming paper.

RIGHTSIZING YOUR WAY OUT OF THE MORASS

Ten years ago I probably couldn't have said this with much certainty, but today it's more true than ever — if you throw something out by mistake, you now can nearly always find the information again on the Web. This means you no longer should hesitate to throw out the paper clogging your file drawers.

Yes, you'll have to go through them, file by file, but the most efficient way to do this is to cull out the paper you do need to run an organized life. Many of the top ten reasons we're drowning in paper revolve around guilt, and in most cases, guilt is a wasted emotion. Try to remember that you didn't request the information coming through your door, so it's okay to toss it (even those personalized "free" address labels and the pennies many charities send with their pitch — use 'em with a clear conscience and then donate your hard-earned money to the good-works group of your choice!). We're grown-ups now. We get to do what we think is best.

Here are the basic steps to powering through those files and the litter on your desk, stuffed in drawers, strewn on the office floor, and scattered throughout your home.

First: Gather all the stray paper to be dealt with in one location, if possible. That means junk mail, bills, even supermarket ads you've stuck on your refrigerator door with magnets. Pull the restaurant menus out of the kitchen drawer, then pile your magazines in one place and your mail-order catalogs in another.

No kidding; corral every scrap of paper in every corner and hidden crevice of every room, and while you're at it, bring along some empty paper grocery bags. The rest of your house will instantly look better, even if your "staging area" looks like the paper Pyramid of Giza!

Second: Take a break. I mean it. Shut the door on your mess and go have a latte, a glass of chardonnay, or take a walk around the block. Set the tone for what comes next by repeating to yourself, "I will spend the next hour or two sorting and purging. I swear I will not read *any* of the material I'm going to throw away!"

Third: Return to the scene, take a deep breath, and write on sticky notes: BILLS, RECEIPTS, TAX-RELATED, PAY STUBS, MEDICAL BILLS & RECORDS, VITAL RECORDS, INSTRUCTION MANUALS, IMPORTANT ADDRESSES, WARRANTIES, REBATES, etc. You may think of several more categories; if so, make sticky notes for them.

Fourth: Follow the advice of all the paper-taming mavens in the organizing biz and just start purging that paper! Against one wall, line up an army of empty paper grocery bags. Assuming you've properly paid your yearly taxes, you can begin to toss the following categories from lists that I've adapted from such excellent organizing how-tos as

Julie Morgenstern's *Organizing from the Inside Out* and Barbara Hemphill's *Taming the Paper Tiger.*

May I add my own suggestion? Throw out these types of paper *without reading anything but the date:*

- Paid bill receipts earlier than the current year
- Notices of expired events and invitations
- Notices of future events you don't wish to attend
- Magazines and catalogs older than three months
- Magazine articles clipped but now stale
- ATM, food, gas, restaurant, gift receipts if they also appear on credit-card statements
- Appeals from charities to whom you do not wish to donate
- Restaurant menus you don't use (most are online now)
- Outdated, unwanted ads and other product solicitations
- Recipes for dishes you haven't made and now hold no special appeal
- Expired coupons
- Coupons that save you less than a dollar
- Coupons for items you rarely buy
- Health information more than six months old
- Closed checking-account receipts and old checks
- Greeting cards that don't meet the "prizewinner" test
- Business cards and addresses you won't take the trouble to enter into your address book or personal data organizer

Fifth: Remove the paper bags containing obvious junk mail to the trash immediately. Buy or borrow a shredder and make confetti out of the cast-off receipts containing any personal information. Then remove them to the trash in a fast trip to the garbage cans.

Sixth: The paper items you didn't throw away can remain near their identifying sticky notes until you begin to rework your filing system.

Seventh: Try to find the time to put yourself on anti–junk mail lists by contacting such sources as www.ecofuture.org and consider pruning the number of magazines and periodicals you allow into your home. You can also register at www.emailpreferenceservice.com to put a finger in the dike of junk mail.

And now take a well-deserved break and congratulate yourself! You are definitely a rightsizing champion on the road to a less-burdened, freer daily existence.

PAPER YOU ACTUALLY LOVE

I have a friend who is an inveterate theatergoer. She saves every playbill from every show she's ever seen and puts them in a handsome brass, two-handled pan, seven inches deep, which she keeps on a little chair near the entrance to the guest bathroom. At the end of every year, she culls out the shows she didn't much like and keeps the new additions on top for her friends to peruse.

It's paper she loves and has designed a way to corral so it's not just piling up in a jumble, gathering dust.

Unique solutions like that can be invented for greeting cards you can't bear to toss or cartoons friends send you or plastic keys from exotic hotels still in their paper sleeves that you're not ready to part with (never leave them in your room as all your personal information is encoded in the magnetic strip on the back!). However, if you can't come up with a *clever* way of organizing your paper memorabilia, it's time to rightsize the stuff using the cleverest receptacle of all: the circular file.

THE PAPER YOU KEEP

When it comes to what is — or should be — in your files, most professional office organizers agree: the "80/20 rule" generally applies. Probably 80 percent of the paper you've filed can be eliminated, while the remaining 20 percent should be better organized for easier access.

There are even rightsizing toughie types that say 90 percent of what we dutifully file away is *never looked at again!* So, before you start tackling what is in *your* dreaded files, here is a list of what to make sure you keep:

- tax returns for the last two years on hand; last seven years on file in the event of an audit

- passports
- wills
- ownership titles and/or deeds to homes, cars, boats, etc.
- birth records
- death certificates
- military service and discharge papers
- marriage license
- divorce records
- adoption records
- naturalization records
- living wills
- powers-of-attorney
- health-proxy documents
- insurance policies
- Social Security and pension-plan proof

Even these "official" documents can be replaced, but not without a stupefying amount of trouble. Your best bet in this realm is to create one file drawer labeled FAMILY DOCUMENTS and keep them handy, should you ever have to make a hasty exit (à la my tsunami scare).

THE SAVVY FILER

Okay, so now you're ready, willing, and pumped up enough to go through you files drawer by drawer. Now that you've nabbed the really important documents from your files, this next little exercise will be about purging only what's been lurking in those folders. Once you've shrunk your paper glut to manageable proportions, you'll have weeded out enough to figure out how you want to set up a new filing system that will keep you rightsized from here on out.

First: Give a call to your accountant or lawyer for advice about what tax and legal papers you must retain, especially from businesses that no longer exist or ones you may be developing. Take notes of this conversation and follow their prescriptions precisely.

Second: Pull those additional "keeper" documents from the files and put them in top-quality legal storage boxes, labeled as to subject, contents, and year. Find a place to house them where you won't trip over them in years to come.

Third: Line up a new phalanx of empty paper bags and tackle the first of your file drawers. Locate the kinds of "maybe" items that should turn into nos. Things like:

- Duplicates of personal documents (if you must, give backup copies to a family member or friend in a neatly labeled folder)
- Drafts of projects that went DOA
- Drafts of letters and proposals that are no longer relevant to your life
- Old expense accounts and supporting documents that your accountant or lawyer said you do not have to retain for your records

Once this category of jettisoned paper is dispensed with, you're now ready to confront the rest. Ace organizer Julie Morgenstern says that if you are faced with files you haven't purged in a while, let this one thought guide you: "Keep only *core information,* those materials you actually use."

By "core" she means a document or record that is at the heart of your business or personal activities. Ask yourself if it will advance a project you're committed to. Do you refer to it regularly, or do you need it for future tax or legal reasons?

Morgenstern say the other key question is, "Would my life/work change if I didn't have this [file or] piece of paper?" If not, deep-six it, she says.

The only thing to add to this is what I've said before and will say again: do not be caught in the trap of starting to *read* every word of papers left in your files as you sort and purge. Instead:

- Glance at the heading on the piece of paper
- Check the date
- Ask "Will my life or work change" without the item?
- Make a speedy decision yes or no.
- Put nos into a paper bag for later shredding or disposing
- Put yesses into a KEEPER pile for later filing

MAYBE . . . MAYBE NOT

Many people become totally paralyzed by the "MAYBE" category, in contrast to the "DON'T HAVE A CLUE" designation, which commits you to ultimately making a final decision. "Maybes" never get resolved and just turn into clutter. In fact, "maybe" is the bane of a rightsizer's existence. Resist the word "perhaps"! Be decisive.

I once kept an entire five-inch-thick folder of brochures about trips sponsored by my university, which of course I never went on because not only were they fabulous worldwide junkets, they were fabulously expensive! I kept thinking, "Maybe we'll win the lottery and go next year. Maybe I'll sell the foreign rights to a book and spend the windfall sailing from Venice to Dubrovnik."

Maybe, schmaybe! If I ever get such a windfall, I'll go online and see what's set to sail once I cash the check! Better to read the yummy brochure, spend a minute fantasizing about it, and toss it into the circular file. I still can dream, and it doesn't take up a centimeter of space.

PAPER RIGHTSIZERS SET GOALS

Set a simple goal for yourself: tackle one or two file drawers at a session, assuming you aren't up against the proverbial time crunch. Be sure you immediately shred the documents you're purging and put the other rejected paper in opaque garbage bags and into the trash ASAP.

When it comes to setting up your new, rightsized files, office Nazis maintain that no one needs more than two drawers in a home filing cabinet. But I find that running a household and running a business life requires more. Whatever the number, the key to the future simplification of your home office depends on the *way* in which you set up your new files.

When I talked to rightsizers who maintain home offices in their post-fifty lives, I was struck by the fact that everybody seems to have his or her own way of organizing and remembering the things put in files — or *not* remembering, as is the case for some of us! If you have files that relate exclusively to your private household (see below), the file designations are pretty obvious. If you are also organizing files for work, it's usually best to keep them in drawers unto themselves. Either way most folks set up files alphabetically throughout or alphabetically by type of activity. In other words files that relate solely to the household, a business (or two), and perhaps leisure activities each have their own drawer or drawers. The tricky part is deciding how to label a file so you can locate the information again.

Kathleen Kendall-Tackett, a health psychologist in New Hampshire, has researched the high level of stress generated within families prone to disorganization. She believes simple techniques can transform a home — or home office — from a clutter zone into a clean and serene place to live and work.

"A frequent mistake is making a filing system much too complex [with] too many categories when a few broad ones will do," she says. As with many organizing experts, she recommends you think about your current life before you start putting labels on file after file. How many balls do you have in the air? For household files she likes the idea of making a folder or even a section of a file drawer for every member of the family. Then, within those personal files, create categories by type of information. Business files, on the other hand, will be organized by types of tasks: administration, sales, marketing, accounting, etc.

Several organizers urge picking a noun first to describe a specific folder, as in "Health — Paid Bills," rather than "Paid Bills — Health." Regardless of nomenclature, everyday categories will probably include topics that refer to the categories on your IRS form such as:

- automobile (maintenance, registration, etc.)
- credit cards
- dividends
- donations
- dues and memberships
- earned income
- electricity
- gasoline
- gifts

- health (bills, doctor files, information)
- home heating
- insurance
- mortgage payments (or rent payments)
- pensions
- Social Security
- telephone (land lines, cell phones, long-distance service)
- travel (personal, professional, information)

This is by no means a complete listing of files you may want to create for rightsizing your personal files, and there is certainly *no* one way to set up files that make your life easier. But it suggests a way of thinking about organizing and simplifying your life.

Cutting-edge rightsizers may choose the digital route to taming the paper in their lives. The contents of files and key documents can now be scanned into your computer hard drive and searched later using services like Google Desktop to find them fast. There are also online storage companies like www.ibackup.com that will keep copies of your documents off-site in files arranged in a hierarchy so you can access them.

Regardless of whether you have paper or use electronic files for ongoing business ventures that you run out of your home, there are volumes on the subject of how to organize a home office and do so efficiently. That includes setting up your organization, with suggestions for color-coding types of files such as administration, business plans, employees, financial, promotion and PR, sales and marketing, and so on.

Several organizational experts vote in favor of *eliminating the center tab* from a "left, center, right" manila folder tabbing system. That way, when you add a tabbed file or remove one, you don't break the nice patterned sequence in the file drawer. This, in turn, wards off doubt about what tabs are lurking, unseen, behind the others.

Another good tip I've heard is to purchase folders with tabs alternating between left and right that are the same color inside and out. That way, you can always maintain your system if you rearrange specific folders by merely turning a "next up" folder inside out and rewriting the proper file name and placing it in its new position.

CONTAIN YOURSELF

The Container Store and its competitors have become almost temples of religion for veteran rightsizers. I certainly have been a worshipper of magazine holders and color-coded file folders. Be warned, though, that there is no point in spending a fortune on baskets, plastic, cardboard, and canvas boxes until you've gotten rid of whatever clutter is clogging your office arteries. An empty plastic butter tub can serve as a "placeholder" receptacle in which to store packs of pens temporarily, or a shoe box can stand in for an archival photo file until you've tamed the mess in your office. Once you've cleared the desk and drawers of the excess, you'll know what type and how many containers you'll ultimately need when you set out to make your working space not only efficient, but beautiful.

Again our familiar mantra: assemble like with like. Pull out every single pen and pencil and highlighter from drawers and cupboards and test each one. If the ball point doesn't write, the felt tip is colorless, or the eraser is shot, toss it out. Collect all your notepads together. Once I gather them from all their hiding places, I'm usually amazed at their volume; I could practically open a stationery store.

The point is to:

- survey the office supplies you already own
- pick the best working gear you have
- toss, recycle, or find homes for the rejects
- find spots within your home office for each category of office supplies that are close to where you use them

Then and only then will you be issued a permission slip to head for your favorite container retailer or go online to put goodies in your electronic shopping cart. Now that you've presumably set a course for clearing out space throughout your present home (and sworn off cluttering the space in any new dwelling), the proper containers for everything from papers to shoes will help you rightsize your world and help keep it that way.

EYES GLAZED OVER

Okay. You've tried your best. Or maybe you're one of the "tough cases," like my great-grandmother, the collector of tuna-fish cans. Sometimes there's no way to get rightsized without professional help. If that's true (at minimum, you'll probably call for help from a professional mover), then choosing the best pros for a particular task becomes job one.

Chapter 10

Step 6 — Call in the Professionals

When and how to hire help to declutter, reorganize, rearrange, retrofit, or move

HELP IS ON THE WAY

There is no shame in discovering you need some assistance — or even a lot of help — in rightsizing your life. At any point in the process, you may decide the smartest move would be to enlist outside support for sorting through those files we've just been discussing. Perhaps you could use a little boost with basic clutter clearing, better organization, or placement of the possessions you've decided to keep. Then again you might need some guidance when it comes to space planning either your present or prospective living quarters. Maybe an interior designer could spruce things up a bit or a retrofit expert could advise on making a house safe for the day when you can't climb the stairs so easily. And it never hurts having a wardrobe guru to consult about getting your clothing, closets, or storage areas into shape for your simpler, sleeker lifestyle.

I JUST CAN'T FACE THE BOXES!

For twenty-seven years former Indianans Joseph and Farrell Malandro lived near the Indianapolis Motor Speedway in a four-bedroom home. Ultimately, the couple reached the point where they'd had enough of the noise and congestion of big-city, race-week life and moved into a 1,600-square-foot condo in a nearby community.

On that first move, says Joe, the couple managed the logistics of planning and packing reasonably well on their own.

"We got rid of things like gardening tools," he says, but admits "we also took a lot with us."

The Malandros' grown children were scattered around the country. The couple had sons in Chicago, Atlanta, and Stockton, California, but their daughter lived in northwestern Florida with her growing family. As Joe and Farrell thought about retirement, Florida seemed like a good idea for their eventual permanent home, and for several years they had rented a place on winter visits so they could see their daughter and grandchildren.

In June 1998 they made the big decision to pull up stakes in Indiana and head for warmer climes. "It was wrenching," Farrell says, "but the logic of the move [finally] convinced us."

However, Mrs. Malandro was a self-described homebody. "My home is the most important thing to me," she readily admits. "For me, it wasn't so much about possessions, but more about leaving family and familiar places."

"The hardest part for me when we left our Indy home," continues Joe, "was getting rid of all the kids' stuff. And the pictures! I couldn't venture a guess how many pictures we had in albums, in stacks, in frames." He worried that sorting through all this would be a burden on his children, but in the end, they took most of their family memorabilia with them as well.

Farrell admits to having even more difficulty than her husband in coping with all the decisions required by these multimoves.

"I don't like change. Every move we've made, I've dragged my feet."

The Malandros had made these initial relocations without much additional help but turned to Beth Warren, owner of Welcome Home Relocation, in the spring of 2005, when they bought a first-floor condo in Tampa, Florida.

"Farrell had developed some health problems," recalls Joe, "and I realized this move would have been hard on me physically to do it alone. I saw an ad [for Warren's services] in our condo association newsletter and called Beth to take the stress off us. We were losing some four hundred square feet [moving to a new place], and I knew we had to make some *serious* compromises."

Now both the Malandros agree; hiring a professional whose skills are tailored to a specific need can be a godsend.

Says Joe, "Beth never pressured us at all. She gave us a choice of the services she offered [packing, unpacking, space planning, dismantling and reinstalling computers, coordinating with the movers, etc.] and an estimate that turned out to be accurate: eighteen hundred dollars for her services and four hundred dollars for the movers, who carted our belongings just a couple of miles across town."

Their new place had significantly less storage, so Joe and Farrell, now in their seventies, were grateful for their move manager's skill in diagramming the new house and working with them on choosing the furniture and household items that would work in their pared-down space. She also guided them in the placement of the goods she'd helped them select from all the possessions they still owned.

"She worked hard on the smaller kitchen with Post-it notes to figure out how much space there'd actually *be* for what items and what we had to toss," says Joe admiringly.

Farrell, a slight woman with red hair and a shy smile, adds, "The movers arrived at eight a.m., and we were in our new home with everything in place by three!"

"I tried to talk to them both as a loving daughter would," recalls Beth, who was convinced that a one-level home at this stage was probably a wise choice for her clients. "My mother was ill for two years, and I understand these health issues. I had to reach deep into my own experience in order to reach *them*."

Beth used blue painter's tape to outline on the floor the dimensions of their new closets and cabinets as a means of graphically showing the Malandros exactly how much space they would have in their new condo. Ultimately the couple selected the "best of the best" from their store of possessions and are now happily installed in smaller living quarters that suit them perfectly.

Says Farrell, "Actually, I feel more at home in this place than in some of the others we've lived. We're close to our family, shopping, and our son-in-law is happy to come over and fix things!"

HELP WITH THE MOVE

In 2002 the National Association of Senior Move managers (www.nasmm.com) designed a code of ethics and set standards for their burgeoning service. The first year there were eight members. Soon there were close to sixty, and the numbers grow monthly.

Moving Solutions owner Margit Novack helped found NASMM. She says rightsizers should look for "quality indicators when hiring someone who will be coming into your home. Find out if they're members of NASMM, adhering to our written standards. Ask if they carry insurance, train their people, pay business taxes. And be aware that a typical job employing a senior move manager currently runs between two thousand and eight thousand dollars — not including movers — depending on the size of the house and the 'density' of the goods to be dealt with." Margit, who recently moved to smaller quarters herself, understands the "misery of moving, but once you've accomplished it well, you've bought yourself a wonderful, new lifestyle."

NASMM full members like Margit must have proof of liability insurance and be vetted by the organization with verified letters of recommendation from satisfied clients. They must be able to perform these sorts of functions:

- packing and unpacking
- arranging estate sales
- estimating space requirements accurately
- space planning

Beth Warren, Margit Novack, and their fellow members of NASMM have as part of their credo the conviction that all the decisions are the *clients'* to make. Professional move managers have a solemn obligation to take anything to the next home that a client elects to transport without berating them. A move manager will point out that something won't fit in the new home (a fact that will soon become patently obvious), but it is the client's sacred right to be injudicious.

Such moves never end, however, because clients of this sort will have to do the purging and sorting all over again. Nevertheless, the decisions about what to take and what to toss are truly up to those making the move. Certainly professional move managers can gently remind their clients they're "paying to pack it, move it, or store it." After all, the pros are there to help people have a successful move.

There is also the American Association of Homes and Services for the Aging (www.aahsa.org), a Washington-based group that represents nonprofit nursing homes and assisted-living and continuing-care communities. If requested, a coordinator provides phone support and keeps track of details during the move but is not on-site for packing and unpacking.

Many corporations hire relocation experts, subcontractors retained to move their executives. Some national moving companies also offer this type of "blue-ribbon service," which is typically contracted through corporations wishing to ease the pain of a move for senior executives and their families. If you're not among the anointed and you need help, you can ask a local organizing specialist if he or she would help you plan and coordinate your move.

The National Association of Professional Organizers (www.napo.com) also offers these sorts of move-management services, along with hosts of people who advertise locally. Whoever you hire to help with rightsizing, be sure that the people who work for them are bonded and on their staff and not subcontractors. If something gets broken, lost, or stolen, you want to know they'll fix it or replace it.

FIX-IT, PLAN-IT, AND DO-IT PROS

Perhaps one of the best ways to determine what kind of outside help you need is first to ask yourself *what problem or problems you are trying to solve.*

The gray areas between people who can assist you in sorting, purging, editing, and then organizing and arranging what's left versus the experts who think through and suggest *better* ways of planning the use of interior space and then fill that space and the surrounding walls with new items and old are sometimes . . . well . . . gray and fuzzy. The best way to see through the haze is to determine whether you need a fix-it pro, a plan-it pro, or a do-it pro.

Fix-it pros help you fix the problems of sorting, purging, editing, and disposing of unwanted or unneeded possessions and then assist in

PROBLEMS AND THE PEOPLE WHO SOLVE THEM

- **Decluttering** is a process that eliminates objects that no longer serve an aesthetic or practical purpose and, in fact, litter the interior landscape. These experts are generally called **clutter** or **decluttering specialists, interior rearrangers,** or professional **organizers. Feng shui experts** approach clutter as obstacles obstructing the balanced flow of energy and offer advice on ways to clear out and dispose of offending objects.
- **Editing** is a process of choosing to keep or reject objects within a collection of similar items such as photographs, clothing, or duck decoys. **Same experts as above.**
- **Organizing** is a process in which you assemble or design systems for groups of objects such as paperwork or clothing that promote ease of daily use. There are **professional organizers** who specialize in **paper management** or **clothing selection** and **closet design;** others concentrate on the general organization of everything from kitchens to home offices to wood shops.
- **Space planning** is a process that determines the most pleasing and efficient use of your square footage when calculating available interior dimensions and the objects contained within either an existing house or a new one. **Interior architects and designers,** along with some **contractors** and professional **move managers,** are trained in this field. **Feng shui experts** are also trained in the ways the use of space affects our energy levels.
- **Rearranging** is a process in which you place the objects you already own in new positions in your house that are both aesthetically pleasing and convenient for their use. **Interior designers,** professional **interior rearrangers,** and **house stagers** are usually the ones who till this field as their specialty.
- **Remodeling** is a process in which you reconfigure interior and exterior space so the overall design and features suit your current needs. **Interior designers** can help with issues within the four walls. **Architects** and **contractors** are experts in dealing with structural changes.
- **Retrofitting** is a process that adds or adapts desired features to an existing space. **Architects, interior designers,** and **contractors** with training in the science of "aging in place" are schooled to handle challenges of accessibility and barrier-free design. Some are certified in this specific field.
- **Interior design** is a process of conceptualizing a plan for improving interior space. This encompasses the color, texture, style of the

walls, flooring, ceiling, and furnishings. There are many talented people in this field, some without the formality of a degree or membership in recognized professional organizations. However, **interior designers** who have recognized credentials should be considered likely bets.

- **Household goods disposal** can be handled by trash haulers, auction houses, home sales experts, charities, consignment stores, tag and estate sales organizers, or online sales outfits like eBay.

organizing what remains. These tend to be professional organizers, move managers, and professional rearrangers.

Plan-it pros help you envision your new and improved environment. They can show you ways to simplify and/or enhance your new surroundings or fix up familiar ones. Interior designers and architects and some contractors fall into this category, along with "crossover" pros, who include experienced professional organizers, interior rearrangers, and move managers.

Do-it pros help you accomplish a specific task at a specific time. Movers, house cleaners, and trash haulers are do-it types who appear with a clear agenda of what they must accomplish and by when.

Fix-it and plan-it pros offer a wide range of expertise, while do-it pros tend to have niche skills only, which, by the way, may be all the expertise you need for a particular job. For instance, if you have a closet chock-full of garments and you don't know how to sort what's in there, a stylish friend, clutter buddy, or clutter-busting fix-it pro might be the answer to the problem. This person could come and help you fix the state of your closet by walking you through the process of deciding your present clothing needs and then guiding your choices.

On the other hand if you want more space in an existing closet or want to add some built-ins to expand its possibilities, then a bona fide plan-it pro such as a closet expert can help you plan better use of existing space or design the new space for your wardrobe.

A do-it pro will be the person hauling wood into your house, hammering nails, and hanging the new clothing rods and installing shelves and drawers. In other words they get the job *done*.

There are situations when you might need fix-it, plan-it, *and* do-it professional help if you find yourself confronted with a number of issues, e.g., overall space problems *and* closets that are bursting at the seams *and* a parallel need to retrofit or remodel your home for someone wheelchair bound.

Hiring various experts to get the job done will, of course, initially cost more, but in the end could save you money. For example, a certified organizer who also does space planning and is willing to call in bona fide designers and contractors should circumstances warrant may also provide a skill level that's more creative, more efficient, and more cost effective.

To orient yourself in the world of rightsizing experts, let's get our arms around some important definitions that are organized by task.

DO YOU REALLY GET WHAT YOU PAY FOR?

The most highly trained professionals, such as interior architects and designers who are members of organizations that have rigorous standards for admission, will tend to price their services higher than others without such specialized training. These are the people who — on paper, at least — have proven skills helping you at a strategic level to improve or update your home for the way you live now. Depending on where they ply their trade, their fees tend to run $100 an hour and up . . . and up. Be sure to ascertain when you hire them exactly how you will be billed for a project and always ask for a detailed time-and-materials breakdown each week as things progress.

In some cases, however, engaging the services of such highly trained people may be overkill. Instead, a collection of qualified and experienced subspecialists could be the perfect fit for your particular situation. For instance, furniture chains like Ethan Allen have staffers whose many years of experience qualify them to help you plan the use of space or render floor plans and consult on color and fabric choices at no charge to the customer. Even a talented friend or acquaintance who has "gone to school on the job" and has become an expert in tasks such as organizing closets, selecting paint and fabric, placing furniture in innovative ways, or sorting through paperwork can come to the rescue in your hour of need.

In other words you don't need an AIA-certified architect to help you decide which of your seventeen ceramic frogs you should keep, or the best place to reposition your potted palm, or how to dig out from under an avalanche of bulging file folders.

On the other hand, you want to be sure you've got the correct specialist to match the job in question and that you're hiring people who not only know their stuff, but who also charge fairly for the services they render.

So, what's a rightsizer to do?

Learn to ask questions, that's what!

HOW TO HIRE A RIGHTSIZING PROFESSIONAL

1. **How do I locate the best rightsizing pro to work with?**

   Once you know the area of expertise you need, you can ask friends for recommendations or check in the Resource Directory in the back of this book as a starting point. Ads in local newspapers or even on a community bulletin board can yield names. Or you can try the Yellow Pages or computer search engines under "organizing products and services."

2. **How many professionals should I interview before making a choice?**

   Your safest route is to interview at least three candidates before selecting one to work with. You can do this on the telephone or by e-mail, asking each person the same list of questions. On the other hand, if you're looking for someone to haul your trash or take your consignment-store item and you like the terms and price, your "interviews" will probably be brief.

3. **What questions should I ask of the rightsizing professional?**

   For professionals who will be rendering higher-priced services, consider asking:

   - How long have you been in this business?
   - Are you a single practitioner or do you have employees? How many?
   - Tell me about how you got into the field.
   - Where did you train for this field?
   - What professional organizations are you a member of?
   - Do you have any certification or training in related areas such as coaching, feng shui, aging in place, or dealing with sufferers of chronic disorganization, etc.?
   - What is the range of services you provide?
   - What are your areas of specialization and expertise?

- Describe your typical client.
- Are you the actual person who will work with me?
- How long do you estimate this job will take?
- Do you give written estimates?
- Describe the way you work and the length of time you spend on-site.
- Are you licensed by the state? Do you need to be? May I know your license or certification number?
- Are you bonded?
- Can you tell me the name of your insurance carrier?
- What questions do you want to ask of *me*?
- Can you provide three *recent* references?

4. How much will it cost?

Fees for various services in the field of rightsizing can vary widely, of course, based on qualifications, competition, location, and the demands of a particular project.

Ask potential hires:

- Will you give me a written list of the services you're providing, together with a written itemized estimate and a projected timetable for getting the job completed?
- Will you give me detailed, written weekly invoices?
- If we don't "click" as client and professional, what is your *cancellation* policy?

CLEAN SWEEP

The first — and often the last — professionals that rightsizers hire are cleaning service people. The questions listed in the "How to Hire" box certainly apply, along with a few specific queries as to how many people are on the crew, what cleaning chemicals will they be using, and whether the cleaners can provide special services, including window washing, baseboard cleaning, and a complete makeover of refrigerators, ovens, and stoves. If the cleaning crew is not conversant in English, ask if there is a supervisor with whom you can communicate as the job goes along.

One suggestion from the National Association of Cleaning Professionals — NACP — (www.cleaningassociation.com) is to help your provider establish a *list* of what you expect them to do. Also ask if the employees are covered by your state's Workers Compensation program. If they aren't, this could be an indication they are paying their employees under the table.

And finally, says the NACP, ask the head of the cleaning service you're considering if he or she does criminal background checks on employees.

That's always a good thing to know about people who are coming into your home, right?

TIPS FOR TRACKING DOWN LOCAL ORGANIZING EXPERTS

Welcome to the burgeoning field of "professional organizer." Just type the words "clutter," "organizers," or "rearrangers" in any computer search engine and hundreds of listings will pop up with intriguing dot-com monikers like ClutterFreeForever, MindOverClutter, and MessiesAnonymous.

As previously mentioned almost anyone can hang out a shingle or buy an Internet domain name and call him- or herself an organizing professional. Your best bet is to first check with friends to see if they have anyone they can suggest to help with various aspects of the getting-your-house-in-order process.

Barring that, start with professional organizing associations, along with national companies like California Closets and the Container Store, who perhaps can suggest candidates in your area that have met at least a minimum standard of qualifications and mastered the necessary skills. Just be sure that with each candidate you pose the questions suggested in the "How to Hire" box on pages 187–188.

National trade associations are a source for leads to local providers of certain kinds of specific services in the area of home improvement. As previously mentioned the **National Association of Professional Organizers** is a nonprofit association with more than thirty-three hundred members throughout the world whose stated mission is to "enhance the lives of clients by designing systems and processes using organizing principles" and then hopefully transferring those organizing skills to *you!*

Other groups in this arena of pruning and purging that can give you leads in your local area include the **Interior Arrangement and Design Association** (www.interiorarrangement.org) and the **Interior Redesign Industry Specialists** (www.weredesign.com). Their contact information can be found in the Resource Directory at the back of this book.

DECORATORS AND DESIGNERS

Who knew that interior *decorators* and interior *designers* are not the same thing?

The pros themselves are very aware of the differences and sometimes quite prickly on the subject. **Designers** are schooled in architecture, layout, and planning. **Decorators** specialize in the aesthetics of room furnishings and the look of the walls that surround them.

Obviously, the art of rearranging the use of existing space and space planning, per se, are closely aligned. So, that puts **Interior Rearrangers** in a camp related to interior designers and decorators. Like full-fledged interior designers, interior rearrangers should ask you about your lifestyle, whether you entertain a lot or a little, need space for overnight guests, or have hobbies with particular space requirements.

Then the good ones start to work their magic, positioning a couch at an angle you'd never imagine would work, clustering a collection of your artwork in a fashion that gives a wall the "wow" treatment, adding a ficus tree here or silk pillow there to create an entirely new look that makes you wonder why *you* never thought of it!

Although some practitioners are trained in all three areas, it's wise to *ask* about these definite distinctions.

The practitioners with the highest academic qualifications (and often higher fees) are typically members of such professional organizations as the **American Society of Interior Design,** based in Washington, D.C. (www.asid.org) and the **International Interior Design Association,** based in Chicago (www.iida.org).

Somewhere within those ranks is a qualified specialist that can help with interior-design issues and the arrangement of the furniture and objects within your home.

SO WHO ARE SPACE PLANNERS?

Just to complicate the issue, professional space planners . . . well, duh . . . plan space. They plan the inside of office buildings, they plan the use of open spaces in cities and parks, and a smaller number plan the inside of houses. Often they're architects, but not always. Many are members of the **American Planning Association** (www.planning.org). In fact 65 percent of the APA's thirty-seven thousand members work for state and local government agencies.

Be assured, though, that there's an abundance of a different breed of space planners who concern themselves primarily with home interiors. My dear friend Cynthia Challed works for a large furniture store in Lodi, California, and is a highly experienced interior designer and space planner, capable of drawing excellent floor plans with a terrific traffic flow and exceptional furniture placement, yet she is not a member of APA.

The point is, a large range of talented people are involved in space planning, and as you explore this world, you'll find that lots of folks who are interested in organizing, designing, and *re*designing residential spaces are, de facto, space planners as well. When you run into such professionals, ask them to explain their orientation and give you

MATCHING YOUR STYLE WITH THE STYLIST

- Make certain the person you're considering hiring really has the time to work with you and is sensitive to your needs.
- Remember, you certainly aren't obligated to buy the additions they might suggest.
- Make certain you feel really comfortable with the person before you sign an agreement.
- Don't engage them if it feels like they're trying to force changes you don't want to make or pressure you to buy items you don't want.
- Do not assume the rearranger knows what you want or need. You have to do your part and communicate your ideas, likes, and dislikes to them.
- Expect to pay by the hour or by the job. Ask up front if there's a fee for a first-time consultation and read any contracts carefully.

a rundown of their experience and various areas of expertise. Visit one of their recent projects. That way you can decide if they're the *type* of space planner that could truly offer you help.

REMODELING AND RETROFITTING FOR THE FUTURE

Here's where we get into the big bucks when it comes to hiring building and remodeling professionals. In fact, Silicon Valley veteran Dan Fritschen, who has a background in both engineering and business, saw a need to help people who were dithering over whether to stay and remodel their house to perfection or to move to a new home. As a result, he created www.remodelormove.com, a Web site that provides (for free to those who register) not only calculators for weighing options but also a probing questionnaire that yields seasoned advice about this difficult decision.

Fritschen, who has bought and remodeled several homes for his own family, saw that "there was no good tool out there to help try to weigh the finances and the emotional factors involved with remodel-

REMODEL OR MOVE

Fritschen's Remodel or Move Web site (www.remodelormove.com) provides these reasons for choosing one option over another.

Move instead of remodel if:	*Remodel instead of move if:*
Your floor plan doesn't suit your current needs	You'll get your dream home
You probably will move in the next few years anyway	You like your neighborhood and neighbors
Your house is the nicest one in your neighborhood, so adding on isn't cost effective	You want to avoid buyer's remorse
Your contractor or architect says "move"	You'll be adding features that will enhance the value of your home
	Your contractor or architect says remodeling is feasible

ing, and then to make a recommendation." Before committing to a major project, check out this method of weighing the pros and cons.

AVOIDING THE CONTRACTOR BLUES

We've all heard the horror stories: The contractor skips with the money and doesn't pay the subs. The work is shoddy, not up to code, doesn't pass inspection. The contractor's license was bogus, yadda, yadda, yadda.

I had one friend who endured a $300,000 nightmare remodeling her house even though the contractor was her cousin. I have another pal who was able to go on a trip during major construction and came back to find the house of her dreams waiting for her.

Maybe it was just luck — good or rotten — but the friend who ended up with the house of her dreams hired someone who'd done a similar feat for a close friend. Therein lies one of the keys to success when hiring a remodeling professional: do plenty of homework before you sign a contractor's contract.

Finding someone who says he or she is a remodeling pro and signing a contract are two separate parts of the process, so be certain you've asked all candidates the full series of questions in the "How to Hire" box on pages 187–188.

GOOD CONTRACTOR'S KARMA

Here's how to find reliable people to remodel your home:

- Ask for referrals from friends, neighbors, coworkers.
- Sidle up to a county inspector and ask for recommendations or names to avoid.
- Ask for recommendations from people who have worked for either you or your friends in the past: real-estate agents, plumbers, gardeners.
- Check with lumberyards that do a lot of business with contractors.
- Check online referral services such as www.servicemagic.com and www.improvenet.com.
- Look in the Yellow Pages under "contractors" or check local newspapers and magazines for ads.
- Confirm the contractor's license number with state authorities.

AGING-IN-PLACE RETROFITTERS

A closely related breed of remodeling professionals specializes in making a house "barrier free." These people can be handypersons or full-fledged builders and contractors, but their main task is retrofitting bathrooms, kitchen counters, and approaches to homes to make them safer for people with disabilities or age-related infirmities.

As we heard earlier, the thinking these days is that good design is good design and the term "universal design" means that anyone can benefit and enjoy layouts that allow the most access with the best safety features and an attractive appearance in the bargain.

Since 1989 the 50+ Housing Council of the National Association of Home Builders (www.nahb.org) has coached more than 1,100 NAHB members involved in seniors housing, mainly through their CAPS program: Certified Aging in Place Specialists.

With America's over-fifty population estimated to hit one hundred million by the year 2010, the active-adult market "represents one of the fastest-growing segments of the housing industry," says a spokesperson for the professional association whose members are primarily builders, developers, and contractors.

To reach this market, NAHB offers its members a program that teaches the technical, business-management, and customer-service skills essential to making quality home modifications for people who wish to remain safely, independently, and comfortably in their own homes as they grow older. CAPS are trained to install grab bars in the bathroom, modify tubs and showers to make them more accessible, adapt other aspects of a house to make it safer and more user friendly. They can also modify steps with ramps so as to offer wheelchairs and walkers an easier approach to a residence.

To find a CAPS specialist in your area, visit www.nahb.org/CAPS. Certainly non-CAPS folks also can provide many of the same services (the certification course consists of three days of instruction), but whomever you interview for the job, don't forget to ask that essential list of questions from the "How to Hire" box on pages 187–188.

MOVING TOWARD A DECENT MOVE

In the next chapter we will highlight specific steps to promote a sane moving experience when departing one home and heading for another, but it's not too soon to wave some yellow caution flags.

Deservedly or not, moving and storage companies do not have the most sterling reputations among the myriad of rightsizing service providers. A highly critical Web site, www.movingscam.com, has something close to three hundred moving companies on its blacklist.

At a minimum, says Tim Walker, founder of MovingScam, "If you don't take precautions up front, [moving] can quickly turn into a nightmare." His free Web site is a wealth of updated information and tips and well worth some time spent cruising around its pages. It even offers several helpful e-articles, including "How to Find a Reputable Mover," "Understanding Estimates," and "How to File Moving Complaints." If you're not particularly computer savvy, ask a friend or relative to download and print copies for you.

For those of us who have moved a few times, moving scams are not news. What is news are the easy measures you can take to ensure that you find a *good* moving professional; I can bear witness that they're out there.

The best and most economical move I ever made was through movers recommended by a real-estate agent who was also a friend. Ask your local real-estate agents for the names of three moving companies with offices in your area. Here's what you're looking for:

- The names of three moving companies that have been in business at least ten years, preferably in the same location
- The DOT and MC license numbers for the companies you are considering (Department of Transportation=DOT#; Motor Carriers=MC#)
- Full company name and DBA (doing business as) names
- Company headquarters address and name of the boss or CEO
- Local and toll-free telephone numbers
- E-mail addresses of your contact and his/her supervisor
- Names of three references who have moved with the company in the last eighteen months
- Guarantee of an on-site estimate in writing

Once you have this information jotted down in your rightsizing notebook, you can compare prospective movers more realistically. Use those DOT and MC numbers to check with the Federal Motor Carrier Safety Administration's Web site, www.safersys.org, where you can learn about a moving company's safety record and confirm it has the proper insurance on file. This government agency also publishes "Your Rights & Responsibilities When You Move," a pamphlet that the law now requires every moving company provide prospective clients.

Consumer watchdogs who follow the moving industry warn against hiring what's known in the trade as a moving broker. Moving maven Tim Walker of MovingScam adds, "Current consumer protection laws related to the movement of household goods only apply to Motor Carriers and not to Household Goods Brokers," so make sure you're dealing with the carrier directly and not someone selling the services of the carrier.

One last place to check is the government's Safety Violation and Consumer Complaints Hotline at 888-368-7238 to ask about the complaint history of the moving companies you're considering.

Walker recommends you set up appointments for the moving estimators to visit your home with your *least* favorite choice arriving first and your leading candidate last. Only sign with companies that are doing the move themselves, not subcontractors. There will no doubt be a range of prices that have to do with one company providing a service that another may not, e.g., the amount of insurance included or the estimated value of your belongings. Your quote should be calculated based on weight, not cubic feet, and you should *never* sign blank paperwork or any contract you haven't read thoroughly.

All this checking may seem like an added burden, considering the stress of moving, but time invested early to vet the moving professionals you're considering and comparing costs and services can save you hours and big bucks. It will also help you avoid the even bigger hassle of an unhappy, misbegotten move.

WHEN THE MOVING VAN PULLS UP TO THE CURB

How does a move made by a rightsizer differ from an average one?

In many ways, actually. Rightsizers are dedicated to simplifying and smoothing the way to a more serene life, not to mention getting there with less angst. Easy systems and approaches to moving can make the transition a lot less stressful than what you might expect. The same goes for potential heartburn when grappling with the subject of off-site and on-site storage.

Read on!

Chapter 11

Step 7 — Stay Sane During Your Rightsizing Move

Secrets to making moving day a happy memory

MOVING TALES

Some people just seem to have the knack of finding, moving to, and living in wonderful places, while doing it all with ease and grace.

The first apartment inhabited by novelist Michael Llewellyn, who was born and raised in Tennessee, was a unit in an apartment house in Atlanta that had been lived in by one of his literary idols, author Margaret Mitchell, when she was writing *Gone with the Wind.*

Later on, when he was working in the ad business in New York City, he resided in a classic 1830s floor-through apartment in an old sailor's inn in Greenwich Village. It was replete with casement windows, French doors, two working fireplaces, and an exposed brick wall in the kitchen.

In the early nineties he returned to his Southern roots and scored a second-floor 1833 masterpiece on celebrated Dauphine Street in New Orleans's French Quarter, featuring fourteen-foot ceilings and a killer view. This home also had a cast-iron "gallery" – nonnatives would call it a balcony – where the clip-clop of carriage horses mingled with riverboat whistles and the muted sounds of jazz wafting from a nearby watering hole.

Why, you ask, would a person with such a charmed life ever move from such a places and maintain that changing locations so often hasn't been particularly stressful?

The final move was motivated by love, of course. Llewellyn, by then in his late fifties, formed a committed relationship with a retired librarian and antiques dealer and, in 2003, decided to pull up stakes and head west. "I was moving into a house that was fully furnished by someone with a really good eye," Michael says, modest about his own highly developed interior-design skills. A former art director and architecture student, Llewellyn remembers, "I had about six months to think about it all and make a plan. I got rid of ninety percent of what I had in New Orleans, selling most of it to friends and neighbors in the Quarter, and donating the rest."

Like so many people age fifty-plus, Michael had done his fair share of collecting, including artifacts from Egypt and pottery by Fitz and Floyd. "I'm also a book lover, but I gave each volume a long, hard look and admitted to myself 'I'm never going to read this book again, but there's somebody else who will.' I donated them to a thrift shop because I can't throw a book out . . . I just can't."

He found a mover through a recommendation from a friend. "The truck showed up, the guys unloaded things carefully, and it all went very well," Michael recalls. In fact his past moves are a case study illustrating the way major transplantations can be accomplished with a minimum of fuss.

So, what are the key factors that make for a sane move?

"You've got to develop a plan and a system," Michael urges. "My moves went as smoothly as they did because both Tom and I were *organized* about it all! There's nothing more stressful than moving, unless it's death, if you don't take the time to organize everything," he adds. "I attribute our success to planning." You make a list, he says, and you check things off. "It's all about *not* procrastinating. Do a task or a chore as soon as you know it's on your list. Also, save yourself some heartbreak and plan on hand carrying your art, family heirlooms, and the everyday necessities like your toothbrush in a couple of car trips, if at all possible. When you don't worry, you don't stress."

In fact, many veterans of multiple moves will tell you it pays to install your precious and/or important items first: set up your kitchen as soon as possible, unpack as much as you can before the furniture arrives if there are built-ins, get the bookshelves assembled early on so you can put things *in* them right away.

Did Michael regret winnowing down his possessions or abandoning any of the unique spaces he'd inhabited over the years? Truth be told, didn't he grow to hate moving? "Absolutely not," he says convincingly, with the air of a man whose writing career has taken him many miles.

WHEN A MOVE DOESN'T GO SO SMOOTHLY

Sometimes, of course, bad things happen to good people during a move. Through no one's fault a truck gets caught in traffic, a mover gets injured, somebody gets sick, or, saddest of all, somebody dies, and decisions must be made in a hurry.

Whenever humans are involved, trouble can walk through the door. But regardless of circumstances, if you do your part and create and execute a reasonable plan to the best of your ability, you have a much better chance of having things go well.

Let's face it, though, even a welcome move usually has its fair share of stress. In fact, the famous Holmes-Rahe stress scale indicates that moving ranks only a few notches below life events like the death of a spouse, divorce, personal injury, taking on a big mortgage, saying good-bye to adult children, or getting fired as a source of high anxiety. Research has shown that these stressors place serious demands upon the adaptive capacities of our minds and bodies. When changing your address is *combined* with some of those same stressors, moving can be . . . well . . . just plain awful!

Yet there are always ways to deal with such situations.

Diane and Lou Commendatore, both in their early sixties, planned their move by the book. In the months leading up to the sale of their house, they held two garage sales, left unwanted items out on their front sidewalk as neighborhood giveaways, and gifted friends and relatives with the treasures from the Commendatores' twenty-three years in the same 2,000-square-foot house.

"We must have gotten rid of about half our stuff," explains Diane about their move to a compact 1,100-square-foot home near their grown children. "We'd been married thirty-five years, so we also owned lots of sentimental things, given us by our parents. Lou kept saying to me, 'You're making me get rid of too many things.' But we're pretty organized people, and our children helped. We made lists so I knew what was going to happen, and when. The move itself was hard work, but I have to say it went really smoothly."

That is until the final push.

Diane was in charge of driving their two cats in one of their cars to their new home. "What a total nightmare!" she recalls. "I had one kitty in the cat carrier and another in a makeshift box taped shut with air holes on top. That darn cat pushed its way out of the box and started yowling nonstop. The insane screeching lasted the entire trip. It was the worst day of my life."

The cats were so unnerved by their journey that they ran away as soon as they arrived at their new home. "One returned in twenty-four hours, and the other finally came back after two days. It was pretty upsetting."

The moral of this chapter of the Commendatores' story? Well, for starters, if you're moving pets, invest in a carrier for each animal. Sometimes trying to save money can end up costing your peace of mind.

The Commendatores' other glitch during the actual move turned out to be far more serious than howling felines. Part of the family's overall plan was to transfer Diane's elderly mother, who had been living in a nursing home near them, to another facility not far from their new place.

"I'd gone around everywhere trying to find one that was acceptable," she explains. "We'd moved in September, and *finally*, in November, I found a place for her. I went up to get her and brought her down with her oxygen tank and clothing and moved her in. She had already been showing signs of disorientation and shortness of breath in the first nursing home and to our shock, she died within three weeks at the new place due to congestive heart failure."

At first Diane was heartsick that their move had hastened her mother's end, and she pressed the doctors for answers. "They told me Mom was in far more serious condition than any of us realized, and it wasn't the move that caused her death. Her heart was simply giving out." Today, two years down the road, the Commendatores believe their decision to rightsize remains the correct one. The loss of Diane's mother on top of the stress of the move was terribly hard, but Diane looks back and counts her blessings.

"Now that some time has passed, I can say it's been a really good move. Our life is much simpler. We love the way we live now, and I don't miss anything we gave away. I love my new part-time job, and I love being with our four grandchildren. The older ones can ride their bikes over to see us, and my daughter Carrie brings the baby in the stroller all the time."

Diane probably would have had a much harder time adjusting to her new life if a nightmarish move had been added to the tragedy of her mother's death. Thanks to their planning and executing their move so well (except for their lapse about the cat carrier), they quickly settled into their new surroundings and eventually recovered from the blow of losing the eldest member of the family. They've been able to accept that they are now at the front of the generational train and see the "changing of the guard" as an inevitable part of the process of saying farewell to one phase of life and planning for another.

MASTERING THE RIGHTSIZED MOVE

Before you pack or move a single item, pull out your camera or buy a disposable one to photograph every room, basement, attic, nook, and cranny of your house and its grounds. Whether you're a clutter bug or a feng shui master, this is the place you called home. Who knows? You may wish to recreate some aspects of your present home in your next place, and shooting photos provides a record of what it looked like. Even if you want to start with a clean slate, there's something essential in saying to yourself, "I lived here, and now I don't."

I myself have a small photo album that chronicles the homes we've lived in and find it both a good reference tool and fun to show to friends and visiting family. My son, a skilled cinematographer, videotaped our Santa Barbara house inside and out prior to the real-estate brokers' open house so we'd always remember it when the place looked its best.

Taking leave of a place may be cause for kicking up your heels or crying your eyes out, but either way capturing it for posterity helps to "close the book gently" (plus it's always a good idea to keep a record on hand for a few years for insurance or tax purposes).

GETTING GEARED UP FOR THE MOVE

Chapter 7 offered a list of the kinds of gear you need for the sorting-purging-editing phase of getting your house in order — a process that comes before packing the boxes for the move. Once you have your actual moving date established, you need to assemble the same sort of "tool kit" to prepare for the physical move itself.

To refresh your memory, here again is the "to-get" list. It includes items you should gather prior to packing even one box.

- Sturdy cartons or large bags labeled KEEP, TRASH, GIFT, DONATE, RECYCLE, REPAIR, SELL, DON'T HAVE A CLUE
- Professional tape dispensers and several rolls of tape
- An ample supply of large, *clear* plastic disposal bags to use when it's important to *see* what's stashed inside; that way good things don't mistakenly get thrown out as trash
- Several boxes of large, *opaque* plastic disposal bags, to be used for trash only

CARTON SMARTS

When it comes to securing the sizeable number of packing boxes needed for a serious move, this is not the time to try to save money with flimsy cartons you rescue from behind your supermarket Dumpster!

Check with your mover or an office-supply store and get yourself some decent moving cartons. You'll need a variety of sizes, so survey the kinds of goods you're transporting and estimate the numbers of each size you'll need for books, housewares, glass packs, clothing, linens, artwork, and so forth. If you're on a strict budget and feel you must buy used ones from a moving company or a friend who's recently relocated, make sure the cartons will hold up under the stress of one more move.

Many items like stemware or china will need to be packed separately. Either start saving newspapers or purchase blank newsprint at the same place you buy your boxes. I am not of the school where you use your towels and sheets as packing material. Who wants to wash and iron all that wrinkled linen in the midst of settling into a new place? No way. A nice big pile of blank newsprint will keep your hands cleaner, your glassware safe, and your spirits up.

Another hot tip: get yourself a professional tape dispenser (or two) and a couple of rolls of wide tape for sealing the boxes top and bottom. Don't stint on this stuff, as you can never have too much, and it wastes precious time to have to run out to buy more.

PREP TIME

If you bought new boxes and need to assemble them, read the printed directions (usually right on the box itself) and follow them precisely. Employing previously used cartons? Then affix large blank labels on two sides so you can write *your* content descriptions, e.g., "Dining Room: placemats, napkins, tablecloths." Take the time to black out old notations that were made by the previous movers whose boxes you've inherited. As you fill the boxes, write clearly and legibly on the new labels you've plastered onto your cartons and *don't* label the tops of the cartons because you can't see them when they're stacked. Instead label *two* sides.

Some boxes need more information on the label than just the contents. If a box is packed with stemware or your grandmother's priceless Wedgwood dessert plates, clearly mark it FRAGILE. If bad things will happen if a carton is put in the truck upside down, mark the box with an arrow pointing to the top and write the word UP.

Some veteran movers like to number boxes and keep a written inventory describing the contents in each box. This is an important option, especially if boxes of goods are going straight to storage and you will be consulting a list from time to time to locate something specific you'd like to pull out for later use. That way, you look at your list, find the item is in box number ten, and then scan the stacked boxes looking only for that number instead of having to read the sides of every carton.

If the move is from one house to another, for me at least it works best simply to label each box thus: "Master Bedroom: blankets" or "Kitchen: steak knives, cooking knives, misc. utensils." That way the movers (even if it's you) know not only where to put the box upon arriving at the new place but also its contents for faster repositioning in your new home.

TOOLS OF THE MOVING TRADE

An army doesn't go to war without its equipment, and the same is true for your premove crew (again, that's usually *you*).

As with the decluttering process, part of preplanning an actual move involves getting yourself a plastic home-products carry canister, a multipocket apron, or a moveable canvas shoe bag that can attach over a door (with each shoe pocket labeled with a black marking pen as to contents). Then, as you did with your sorting/purging/editing projects, assemble the following "tools" to make the job of packing that much easier:

- reading glasses if you use them
- retractable measuring tape
- felt-tip pens
- small scissors
- Phillips and standard screwdrivers
- a small hammer
- a box cutter with a safety catch
- sticky notes
- a packet of plain, white 3″ × 5″ self-adhesive labels
- small notepad and pen
- self-stick color-coded dots
- packing tape and dispenser
- a list of useful telephone numbers you're likely to call
- a cell phone, if you have one
- a small bottled water
- an energy bar or two

Reminder To preserve your sanity, return these tools to the same place after every use. When the move is completed, put these items in a box marked: **OPEN IMMEDIATELY — UNPACKING TOOLS!** Be sure that the movers put it on the moving truck *last*, as it's going to be the *first* thing you'll want to find when the movers arrive at your new place. Another choice is to leave nothing to chance and, assuming you're not trying to pass through a Homeland Security checkpoint, keep your mover's tool kit with you at all times and don't even put it on the truck.

MOVER'S FIRST AID

In addition to your moving tool kit, you need a mover's first-aid kit. This should consist of a duffle or tote bag with a tag tied to it sporting a big red cross. Keep this bag stashed in the island of sanity you set up back in chapter 7.

Inside the bag place the following:

- a local phone directory on the bottom of the bag
- your rightsizing notebook with floor plans
- a bottle of aspirin or the painkiller of your choice
- a couple of paper cups
- a small bottle of water and/or soda
- a box of Band-Aids
- an extra pair of scissors
- a second pair of reading glasses if you use them
- an extra box cutter with a safety latch
- a utility knife
- your personal phone book or electronic address book
- a roll of toilet paper
- a roll of paper towels
- a small-size bottle of glass cleaner
- tea bags and/or ground coffee and creamer
- sugar, if you take it in your coffee or tea
- a lightbulb or two
- a small flashlight
- the battery charger for your cell phone

Most of these items are backup for when you've misplaced something vital. Others will simply come in handy from time to time during the packing and moving process.

GETAWAY BAG

The third bag you'll prepack is a small traveling suitcase that you'll keep with you as you bid your final farewells to your old place and head for the new. It contains:

- nightclothes
- a change of underwear
- makeup or shaving gear
- the usual toiletries
- prescription medicines
- an easy change of clothes
- an extra pair of shoes
- a raincoat and/or small umbrella
- sunglasses
- jewelry

Even if you're just moving down the street, everyone wants to be able to brush his or her teeth or find a clean pair of underwear amid the chaos of moving into a new home. Put this "overnighter" in your locked car or keep it with your mover's first-aid bag. Take *both* bags and your purse or wallet when you walk away for the last time.

ANOTHER ISLAND OF SANITY

More preplanning and preparation! Before you commence the packing process, you will want to set up an additional island of sanity.

As outlined in chapter 7, your first island of sanity, that little corner in the kitchen, bedroom, or elsewhere that provides a safe haven from the packing chaos, is the place where you can sit down, have a cup of tea, make a phone call, and take a deep breath to recover your . . . uh . . . sanity. As noted, this is the spot to keep your mover's first-aid kit, as you may need to take an aspirin or to look up an address. It will give you a great boost to have everything you need at your fingertips in spite of the disarray that probably has taken over the rest of your home.

Now you should create a second island of sanity, where you will park the things (other than furniture) that are *not* making the journey with you. Select a space — a less-trafficked bedroom, covered porch, empty pantry, etc. — and put the boxes or bags you've labeled TRASH, DONATE, GIFT, RECYCLE, REPAIR, SELL, DON'T HAVE A CLUE in this designated space, leaving enough room to move around.

As you encounter items during the packing process you don't want to take with you, bring them to this "holding area" and place them in the appropriate box or bag for later removal. Keep a set of adhesive labels and felt pens handy to attach peel-off IDs to specific items, noting the name of the recipient, if there is one. For those of us with minds like sieves, it helps to have something jog our memory about what item we've already decided to give to whom!

With the DON'T HAVE A CLUE pile, once you've come up with a solution about a particular item, you'll eventually file it in one of the other designated receptacles or will take it back to the packing area to be included in the move.

PLAYING TAG

Before a single box is packed, deal with the furniture first. Get out those adhesive **dots** we had so much fun with earlier. I like to tag the furniture that is going into the moving truck with green dots, and I put red dots on the furniture that's headed somewhere else, like to Goodwill or to a nephew.

Additionally, it's probably a good idea to add a sticky note on the "keepers" you've marked with green dots. Write the room designation for each item and affix it securely with painter's tape on the piece of furniture or lamp in an obvious spot where the moving crew can see it and put the item in the appropriate room in the other house. If you know the ultimate destination of whatever furniture and household items you'll *not* be taking and have marked with the red dots, you can put a taped sticky note on them, too ("Cousin Joan," "Salvation Army," "The kids," etc.) which will facilitate their proper removal later.

For furniture such as beds that is going to be dismantled, a major way to prevent hassles is to provide clear plastic zip bags for the hardware required to put the piece back together again: screws, nuts, and bolts. Label these bags "Master Bed Hardware" or "Den Shelves Hardware," etc. Put all these plastic bags into one box labeled IMPORTANT! Hardware for Furniture Reconstruction! (Your screwdrivers are in your tool kit, remember?)

In my own moves I hand carried this precious hardware box to my new home on the theory that "what can go wrong will go wrong," and thus, it never did.

THE FIRST BOX PACKED

Let's assume that you've completed your sorting, purging, and editing and you've labeled the furniture as to final destination.

What carton to pack first, you wonder?

Unless you're doing a "blitz pack" because you have to be out of your house pronto, you should probably pack the household items you'll need *least* first.

That generally means you'll initially pack up a guest bedroom or guest bathroom, perhaps a dining room or linen closet. If you suddenly discover that you "forgot" to sort/purge/edit a group of items when you get to packing them, remember our rightsizing mantra:

- Do I use it?
- Do I love it?
- Will it work in the new place?

It's still not too late to take things into island of sanity #2 and put them in the proper "bye-bye box" or to find a home for that ratty sofa somewhere other than your new place.

BLITZ PACKING

You may recall Paula Skinner, who had to pack up her 7,000-square-foot house in Charleston in two weeks' time because the new owners planned a big birthday bash. She and her friends did what she dubbed "a blitz pack," which requires quick decision making, firmly grounded in reality.

The main question becomes what can you get rid of fastest? The inventory tends to be pretty long, but basically it's stuff you haven't used for all sorts of reasons. (Nobody cares what those reasons are anymore!) Here are just a few of the items that belong on the "DON'T EVEN *THINK* ABOUT TAKING IT" list:

- shabby patio furniture
- half-empty bottles of suntan lotion, eyewash, digestive aids, and other medicine cabinet no-nos
- calcified steam irons
- books you haven't opened in five years
- the box full of papers from two jobs ago
- Halloween decorations not used in two years
- old cans of paint, varnish, or thinner
- outdated roadmaps
- saved magazines you never read
- clippings you never filed
- checks from closed bank accounts (shred them)
- hardwood floor cleaner (when you'll have wall-to-wall carpets)
- pull-down shades that won't fit new windows
- skis you haven't used since your knee operation
- off-brand bottles of booze

You get the idea. With any luck these kinds of items were purged before the packing process began, but if not, don't be tempted to throw this stuff into a box and "deal with it later." Deal with it now, and don't let it clutter up your next dwelling. Be strong. Be brave. In fact, be fearless! Stick to your moving mantra, and I know you'll do the right thing: get rid of it!

AT LONG LAST — MOVING WEEK!

The good news is that if you're willing to approach moving the rightsizing way with the right preplanning and organization, you'll go a long way toward making the week you move much smoother than it would be otherwise.

In my travels around the country interviewing rightsizers and wannabes, the *single most important factor* determining the success of a move had to do with facing reality at a fairly early stage in the process and being able to let go of possessions that had no real use in the new abode. If that was accomplished, the actual moving day became a well-oiled machine.

Widower Don Pickard, now in his seventies and living in the Sunbelt, retired from a long career in senior management for several major moving companies. His work took him from California to Washington, D.C.; to Alexandria, Virginia; and finally to Florida, where he now serves as a consultant to the industry and conducts visual surveys of homes where corporate executives are relocating. He also gives free seminars to people on fixed incomes who are preparing to move into retirement communities.

Pickard does his best to convince both groups about the complications created when people try to cram too much into a space that won't accommodate it.

Cautions Don, "Moving too many boxes of possessions simply wastes time and money and often requires additional rearrangement of furniture, especially if you find yourself trying to make too many things fit in a small space. This increases the cost of the move and sometimes results in people having to acquire extra storage space at extra cost to deal with the surplus." (See storage issues discussed in chapter 12.)

The second determining success factor has to do with developing a plan and timetable and being organized and disciplined enough to follow through on it.

Pickard in his travels has observed that "most people do not allow enough time to complete the monumental task of sifting through twenty, thirty, or forty years' worth of possessions." He's become an expert at spotting what he calls the "stumbling blocks" to a sensible move. "It's always the files, the pictures, the memorabilia, the books, the collections, the decorations, the small things that are the hardest to eliminate and, by far, take the most time to deal with."

Don even freely admits he's suffering from the same problem himself.

"Since I lost my wife, I now have a lot of personal sorting and disposing to do. Each piece I handle and look at has a history and emotions attached to it. You even find yourself crying while performing this task."

The heartaches and headaches can really get intense when it comes time to pack and move possessions for which there isn't enough room or which simply have no useful purpose.

If you're reading this book with enough lead time, start dealing with Don's list of stumbling blocks immediately, even if you spend only one day a month winnowing your files, pictures, books, and so forth. As suggested in chapter 4, you need to give a cold, hard look at everything you own and to develop a timetable for sorting/purging/editing. Jot down specific dates in your calendar to devote to the job of preparation and to preplanning your move.

If your moving deadline is looming, then organize a crew to consult with you during the process of implementing your new credo: "Do I use it; do I love it; will it suit me or my new place?" If you waver, they often stand firm or act as a sounding board. Together you can power through these various categories *before* you start filling up the boxes.

COUNTDOWN TO A RIGHTSIZED MOVE

Keep this list close by as you prepare for your move. Most things on the list are simply common sense, but there may be a few suggestions you haven't thought of.

1. Contact movers for an in-home estimate six to eight weeks before the move. Ask for a soup-to-nuts cost analysis, even if you plan to pack yourself. If you run out of time, at least you'll know what you're in for. (Save all your receipts for taxes.)
2. Book your movers *at least* three to four weeks in advance. If you plan a summer move, the busiest time of the year, make that five to six weeks in advance.
3. If possible move on a weekday, when utilities, banks, and government offices are open. Some urban buildings forbid moving on weekends, so check with the landlord, condo association, or co-op board before scheduling your move. Plan to be present during the move the entire day.

4. Collect all your important records (passports, birth certificates, insurance documents, medical and dental records, veterinary records, etc.) in one container and keep it with you.
5. Close local bank accounts and open new ones as needed.
6. Contact all utilities to arrange the cutoff dates for services and provide a new address where the final bills will be sent. Set up new utility accounts as needed.
7. Give your new address to the post office as well as your primary contacts.
8. Prepack and hand carry as many precious items as you can.
9. Pick up your final batch of dry cleaning before you move.
10. Gas up your car and have it tuned if you plan on driving it any distance.

A moving postscript: don't forget to take your documents file, your rightsizing first-aid kit, your rightsizing tool kit, and your getaway overnight bag with you as you walk out the door. If it makes you feel more secure and you have the room, also don't trust the box of hardware you'll need for reassembling your bed to the moving truck; take that, too!

THE MOVERS ARE AT THE DOOR

Keep your floor plan or detailed blueprint close by and make copies to post at the entrance to each room or to give to any friends who may be helping you on moving day. This way you can accurately instruct the movers which household items should be removed from the old house and where they should be placed in the new. If you've labeled your boxes and the big furniture pieces as recommended above, there should be a minimum of confusion.

Another "traffic-management" tip is to put identifying placards for the mover's benefit at the entrance to each room in your new home: "Master Bedroom," "Guest Bedroom," "Home Office," "Attic Upstairs," "Back Porch." What may seem obvious to you may not be so to moving crews who've been in scores of houses where the dining room was used as an office or the second bedroom was the baby's nursery or the finished basement was the guestroom. The more the crew knows about your intentions (even if they're friendly volunteers), the less often they have to pause while carrying a couch on their backs to ask *you* questions. This, in turn, frees you up for other important activities, like telling the cable guy where to hook up the TV.

AND SPEAKING OF MOVING BUDDIES

If you're lucky enough to have friends to help (or even go the hire-a-pal route, where you pay friends or relatives for their time), you greatly improve your moving karma. However, just as too many cooks spoil the broth, be sure to assign your worker bees specific tasks to avoid playing bumper cars with the professional movers.

See "The Rightsizing Brigade" box for a rundown of the obvious "jobs" you can dole out to your friends willing to help you pack. Do your best to match their talents to the task at hand.

THE RIGHTSIZING BRIGADE

Position	*Helps pack*
The Garden Guru	potted plants (load last; unload first to avoid crushing and wilting), garden tools
The Fashionista	clothing and accessories
The Kitchen King/Queen	pots, pans, utensils, plates, glassware
The Librarian	books or home-office files, papers
The Geek	computers, stereos, TVs, CDs, DVDs, faxes, scanners
The Curator	paintings, photographs, objets d'art
The Handyperson	tools, garage, basement, attic

DEALING WITH LEFTOVERS

The boxes are packed with the possessions you want to take with you, but there's all that stuff still waiting in your island of sanity #2 that threatens to turn it into the island of chaos.

Now's the time to turn your abode into Party Central. Invite the recipients of your labeled largesse to come pick up the items they're going to buy or take as gifts. Anything else that didn't get packed by this time is also assembled under a sign: "I'M FREE!" Invite your neighbors to drop by (even those to whom you've never spoken) and see if there's anything they'd like.

There's one more outlet for last-minute disposal. Many towns have a tradition whereby you put items you're "releasing to the universe" near your front curb. You'll probably be amazed at how fast they disappear when they bear that welcome sign, "I'M FREE!" Make sure your town has no ordinance against this practice (what killjoys!) and set out your discards a few days ahead of your move, if possible, so you'll know if you need to make other arrangements for removal.

Previous chapters have gone into detail about the proper disposal of hazardous items and other problematic possessions, so if you need a refresher course, check back to chapter 7.

CLEANUP CREWS

Once your household goods and the leftovers are removed from your home, down to the last paper clip, a cleanup crew should be poised to descend upon your old place so you can leave it in immaculate condition. If this crew consists of *you* and your volunteer brigade, try to arrange your timetable to allow for a day, or at least a night's sleep, so you can recover from the rigors of the move.

If you've hired someone to do the dirty work, give them a call as the move is progressing to update them about how things are going and to confirm the times you want them to show up after you vacate the premises. Review chapter 10 to make sure everybody's on the same page about what the cleaners will be doing, how much it will cost, and the time it will take to complete the job.

If you have to be on your way immediately and can't supervise the cleanup, try to enlist a friend to do the follow-up on this last phase of your move to avoid later hassles from your landlord or the new owners. Make sure someone takes pictures of every empty room you've left in pristine condition to prove you've held up your end of the bargain and have left the place in "broom clean" condition, as many contracts require.

TO STORE OR NOT TO STORE

If everything that's useful and meaningful to you is packed neatly in labeled boxes and loaded on the moving truck, then what do you do with those leftover items you simply can't part with, at least for now?

And what if there are a few surprises waiting for you at your new place, like a love seat that crowds the room, too many pots and pans for the kitchen cupboards, or other storage problems — the kind of things that must be solved or the move won't look like such a good idea after all?

Good question.

And there's also the problem of maintaining your newly rightsized life. This is especially true if you've had to struggle hard to declutter and organize yourself — perhaps for the first time ever. What steps can you take to keep it from piling up again? You can read chapter 12.

PART III

The Time of Your Life

REVELING IN A RIGHTSIZED WORLD

Chapter 12

How Can I Maintain My Rightsized Life?

Sustaining your simplified surroundings

OLD CLUTTER HABITS DIE HARD!

Once you've lived in a rightsized environment, you know why you like it. You feel calmer, more serene, more in control of your life, and less distracted by "things," especially untidy things (better known as clutter). In *un*cluttered surroundings you're better able to focus on what matters most, which generally boils down to just plain living your life with friends and family, using your creativity in ways that give you pleasure, and generally enjoying the world around you, minute by minute.

The difficulty, of course, is maintaining a rightsized world after you've done all the work to create one!

The quest for answers on how best to sustain a post–rightsized world led me to the door of Gail John, a professional organizer who's encountered a few bumps in her own journey to arrive at the type of life she currently enjoys. Meeting her, you sense at once that she possesses a profound sense of serenity despite revamping her living quarters to fit her drastically changed circumstances.

For years she had a successful career in both the wholesale and retail sides of the clothing business, an industry that was extensively transformed when American companies sent the majority of manufacturing overseas.

"My business changed overnight," Gail recalls. "The brand-name company I'd worked for for a long time suddenly consolidated. What jobs that were left went to New York, and I didn't want to uproot my entire life to move thousands of miles."

In the aftermath of a divorce that had added to the turmoil, Gail took any job she could get, from event planner to bank teller to tour guide. Despite her experience and training, the positions she got offered low pay and no benefits. She even did a stint as a waitress while she tried to regroup.

All Gail's life her friends and family had told her, "'You are so *organized!*'" she relates with a smile. "I've always liked to rearrange houses and quirky spaces. If you look in my wallet, all the dollar bills are facing the same way. As I kid I liked to draw floor plans."

In the autumn of 2005, Gail put her natural inclinations together with her fashion and design sensibilities to found Get It Done, offering her services as a professional organizer, home-office consultant, and room rearranger to her community at large.

"My greatest thrill is thinking out of the box to solve organization and design problems," she relates. Once an everyday neatnik, she's now become a professional rightsizer.

Gail's first clients could plainly see that she'd already solved her own design problems when she elected to live in 425 square feet, a one-room garret with an outside entrance atop an old sea captain's house.

The room, which was probably once an attic, has two alcoves — one large enough for a queen-size bed with a raw silk coverlet and an attractive scattering of pillows and another nook that serves as her home office. It has room for a small desk angled from the wall, a slim laptop, and an unobtrusive portable printer placed below eye level.

In the kitchenette two small garbage cans are disguised out of sight in an antique copper washing tub with a fitted metal top; a fabric-covered box covers her answering machine. Framed art camouflages the doors that open into storage spaces tucked behind the walls of the odd-angled room.

On the evening I visited her hideaway, ivory candles positioned on her small dining table cast a magical golden glow to the four corners of the room. Gail's private realm was utterly free of clutter and exuded a calming serenity yet still provided distinct areas for cooking, eating, socializing, sleeping, working, and bathing.

"This is my sanctuary," she said softly, adding that she'd lived in this restricted space for years now — and loved it. "I don't want to see technology here. This place is almost like being aboard a boat, or tucked away in a cabin somewhere. I feel safe, protected, free from noise and bother."

Gail's home is rightsized for a woman whom life has buffeted about a bit, and yet she clearly thrives in this small world of her own creation. She's found a way to use what she knows of organization and design to craft an orderly oasis for herself as a woman and a professional while helping her clients with homes both big and small to fashion their own level of simplicity and calm. She resonates to her diminutive universe and says that, in her case, "less is definitely more."

WHY MORE MAY BE *LESS*

Barry Schwartz is a professor of psychology at Swarthmore College and the author of *The Paradox of Choice: Why More Is Less.* Schwartz believes that the freedom to buy, buy, buy has left Americans increasingly bewildered — not liberated.

In fact, his survey of a number of studies regarding how consumers feel about the enormous choices facing them in the marketplace suggests that we are increasingly overwhelmed by all these choices. What has resulted, postulates the good doctor, is choice anxiety! Schwartz backs up his theories by pointing to, among many examples, the opt-out phenomenon that occurred when people were given a plethora of 401(k) investment options (often they didn't choose any, despite tax advantages) and the panicked reactions of senior citizens to the multiple drug-plan choices they face.

So the assumption that more choice means more freedom and that more freedom makes us happier is false, Schwartz says. Unless we are our own environmental watchdog, we will have problems maintaining our hard-won rightsized world. If we mindlessly allow the cycle to start all over again by continually buying more, the result is likely to be, in Schwartz's view, "stress, anxiety and dissatisfaction."

Conversely, can simplifying your life by paring down to only the items you use and love, as Gail John has managed to do, offer a path toward serenity and a true sense of home? Let us not forget that the onslaught of "Buy Me!" is relentless. Once we've gone to all this trouble to rightsize our lives, how do we prevent our basements, attics, and back cupboards from filling up again?

On the evening of my visit to Gail's tiny upstairs aerie, I couldn't help but be entranced by the allure of her cozy space. Nonetheless, there was one question I had to ask since I currently live in three times her space and continually struggle to acquire the habit of "a place for everything and everything in its place."

"It's just beautiful," I murmured appreciatively, "but it's awfully small. How do you *keep* it this way?"

"If something new comes into my space," she says, her soft voice suddenly assuming the timbre of a mother superior, "something else *departs.*"

Gail John and the other organizing specialists I've consulted coast-to-coast say each of us needs to develop an articulated plan to ensure that surroundings *stay* simplified — whether you have one room or many. Following is a summary of the things I've learned.

Five Minutes in the Morning

Make your bed as soon as you get out of it. Take five minutes in the morning to put your inner sanctum to rights, and the rest of your bedroom will be well on its way to appearing clutter free. One easy way to keep your closet appearing reasonably in order is to have hangers that look alike. Spend another two minutes gathering up abandoned clothing, disposing of old newspapers and magazines, and taking out used glasses and dishware to the kitchen. The amount of time spent tidying isn't as important as doing it just a few minutes a day.

Deal Daily with the Mail

Designate an "opening-the-mail" area with a wastebasket nearby. The number-one rule is "touch it only once" to save a lot of time later on. Stop saying to yourself, "I'll put it here just for now." "Now" turns into days, right? So, as soon as the mail arrives, take five minutes to open it, trash the junk and excess envelopes, and sort it into piles according to addressee. Put saved catalogs in one basket, magazines and newsletters in another, and take bills to the desk where you pay them (and put them neatly in a pile, slot, or basket until you can get to them). If you don't pay your bills immediately, write the date by which you must mail it in the corner where the stamp goes and then stack or file these envelopes by deadline.

Reading Matter Matters

Put daily newspapers in a receptacle as soon as they are read. On the same day each week, put the pile in the paper recycling bin or basket. Resist bringing paper into your house from events you've attended. Ask yourself, "Will I ever *really* look at this museum guide or conference rundown again?" Don't accept the subscription offer of "one free year" for a magazine that you may not even have time to read. Just remember that for each item in your mailbox, you have to bring it into your home, stash it somewhere, maybe read it, and take it out again. Like marriage, a subscription is a big commitment . . . so think twice before agreeing to it.

A Room with a Wastebasket

Purchase a wastebasket for every room in your home. Train yourself to constantly use these "circular files" as the paper flows into your home. Think of these disposal receptacles as part of the decor; they should fit with the overall design scheme, which could mean that you choose a leather one in the den, wicker in the bathroom, etc. One or two times a week, just before leaving your home, get a big garbage bag and circulate through the house emptying the wastebaskets in one fell swoop. Then, on your way to another appointment, put the paper trash into the bin outside your home. Voila! Your entire place looks tidier.

Darn It! Where Are My . . .?

Keep keys and reading glasses in the same spot. Pick one location where you tend to set down your keys and designate a permanent container for them in that spot. Some people put attractive baskets or bowls standing side by side to hold both keys *and* reading glasses, if you use them. An alternative is to employ a key box or hook system with labels so the errant devils end up in the same resting place each time. If you use this system, designate some spot nearby as the place where your extra pairs of glasses will live. The same goes for your cell phone, spare change, or your I.D. badge. Select a convenient location to stow the items that travel in and out of your house most days and be *consistent* about putting them there!

Store Items Where You Use Them

Train yourself to put things away in places nearest their use. Select locations for the items you use most frequently that are adjacent to the places you're apt to use them. This means you put the poultry shears in a kitchen drawer near the cutting board or stash your toothpaste next to your toothbrush in the bathroom. If you're always looking for a safety pin, gather all of them in one place and put them in a small box in the corner of your sock drawer and then train yourself to put new ones there when they come into your house. The same goes for loose change. Don't leave it *on* the bureau but *in* a receptacle. Lots of supermarkets have machines that will quickly sort the collection you've kept in a jar (for a fee) and give you paper money in return.

Parking Karma

Find "parking places" for items on their way somewhere else. Household items that become clutter are often things that are heading for a room upstairs, the garage, a shed at the back of your property, a closet, dresser, your home office, or the attic. Collect them in locations that remind you to take them to the place where they "live." In home-furnishing stores, container stores, and online sites, you can find baskets designed to snug onto two steps of your stairway where you can park items that are heading for higher ground. Wall hooks are a good choice for clothing that can rest until restored to a permanent home in a hall or bedroom closet. Newspaper caddies fall into this category, as do in-and-out baskets for mail and pending bills. (FYI: the floor is never considered a proper parking place.)

Instant Clutter Busters

Cut down clutter where it's piled up. Don't just leave a dirty plate in the sink. Take three seconds either to wash it and put it in the dish drain or stow it in the dishwasher, out of sight. Rinse that glass after you use it. Maybe even dry it and put it back in the cupboard. That way disgustingly dirty dishware never piles up. Put away that roll of stamps as soon as you address your bills. Hang up your coat the moment you walk in the door. Take ten minutes before bed to put away things that were left out during the day. Time-study experts say that if you perform a task twenty-one days in a row, it becomes a habit. Keeping clutter at bay is exactly that: a habit, so get into it!

Mini Decluttering Projects

Set up "destination boxes" before you tackle any decluttering job. For mini-decluttering sessions, use the aforementioned box or plastic bag system with these labels: TRASH, DONATE, GIFT, RECYCLE, TRANSFER, REPAIR, SELL, and DON'T HAVE A CLUE. Get the fruits of your editing efforts out of your living space ASAP. If you need to do a bigger purge of a closet or cupboard, don't buy the organizational containers until after you've completed the sorting process; otherwise the new containers are in danger of becoming simply more clutter!

Keep in Mind the Cluster Theory

Keep like-with-like items in the same location: jewelry, ski clothes, kitchen knives, etc. Whatever the category — whether it's items for wrapping packages or products for putting on makeup — cluster the objects in close proximity to each other so you know what you have and can then corral them in appropriate containers to be able to use them efficiently.

The Big Purge and Merge

Every three months purge your magazine and catalog pile. Take ten minutes and cull out catalogs and magazines that are fewer than three months old. You haven't read them thus far, and it's highly unlikely you'll read them in the future. Get the rejects out of the house pronto. And don't fret. If there's an article you want to find later, jot down the date and page number in your date book or rightsizing notebook. You can always recover it online or head for your local library and quickly look up the back issue.

A Permanent Cure for Pack-Rat Syndrome

Save only what you use regularly. Rightsizers stay "clean" by halting the habit of saving things "because I might need it someday." This includes shopping bags, rubber bands, and sturdy boxes you think you want to keep handy to mail something next month. Limit yourself to no more than five shopping bags, ten vegetable plastic bags, ten rubber bands, and a few, small boxes at a time and store them in accessible places so you'll remember to *use* them! Do not get sucked back into saving restaurant menus, church bulletins, conference material, and playbills. If you save and recycle decorative ribbons (I do), designate a specific place for them among your wrapping supplies.

Magnet Madness

Beware of multiplying magnets. I know this may be heresy in some homes, but bona fide rightsizers resist the temptation to start collecting magnets for their refrigerators. These creatures tend to have babies overnight . . . and then you start attaching little mementos with the quote of the week, so-so photographs of your friends, grandkids' oversize artwork, recipes, cartoons. Soon what starts out as a collection of sweet memorabilia turns into a rat's nest. If you must, retain one or two of your favorite magnets to tack up truly important reminders in plain view. The one I saved?

BEWARE
PICKPOCKETS
and
LOOSE WOMEN
New Orleans Police Dept.

I think I enjoy that magnet even more than ever as it sits like a solitary sentinel on my fridge.

Generous to a Fault

If you're saving an item for a friend or family member, box it up and send it. Make every day a holiday and bestow your gift as soon as you decide you're going to part with it rather than allowing it to languish somewhere in your home. If the person lives nearby, store it in the trunk of your car so you'll have it the next time you see him or her. The same holds true for news and magazine clippings. Keep a stack of envelopes in the area where you pay your bills and pop those babies into a mailer, put stamps on them, and send them on their way! If you haven't done this within one week of clipping the item, toss it and tell the erstwhile recipient to look for it online or at the library. If it's important enough to you, you'll send it. If it's important enough to them, they'll track it down on their end.

Rightsizing New Purchases

Think twice before adding anything to your rightsized life. This may be the toughest rule of all, because it includes everything: new magazine subscriptions, a new shirt, a new waffle maker when you haven't used your old one in six months. If you can't resist buying something, then make a pact with yourself that you'll get rid of something else. This is also known as the sacred "something in/something out" rule. Know the difference between **shopping** and **buying.** If you need something and you've written it on a list, that's buying. If you just wander around without a list, you're shopping . . . and shopping is what brings in the clutter. It's also likely to be the wrong size, a duplicate that you forgot you already owned, or something you really didn't need in the first place.

When Things Are Kaputsky

When something breaks, have it repaired or get rid of it. Raise your right hand and repeat this pledge in front of your bathroom mirror: "I will never put a scratched CD or burnt-out vacuum cleaner in the back of the closet *ever again!*" If the glass in the picture frame cracks or the strap on the dog harness shears off, you will either immediately go to the framer or the shoe cobbler and get these items repaired — *or* you will deep-six them in the trash.

Stop Collecting, I Want to Get Off!

Declare a moratorium if you've stopped collecting. Let friends and family know if you no longer collect some formerly favored item the second you've made this life-altering decision. If the holidays roll around and someone "forgets" or gives you a duplicate of something you already own, keep the best one and pass the other one on to someone who can make good use of it. Try not to fall into the guilt trap. The world will not end if you decide to forgo adding anything more to what you already have in abundance. In fact, when you pare down to the best of the best, chances are excellent you will appreciate the select few treasures you've kept more each day.

HIGH (POWERED) MAINTENANCE

Gail John and I aren't the only ones who sound like Attila the Hen on the subject of keeping clutter at bay every day. Cindy Glovinsky, author of *Making Peace with the Things in Your Life,* recommends putting a sign somewhere (bathroom mirror, refrigerator) that says, "DO IT NOW!" and keeping it there until the suggestions of the sort listed here have become ingrained habits. A habit, remember, is just something you do every day for twenty-one days in a row.

Right after my visit with Gail John in her garret and our discussion about techniques for maintaining the serenity and simplicity of one's environment, I padded down the outside staircase and through a small garden filled with exotic plants that had been brought back decades earlier by the home's seafaring former owner. The air was pungent with star jasmine and flowering lavender. A profusion of white calla lilies bordered the moss-covered brick path. I found myself mulling over the catechism of ideas Gail and other organizers I'd consulted had shared so generously.

Suddenly the thought sprang into my head: maintaining a rightsized world, like prayer, is a daily discipline. It's inspiring to know it takes only twenty-one days to make it a permanent way of life.

THE CONTINUING CURSE OF ACCUMULATION

Let's face it. Given our acquisitive propensities, it's hard to keep clutter at bay, or at least it is for some of us. In my own home everything is in order, and then mysteriously, I look around and there are piles of mail at the entrance hall, clothes not hung up, and simply too much stuff bulging out of closets and cupboards.

Americans are known around the world as the major consumers on the planet, generating nearly two hundred million tons of household garbage a year. Another indication of the astonishing amount of material goods we accumulate can be measured by the number of us who don't even keep our earthly possessions in our homes — storing our excess stuff off-site!

Self-storage is now a $15 billion dollar industry with some thirty-nine thousand facilities nationwide.

"Americans like to keep their stuff," says Tim Dietz, spokesman for the Self Storage Association, noting in the last decade alone that the number of self-storage facilities nationwide has grown about 70 percent.

Since we seem firmly rooted in our inclination to *pay* to store things we no longer use, what's a rightsizing novice to do to maintain a clutter-free life in the face of this seemingly irresistible trend? Fortunately, there's plenty you can do.

Earlier I described the five containers of off-site storage my husband and I were forced to deal with once his company stopped paying the storage bills. We had moved all our worldly possessions from southern to northern California without a thorough purging and, thus, had mountains of household and personal items that were of absolutely no use to us in our current circumstances.

Frankly, I wouldn't wish that sorting job on my worst enemy, so for you I've tried to gather together the best thinking from the most knowledgeable people I know to examine the question of whether to store possessions in places other than where you live.

Winifred Gallagher writes extensively on the subject of environmental psychology. She makes a pithy comment in *House Thinking: A Room-by-Room Look at How We Live*. She says, "One reason the American home in general and the bedroom in particular grow bigger as our households become smaller is that the spoils of our unparalleled consumerism require more and more storage space."

She wryly observes that a spate of reality television shows is devoted to the "problem" of coping with too much stuff. "After they've forced people to face their jammed closets and drawers and figure out what has to go, the host-experts freshen up the suddenly spacious home." But do the homeowners keep it tidy after the camera crew departs?

Not without storage space, they don't. Cultural critic that she is, Gallagher finds the vogue of "faux simplicity" that requires expensive — and extensive — built-ins rather amusing, adding that it is "a simplicity that looks perfect . . . [and] costs big money."

STORAGE — A BIG-TICKET ITEM

Built-in storage on-site, as well as self-storage away from your home, is going to cost you either way, and there are plenty of rightsizers who think such storage is worth every penny.

The most sensible way to keep the costs down and maintain your rightsized life is to do what the experts cited in this book have been saying all along: surround yourselves with only the things you use and love, and you won't have so much to store! This alone will go far in helping to maintain your newly rightsized life.

But that usually means unloading a goodly number of the possessions you have accumulated in a half century or so of living so you can get your household down to reasonable proportions. Once you've done that, however, seeking proper storage becomes a legitimate quest as a means of maintaining your rightsized life, and one for which there are some marvelously ingenious solutions.

Entire books have been written about the best ways to make the most of storage space you have inside your home, regardless of its size. What follows here is the short course on in-house storage, and some of it may sound mighty familiar.

Storage in the Home

Assuming you have already culled, purged, donated, and/or sold those items for which you have no use (or room) in your current household, we can begin to think about seeking storage solutions for the wares that remain.

Here is where clever built-ins come into play — such as drawers fitted into unused space in corners, pullout shelves tucked into free space under a set of stairs, linens and clothing stored under a window seat, shelving to display books or objets d'art crafted floor to ceiling and around windows. If you are really prepared to go upscale, the White Conveyor Belt company, which supplies revolving equipment to dry-cleaning establishments, has created a mini revolving electric conveyer belt for hanging clothes in narrow closets that costs about $2,500.

Another approach to squeezing storage space out of unexpected places is to use dual-purpose furniture: ottomans with space for bedding, entrance-hall benches with hinged tops for boots and sports equipment, tables with long-skirted cloths disguising storage shelving out of sight.

If your storage issues confound you, perhaps you need professional help (see chapter 10). There is an entire industry dedicated to solving your problems: space planners, expert organizers, and contractors and carpenters who specialize in making the best use of the space you have and finding interior space you didn't know you had under your roof.

When it comes to storing books, your volumes are useless unless they are easily accessible. If you have books you simply refuse to part with packed in boxes in your basement or attic or the trunk of your car, your best bet is to look for a room that could be enhanced with floor-to-ceiling bookshelves. A sliding ladder allows access to the top shelves and affords a genuine "library look" if you want to make the investment.

An alternative to the big built-ins is to parse your books in smaller groupings — cookbooks in the kitchen, novels near your bed, nonfiction in smaller sets of shelves in the living room.

But books in boxes? Bad idea.

Media Storage

If you have substantial collections of DVDs, CDs, and videotapes — not to mention the equipment to play them on — you are definitely heading for the pricey territory of "home-entertainment containment." Unless you have the latest flat-panel television or have all your CDs stored on an iPod, you'll probably want an entertainment armoire or possibly a hanging bracket close to the ceiling to house your TV. There are custom towers for your stereo equipment and all manner of freestanding or built-in options to choose from. Whatever path you take, be sure that there is plenty of ventilation to avoid the kind of heat buildup that can eventually KO your audio and video gear.

Clever Kitchens

Drawer dividers are your friends and can be the easiest route to bringing order out of chaos. If you're looking for storage solutions for a specific problem, check out the *Home Storage Idea Book* (see the Resource Directory) and others like it that offer all sorts of "Why didn't *I* think of that?" suggestions. My all-time favorite adapts the magnetic strips normally employed to hold carving knives to secure round, metal boxes with clear plastic tops filled with spices. What a concept! You can actually *see* that saffron and may be inspired to use it before you turn one hundred!

Meanwhile, ask yourself, "How many frying pans do I actually use?" and nest and store the best of them with all your other "chosen few" metal cooking implements. The same goes for glass or white ovenproof dishes. Keep them together in one cupboard, and if you're not using a couple of them, don't push them to the back. Pass them on to a person who can make better use of them than you — and presto! You'll free up some storage space.

Clogged Closets

In many rightsized homes inhabited by people who once dwelled in larger spaces, closets are often the spots where reality suddenly intrudes. In your former house you could put out-of-season clothing off to the sides and line up the outfits appropriate for the current season in the middle at eye level. This is not going to work if space is at a premium. Fortunately there are a couple of alternatives, especially if you remind yourself that your goal is to be able to spot an item you wish to wear and reach in and grab it without having a wrestling match.

Every season, arrange your closet with the clothes you wear the most frequently at that time of year hanging right in front of you when you open the closet door. When the season changes, change out your wardrobe and put the clothes appropriate for the new season that you like best and wear the most closest at hand. (Pitch the things you didn't wear that year.)

To make room for the system just described, store your out-of-season wardrobe in garment bags hanging on standing racks in the basement or attic or in airtight plastic or in vacuum-compressed plastic bags designed to fit under the bed or on high shelves. A few warnings: be sure there is no mildew in the areas where you plan to store your seasonal garments, and if you use hanging garment bags, purchase the type with at least one clear plastic panel so the contents are visible. That way, you can avoid the hassle of pulling out all the clothing packed inside to find the one stored item of clothing you're looking for.

If unmanageable closet space continues to give you migraines, there are national companies happy to help you solve your problems and retrofit the interior to gain optimum efficiency (see the Resource Directory). Or head for my personal favorite, the Container Store, where you can get free advice or do-it-yourself tips.

Meanwhile, the key thing to remember is that if your clothing or jewelry isn't visible, chances are you won't wear much of it. Jettison those wire hangers and replace them with uniform plastic and/or padded hangers (wood, if it's in your budget), which generally take up less space than an odd assortment of hangers that don't snug together neatly. Hangers that are all the same size and color have the added advantage of simply looking neater. They also help you group various types of clothing together to make them easier to find, especially when you're dressing in a hurry. And to avoid "bathroom buildup," consider installing a multiprong hook on the back of the door on which to hang nightclothes.

Messy Drawers Be Gone!

If you store your jewelry or tuxedo studs in silk or velvet pouches, consider investing in a label machine (I bought a Brother P-touch and never looked back). It may seem like an extravagance, but you will love knowing instantly what bauble is in each bag, and the clarity of the print will probably inspire you to label file folders, linen cupboard shelves, and all manner of items in your household for easy identification and accessibility.

Shoe Fetishes

According to closet mavens I've consulted, lining up shoes on the floor can be worse than no storage at all. Your intended left shoe has a way of migrating to a galaxy far, far away from your right one just when you're racing for an important appointment. Some people swear by those shoe racks that telescope to fit the space on your closet floor, but in my experience, the shoes eventually fall off, so I vote for several alternative solutions.

If clear plastic shoe boxes aren't practical or are beyond your budget, label the end of the original cardboard shoe boxes for easy identification and store them (ideally) on an easily accessible shelf. One shoe fanatic I know took a close-up picture of each shoe style and pasted it on the end for even easier identification.

Another alternative for storing shoes is to purchase a large-size shoe bag to hang on the back of your closet door. If bureau drawers are in short supply, such a bag is also handy for storing pantyhose, underwear, or socks.

Garage No More

Many rightsizers get a shock when it dawns on them that they may not have the all-purpose garage anymore as their backup storage system. Even if the family's ultimate "holding area" is still available, it may have room for only one car or have morphed into a carport. This, in turn, means that you'll have to dispose of (or find new homes for) items that used to be conveniently stashed there.

If you don't have a garden to take care of anymore, you won't need spades and hoes. The same goes for old sporting equipment, luggage with nonfunctioning wheels, or excessive amounts of household tools. It's probably a good idea to own a three-tiered toolbox to house your best hammer, Phillips and standard screwdrivers, pliers, jumper cables, and so forth. I, for one, will never surrender my compact electric drill. Back pantries, utility closets, and the rear of front-hall closets often become the rightsizer's "new garage," and their contents must be pruned accordingly.

OFF-SITE (TEMPORARY) STORAGE SOLUTIONS

We've already learned that storage for surplus household goods outside the home is one of the fastest-growing industries in America. There's no doubt that sometimes finding a home-away-from home for possessions is a godsend. Often, however, a personal storage locker becomes a wasteful expense simply because the owner can't embrace the need for "letting things go." That's especially true if someone else is paying the freight. But just as my husband and I discovered, eventually there will be a day of reckoning.

What is so insidious about off-site storage is that we pay good money to house property for which we and other family members have no use now and perhaps forever. When harsh daylight finally reveals what's lurking in the darkness, it's definitely not a pretty sight.

Maureen Murdock writes memoirs that have won awards and earned her a devoted following. She sent me an unpublished essay she wrote entitled "The Dead Mother's Storage Unit" in hopes it will remind others to think carefully before they commit household goods that will languish a long time in the darkness of a storage bin.

"I couldn't even cross the threshold into the storage unit," she writes. "Something stopped me cold. After unlocking the door, I looked inside at the boxes stacked up to the ceiling and slammed the door shut. I couldn't wait to get out of there."

The storage unit, Maureen relates, had been rented four years earlier, just after the death of her mother, in New Jersey. It contained the belongings Maureen had elected to keep but hadn't the heart to sort through. Years went by, until the time she finally determined she must evaluate the many possessions she'd paid to store in a 5½ × 11-foot space.

"The next day I went back and tried again," she recalls. "I only had an hour and a half before meeting [a friend] for lunch. I scheduled it that way; I figured that if I approached the task in small increments, I might avoid a panic attack."

The first box Maureen opened was her mother's straw sewing kit. The next box raised the hackles on her neck.

"On the top of an assortment of items from her dressing room was the white porcelain powder puff case she always had on her vanity table next to her hand mirror and brush . . . I opened it and found a used tawny rose powder puff still holding the indentation of her cheek. I tossed it away quickly, as if I'd burned my hand . . . I am removing her treasured things [as if] out of a coffin which has been waiting for me since her death."

THE SURREAL WORLD OF OFF-SITE STORAGE

Like Maureen's, most stories about storing household goods seem to have an element of mild madness to them. One couple I know spent more than $36,000 to store the contents of a house whose style completely clashed with the decor of their next home and then sold nearly every stick at a huge loss.

Another good friend maintains four separate off-site storage lockers with possessions she and her husband can't bring themselves to part with, but for which they have no room in their new, streamlined lifestyle. One storage locker contains only clothing that she and her husband can't fit into any longer. When I suggested that she photograph the beloved outfits she'd worn when she was several sizes smaller, she laughed sheepishly and replied, "I've become emotionally attached to the pieces I've worn on special occasions. They looked great then, and made me feel wonderful. Taking pictures before I send them off just won't do it for me, I'm afraid."

The best I could do was persuade her to store them in special plastic bags, suck the air out of them with her vacuum cleaner hose, and stow them under the bed. At least that way, they could reduce down to three off-site storage lockers.

The most amazing tale on the subject of storage came from the forklift operator who hauled our own five containers of goods out of the darkness at Nor-Cal storage in San Jose, California. He got a real kick out of telling me about a family that had kept *ten* containers of household possessions at that same storage facility for more than twenty years. Now, *that* is nuts.

To be sure, there are instances when off-site storage makes perfect sense. This is especially true when a clear plan for the future has been formulated so there is an endgame to the storage "solution."

WHEN STORAGE MAKES SENSE

Really Good Reasons to Store Off-Site

- You will be remodeling your new space, and your furniture would hinder the project.
- You have some valuable possessions you plan to sell within six months or give to relatives at a specific time in the future.

Pretty Good Reasons to Store Off-Site

- Your adult children have no room for possessions they truly want and plan to retrieve "sometime soon." You set a deadline, and they agree.
- Your adult child or grandchild has no room for possessions he/she truly wants, and you're willing to foot the bill — or he or she is. Everyone agrees that this "solution" will be *reviewed* in six months.

Off-Site Storage Primer

If you plan to store goods outside the home, before you start packing those boxes imagine that someone else is surveying your possessions. Consider storing only the things you think your children, nieces, or nephews wouldn't throw out if they were in charge.

Be aware that the best rental storage units are those that are easy to access and can be visited 24/7, whenever the need arises. Make sure to lease one that is free from danger of flooding or theft.

Store your items in sturdy boxes or plastic bins with the contents clearly labeled and facing out for easy readability. Put the boxes you might need to open on the top so you can get to them more readily. Do not store paint, aerosols, gasoline, or any hazardous materials in these rented units.

As you pack for storage, number the containers as well as label their contents in the order in which you put them into the storage locker. Jot down a brief inventory corresponding to those numbered cartons for reference so you can locate things with ease and keep the inventory at home with your lists of what you've stored in your safe-deposit box at the bank.

Research the tax laws in your state and shred state tax documents once the books are closed on those years. The IRS has six years to audit federal filings (except in cases of suspected fraud), so after seven years, feel free to shred and toss. For tax returns and receipts you are retaining, store in large manila envelopes and label each by year. Put all the envelopes together (with the most recent years on top) in a waterproof plastic filing cabinet with a snap-top lid and label the visible end "RECENT TAX RETURNS." Check www.irs.gov for records regulations if you have further questions.

Important documents such as marriage, death, and birth certificates; wills; health-care directives; property deeds; real-estate sales and purchasing agreements; mortgages; leases; trust papers; stock certificates; and bonds belong in a fireproof lockbox or a safe-deposit box at a bank with an inventory of the contents kept in a file at home.

To avoid forgetting your storage (and having your goods auctioned off), put the monthly bill on a credit or ATM card so the fee is automatically paid. To get the most out of rented storage space, install large vinyl hooks to hang large items such as bicycles, lawn chairs, and garden rakes from the ceiling. Stand large furniture, like couches, on their ends if the ceiling height allows. Quilted padding protects best.

Visiting Your Storage

Keep a sturdy stepladder and flashlight in your rented storage locker so you have easier access to the hard-to-reach containers. Label the keys to your rented storage locker for your own use and give a labeled duplicate key to a trusted friend or relative. If you use a combination lock, record the secret code on the inventory that you keep on file at home.

After six months of storing (and paying for) your goods, do another survey, and if you didn't miss certain items, sell or dispose of them. Your goal? Get rid of off-site storage entirely!

In fact, the very concept of reviewing the state-of-your-storage situation at a specific date in the future brings us to the subject of our next chapter. What if you need to rightsize your life *again* in a few years?

The upside to this, of course, is that when that time comes, you'll be an old hand at figuring out how to continue to simplify your surroundings while keeping the things that matter most.

With a little help, of course.

Chapter 13

What If I Need to Rightsize Again in a Few Years?

Revisiting your rightsizing scenario

SERIAL RIGHTSIZERS UNITE!

My husband tells friends that it took six rather painful moves (starting with my emotional meltdown when he attempted to chuck our grown son's baby rocking chair into the Dumpster at our first storage facility) for us to get our rightsizing "right" — and truthfully, he's on the mark.

Remember, now . . . we had lived in the same house in Southern California for twenty-two years and then suddenly, in our mid-fifties, became virtual nomads as we sought to find a place to call home during the dot-com frenzy raging in the Bay Area as the new century began. After the third move in as many years, we joked that we'd inadvertently become "serial rightsizers" because our circumstances kept changing.

Looking back, there were a variety of reasons for taking so long to assemble our most useful and loved possessions under one roof, one that contained the correct amount of square footage to suit us at our current age and stage. Several of those six moves would have been far less arduous if I'd had a road map like the one offered within these pages instead of continuing to haul with us many of our earthly goods that had no earthly purpose in our lives anymore.

This fact alone — not disposing of enough during a move — certainly constitutes one reason people might go through the rightsizing process more than once.

On the other hand, things happen. Life happens. Who could have anticipated that the San Francisco condo we purchased (rather too quickly) would feature a gun-toting next-door neighbor who declined to take his meds? Or that two years later a house we rented on a hill in our charming town on the San Francisco Bay had a creek running underneath it that soaked our garaged belongings and puddled in our street — big time — during the rainy season?

Oh, well. Live and learn.

With each move we *did* learn a lot, and the fruits of that "wisdom," combined with the experiences of the many families I've interviewed for this effort, have brought me to the conclusion that, as my late father/writer was wont to say, "The crazy things that happen are all part of the rich tapestry of life." Given this truth, it could very well be that you — like us — will find yourself rightsizing your life more than one time.

WHAT *REALLY* MATTERS MOST

Henry Van Gieson, seventy-three, and his wife of twenty-three years, Linda Little, sixty-five, admit somewhat ruefully to having been serial rightsizers. They've been on the move during most of their post-retirement years — from a place in Seattle; to a home on the Northern Neck of Virginia; to a gated community in New Bern, North Carolina; to a house in Ft. Myers, Florida; to a condo in that same town. They did all this while living three to six months a year in their 380-square-foot RV, either traveling on the road or, more recently, staying put in an RV resort in the mountains of North Carolina, where they escape the Florida summer heat.

"We were the first of all our friends to retire," notes Linda, "so we really did it by trial and error."

Adds Van, "We retired with absolutely no planning and no idea where we would live and no notion what we would do with our remaining time. The only considerations at the outset were a perceived desire to live near the kids and grandchildren, to have a waterfront home to ensure our boating activities, and to live in weather that was better than Seattle, Washington," where Van worked twenty years for Boeing.

"It has taken us ten years to get where we are," agrees Linda, noting that their current condo community is probably not the last place they'll live. "At some point," she says matter-of-factly, "one or both of us may have to go into assisted living and eventually a nursing home or hospice. For now our current situation here in Florida suits our lifestyle and interests. Health, of course, is the biggest unknown."

Before Van did his stint at the aerospace giant, he'd spent twenty years in the air force. Linda had been in computer-industry sales and management for two decades, so the idea of relocating wasn't something that scared them.

Says Linda with a laugh, "We downsized when we moved to North Carolina, then upsized when my mother-in-law came to live with us, then downsized again to the square footage we had before she arrived. You could say we downsize *every year* when we go to live in our RV!"

RIGHTSIZING LESSONS LEARNED

We can see from the Van Gieson–Littles' saga that for many people rightsizing will continue to be a process, not a single event. A living situation that works well for someone age fifty or sixty may not add up when they hit their seventies or eighties. It is also very likely that the seventy-seven million baby boomers and those on either side of this enormous population bulge will make more than one rightsizing move. In fact, *Where to Retire* magazine reported in 2005 that seven hundred thousand Americans move to new towns to retire every year.

Designers and retirement planners alike will tell you that it's probably a good idea to think in terms of five- to fifteen-year increments when considering the future. If there are significant age differences within a group of people rightsizing together, individual needs may take a sharp turn in a new direction at some point, and special requirements or preferences may become important factors when choosing among a number of housing options as the years go by.

As Van and Linda reflect on their last fifteen years, they now consider the need for planning and thinking ahead in a much more favorable light.

"It's best to talk to friends who are ahead of you in the process to get feedback on places, people, and things to do when you're thinking about making a change," recommends Linda.

"We have lived in five different homes while searching for a formula that works for us," recalls Van. "Not everyone will agree with us, but our economic situation and our lifestyle preferences played a major part in the decisions we've made along the way."

Chimes in Linda, "It took us a while to figure out that there wasn't one ideal location for us."

Both Linda and Van recognize that electing to live half of each year in an RV isn't everyone's notion of an idyllic lifestyle, but being on the road so much has taught them some valuable lessons.

For instance, Linda studies the Yellow Pages of the local telephone book or uses the Internet to make sure the new places have what they want in terms of social, cultural, and physical amenities — like shopping! "And don't forget to find out if there's a decent hospital nearby," she advises.

Van wrote a summary he dubbed "What I think we have learned over the last eleven years as our retirement situation evolved" — recommendations from a road warrior that I think are worth passing on, especially if you are considering rightsizing for a second or third time:

- Convenient medical care becomes increasingly important as we age. Living in the boondocks on top of a mountain with a view just won't do!
- Be sure you know if you're the babysitting type. Of course everyone loves the kids and grandkids, but getting together once or twice a year may work fine, too.
- For some people, there is no one place for year-round living. In our price range, a summer place (our RV in North Carolina) and a winter place (a condo in Florida) was one solution.
- By and large, the weather, people, and available amenities have provided the biggest reasons for moving more than once after retirement.
- Friends and climate are far more important than material possessions.

The Van Gieson–Littles had recently come through a harrowing hurricane season in Florida, during which they learned the value of having compatible friends and neighbors. Notes Linda emphatically, "Mother Nature can be very unfriendly at times to those electing waterfront homes," implying that the older one gets, the less a person feels like putting up storm shutters and evacuating hundreds of miles north.

Reflecting on their multiple rightsizing odysseys, I asked Linda for some final words of wisdom.

"I would recommend that people at midlife and beyond start planning *early*. Our lessons learned may not be useful to everyone, but some thoughtful planning should shorten the time required to get it right."

And avoid too many unnecessary moves.

WHEN DO YOU KNOW IT'S TIME FOR ANOTHER CHANGE?

Not everyone moves to a new location when it's time for a change in personal surroundings after age fifty — or sixty and up. Sometimes people stay put and make a midcourse correction right where they are.

John and Nancy Durien are in their early sixties and have long been thinking about rightsizing in terms of ten-year chunks. They'd considered the idea of moving on several occasions as their children began to leave the nest but in the end stayed where they were. Instead they added a 900-square-foot addition to their home of many years in Monterey, California.

"We've had a hard time explaining to people why we were *adding* to our home at this stage of our lives, going through the mess of remodeling, especially with a big wedding in the middle of everything," acknowledges Nancy. "The fact was, we wanted to provide space for our grown kids and their families during the holidays — which they tend to spend with us. We wanted more closets, larger bathrooms, some clutter control, and room for a new grand piano." The Duriens say they've "gambled that a family inheritance will help us pay off the loan."

The Duriens redesigned their physical surroundings in their early sixties to suit their changing needs but declined to confront other key aspects of rightsizing.

"We're pack rats," admits Nancy, who came to understand this fact when the Duriens began the process of remodeling. "We're still bogged down in paperwork and the clutter. That paperwork drives one of us absolutely nuts, but doesn't bother the other one. I know that scaling down our belongings is certainly in our future."

Rightsizing for the Duriens in their sixties has meant *scaling up* to make room for the expanding families of their adult children, with whom they are close, by creating a place where everyone can gather in more comfort for the holidays. Rightsizing for this couple in their seventies or eighties is obviously going to mean something quite different: sorting, purging, editing, and no doubt, *scaling down.* Meanwhile, they've made the rightsizing adjustments that allow them to "keep on keeping on" in a wonderful home filled with what matters most to *them:* their extended family.

TIME FOR A RIGHTSIZING CHECKUP

When do you know it's time to rightsize again? In the same way you sensed it the first time around: something has or is *changing.* This, of course, can run the gamut of life events. See if any of the following reasons resonate.

Twelve Good Reasons to Rightsize Again

1. You're tired of maintaining your home, yard, pool, etc.
2. Your finances just don't add up anymore since you left full-time employment, and taxes and maintenance are eating into your nest egg.
3. Your current home would be fine — with a few important adjustments that suit your age and stage.
4. Your adult children and grandchildren have moved significant distances from the family home and aren't visiting as often as they used to, so maintaining a house that accommodates them is no longer a priority.
5. Your adult children have moved to a new location, had babies, and want you nearby, and you want to be close.

6. You yearn for more cultural stimulation or wish to be near others with similar interests.
7. Harsh weather has finally got your goat. You yearn to live in a place where you can wear shorts all year round.
8. Illness or accident suddenly requires constant care, and you need to live closer to service vendors who can provide medical and personal necessities.
9. You don't wish to — or can't any longer — drive a car and would like to live near public transportation.
10. You're bored with the choices you made a few years ago and crave a new life adventure.
11. Your life partner has passed away or abandoned ship, and the home you shared either is too difficult to maintain alone, too expensive, or holds too many memories.
12. You feel it's time to move to a place where you know that — if you needed it — there's medical care built into your living arrangements.

WHAT *REALLY* MATTERS MOST AS THE YEARS GO BY

Dr. Sage Bennet is a counselor and retreat leader with a special interest in the possibilities for growth among people experiencing life's transitions common to people fifty and older.

"Moving from one stage of life to another is not always easy," she says, recalling a particular client who was contemplating the decision to retire. The client took the plunge but wasn't prepared for the mixed feelings that followed. She thought she'd be elated but instead experienced a period of profound sadness.

Bennet wasn't surprised. "Changing jobs, beginning and ending relationships, seeing our children leave home, or [facing] death all require a process of letting go, of experiencing a myriad of feelings. While these can be enriching, they may not be comfortable."

As we age, she says, we will *all* be faced with serial transitions that, in turn, may prompt our having to rightsize our lives more than once. Each and every transition requires us to let go of something. In the case of Bennet's retiring client, "she had to release thirty years of work that she loved. She also had to redefine herself and realize she is something greater than the role she played during her career."

Perhaps the key rightsizing principle to remember if circumstances require us to adapt our living situations more than once is: we are *more* than the sum of our professional lives or the goods we arrange in the homes where we live. Coming to this realization will require that we be patient with ourselves while we strive to obtain the most important thing of all: a feeling of serenity and contentment with life — just as it is.

Bennet believes that "the challenge of transitions helps us cultivate spiritual qualities within. We learn to honor feelings and to grieve loss . . . to [welcome] self-discovery and the courage to embrace the new." When we make room for the new through the process of rightsizing our lives, many wonderful things can happen at almost any age.

THERE'S NO PLACE LIKE A RIGHTSIZED HOME

Judith Ottoson is a cutting-edge baby boomer, among the first of that generation to turn sixty, in January 2006. Like many women of her generation, she combined a high-level career with her family role. She and her husband of twenty-four years, Lawrence Green, shared similar professions: he, a leading advocate for public health; and she, an educator specializing in evaluation and public policy.

Both with doctorates and the parents of two daughters born to Larry and his first wife, the couple led a life typical of roving academics, buffeted by the winds of unpredictable government grants, the upheaval in American health-care practices, tenure politics on the nation's college campuses, and the ups and downs of dual career tracks. They shared a burning desire to work in areas where their advanced degrees from UC Berkeley and Harvard would be put to best use helping the country sort out its problems promoting decent health care for its citizens.

A move in 1999 took them from the University of British Columbia to Atlanta, where Larry worked for the Centers for Disease Control and taught at Emory University, while Judith assumed a professorship of public policy at Georgia State University.

A decade earlier, in 1988, while both had jobs in the Bay Area, the couple had bought their "dream house" in a unique San Francisco neighborhood called St. Francis Wood. One of America's earliest planned developments, created in the 1920s, each home was designed by an architect to meet the strict codes of the homeowners' association. The Ottoson-Green abode was a 1,750-square-foot, steep-roofed cottage with a glimpse of the Pacific Ocean a mile or so in the distance.

"The first major thing we had to do to get insurance was an earthquake retrofit," Judith recalls. "We bolted the house to the foundation, finishing the job at ten a.m. on the morning of the big quake that hit during the 1989 World Series game at around five p.m. that night!"

The house survived, and the next year the couple went ahead with their first effort at rightsizing their home to "make the house ours," explains Judith. Their daughters had headed off to college. "We wanted to adapt our home for the two of us, though we also designed in flexibility so there was room for Beth and Jennifer when they came for visits." That meant creating a home office, painting, and accomplishing deferred maintenance work.

The remodel had just been completed when the management structure at the foundation where Larry worked as a vice president went through a convulsive upheaval.

"Larry picked me up at the airport after I'd flown home from giving a lecture somewhere, and he said, 'Big news. We're going to have to move.'"

They quickly prepared their newly renovated house for renters and headed north to Canada, each to accept joint appointments at the University of British Columbia, where they remained for eight years.

"At first we tried to sell the San Francisco house, but the market had tanked, so we just kept it rented to pay the mortgage and maintenance. We'd bought a place in Vancouver and still had kids in college. It was a harrowing time financially, but we held on."

When the couple moved on to Atlanta to Larry's job at the CDC, "we clung to the idea that one day we'd be able to come home to San

Francisco. This was pretty strange, in a way, because I'm originally from Minneapolis, and Larry has worked all over the world, but this little house in California seemed so right for us."

Thirteen years after they'd left California, the Ottoson-Greens finished their stints in Atlanta and were faced with consolidating four offices into one home office and figuring out what to do with the collections they had amassed in their travels.

On my visit to St. Francis Wood, I spotted a blue port-a-potty in front of the house that told me the home was clearly in the throes of its second remodel in fifteen years. Amid the construction workers' tools and painters' drop cloths, I caught glimpses of a collection of African musical instruments, a two-foot-tall puppet from Indonesia, a wall full of miniature house facades fashioned in clay representing the many places the couple had worked or visited as public-health educators: New Orleans, Cairo, Sweden, Brazil, Paris, and of course, San Francisco.

"When Larry and I returned to the West Coast from Atlanta, we considered putting on a second story to accommodate our lives as they had evolved. We were both going to continue teaching and consulting — but at a much reduced pace — and thus we'd *both* need offices at home and plenty of storage for our reference books and files, especially for all the articles we'd written over the years. Another requirement: our daughters now had children of their own, so we wanted room for them and their husbands to visit, but Larry and I didn't want to rattle around in a too-big house."

Judith points to the ceiling. "The estimates for a second story came in hundreds of thousands of dollars more than we were prepared to invest. We'd educated our children, managed to pay off the mortgage, thanks to renting out the place all those years, and we didn't want to go into debt for the rest of our lives doing the addition."

Meanwhile, half a flight of stairs above the main living level are three bedrooms, including a master with its bumped-out, enclosed sun porch; a small room that presently serves single guests; and a good-size bedroom that had been turned into their joint home office. Judith indicated two desks positioned on opposite walls of the converted bedroom.

"We consolidated the four offices we had in Atlanta to one shared space. At first this worried me, but it's worked out amazingly well." She sat down at her desk. "See, our office chairs are on casters, so we can slide across the floor for a quick conference — or a kiss."

Judith points to the ceiling and triumphantly pulls on the cord dangling within reach. Down comes a set of stairs that stretches into an attic space over our heads.

"Welcome to the family library 'stacks,'" she jokes, referring to the rows of shelving at libraries where collections of books are stored. "When we were contemplating building up instead of down, we realized there was at least seven hundred and fifty square feet of unfinished space up here that we could utilize for the books we still need in our work. There's also plenty of room to store our long-term files and the articles we've written over the years . . . Larry, much more than I, by the way," she adds, laughing.

We climb up into the eaves. Judith points to a section of the roof that she informed me faced the ocean view.

"We may not have gotten our dream second story, but we're putting in a big picture window right *there!*" she says with a pleased smile. "As long as I'm able, I can come up here with a cup of tea and take in the treetop glimpse of the Pacific — or the fog, depending. I'm sure there'll be a day when I won't be able to climb up here . . . but for the next twenty years, it'll be just what we've always wanted! Talk about *rightsizing!*" she says with a palpable sense of joy that obviously comes from her gratitude that they held on to their precious gem over the years.

We climb down the ladder, returning to the communal home office, and Judith gestures to the hardwood floor.

"One day, when we'd accepted the fact that a second story was financially prohibitive, we looked at each other and said, 'We'll redo the basement and call it the Garden Suite.' Our main goal was to reclaim every inch of space in this house to make it right for the way we live *now*, and the way it will undoubtedly be in the future when we're old."

The architect they'd hired ordered additional support beams installed downstairs, and since the house perched on a small incline, the owners commanded the construction crew to blow out the western basement wall that faced the garden. As if by magic the house gained 450 square feet of living space that mostly serves as guest quarters for their extended family and visitors. When in residence they'll find themselves in a charming space with a marble bathroom and French doors opening onto a redwood deck that faces the garden and a distant view of the sea.

"We made the stair treads down to the new suite wide and the stairs not too steep to accommodate one of those elevator chairs, eventually, so Larry and I could live down here one day," Judith demonstrates, pointing to the straight banister. "The caregivers will get the old master bedroom or the office."

When we return to the living room, Judith glances around at the chaos that will reign for only a few more weeks while the construction crew finishes the job.

"We were so upset when we couldn't sell this house way back when, and now look at how it all turned out! We've managed to reconfigure the same house *twice* with two different sets of goals in mind — and it's going to be perfect for us."

Serial rightsizers, indeed!

RIGHTSIZING AS A WAY OF LIFE

Early in this journey we've taken together, I mentioned how hard it was for me to acknowledge that the adorable, handmade rocking chair that had belonged to my grown son didn't have a place in our lives anymore. Jamie, a film and TV editor and producer, lived in a New York one-room studio with high-tech everything, including industrial-wire shelving and state-of-the-art media equipment. A toddler's wooden rocker with a petit-point seat stitched by his mom was probably not the fashion accent he needed at his stage of bachelorhood.

Even so, I simply could not allow that little chair to be thrown into the Dumpster or be passed on to an anonymous recipient, however worthy. I stowed it in the small storage locker we secured near our new home and tried also to put it out of my mind.

One weekend when my adored second cousin was visiting with her new baby girl, she and her husband suddenly grew very solemn over the Sunday morning pancakes I had produced from my galley kitchen. David nervously cleared his throat and then blurted out, "Alison and I want you and Tony to become Gracie's godparents."

Emotion clogged my throat, and I gazed across the dining table at my husband, who had tears in his eyes as well. We were both utterly undone by the sweetness of the request and the honor we felt having been asked to assume such a role.

And I knew at that moment exactly who was going to receive that little rocking chair — with the proviso, of course, that it would be passed on to the firstborn child of my son and his future wife, whenever and *if* ever that should come to pass.

What sage said it? "Nothing stays the same." Often I think of that heart-wrenching song from *Fiddler on the Roof*: "Sunrise, sunset, swiftly flow the days . . ."

There's simply no avoiding the obvious. Every day we're one day older and, we hope, one day wiser about the need to remain conscious of the ways in which surroundings make us feel the way we do. We can also remind ourselves to continue adapting our homes and their contents to accommodate various stages and needs as we grow older.

Rightsizing as a way of life means that we never stop asking ourselves and others for whom we may be responsible, "What matters most right now?"

Often the answers to that question will, in turn, provide the guidance needed to make informed choices and appropriate adjustments in the way a home can serve the needs of the people who dwell within. For us, at the present moment, rightsizing means pricisely 1,375 square feet of scenic bliss, with the San Francisco Bay serving as our front yard (no lawn to mow). We own one couch and a sofa bed for guests. We have a new, economy-size dog — a jaunty little Cavalier King Charles spaniel. We drive a "baby" SUV that gets close to thirty miles to the gallon. I write on a laptop, having junked my desktop computer and large keyboard. I unloaded a lot of nonoriginal art and kept only the books I'll reread someday. I asked my husband to toss twenty-six cartons of old radio scripts from my seventeen years with KABC in Los Angeles into the Dumpster a few years ago, and I did the same for his dead files. Those chapters are finished and new ones begun.

THE PAST IS THE FUTURE, AND THE FUTURE IS THE PAST

The owners of the home in St. Francis Wood shared a very private moment with me on the day I visited their new/old house.

Down in the remodeled basement level, Judith Ottoson gestured to an expanse of drywall that recently had been plastered and painted in their new Garden Suite addition.

"We feel so grateful that we had this home to come back to. Before we sealed up that wall, we decided to put in our version of a time capsule," she disclosed, lowering her voice a notch. "We put a note handwritten on our stationery in a ziplock plastic bag, along with a picture of Larry and me, the girls, their husbands, and the grandchildren. Then we had the men close it up inside that wall."

"What did the note say?" I asked.

I was consumed with curiosity about what an academic couple, steeped in the history of health science, would want posterity to know about them. For me their approach to weighing their options regarding the final third of life had become emblematic of the rightsizing principles I've come to believe in so fervently.

Judith, a tall, energetic, attractive woman, was dressed in trim slacks and a sage green sweater the color of her eyes. She smiled a bit wistfully and recited what the message in the time capsule said:

TO THE FUTURE RESIDENTS OF THIS HOME
We made this house right for us
and lived here in peace and love.
We wish you the same . . .
Judith Ottoson and Lawrence Green

And that, dear reader, is what I wish for you as you begin the journey of rightsizing your life, keeping the things that matter most.

May you live in peace and love, wherever that turns out to be.

Rightsizing Resource Directory

Visit www.rightsizingyourlife.com for Resource Updates

NOTE: Every effort has been made to provide correct information in this directory; however, no responsibility is assumed for the accuracy, timeliness, or completeness of any listing. Readers should make their own inquiries to confirm details. The following listings are provided for information purposes only; no endorsement is made or implied. Items are listed alphabetically by topic.

- **CLUTTER/DECLUTTERING/SORTING (see also Organizing and Rearranging)**

Books

Campbell, Jeff. *Clutter Control: Putting Your Home on a Diet.* New York: Dell, 1992.

Eisenberg, Ronni, with Kate Kelly. *Organize Your Office!* Rev. ed. New York: Hyperion, 1998.

Ingham, Vickie Leigh, ed. *Clutter Cutters: Store It with Style; What to Toss, What to Keep.* Des Moines, IA: Meredith Books/Better Homes and Gardens, 2004.

Kingston, Karen. *Clear Your Clutter with Feng Shui.* New York: Broadway Books, 1999.

Smallin, Donna. *Unclutter Your Home: 7 Simple Steps – 700 Tips & Ideas.* North Adams, MA: Storey, 1999.

Web Sites and Organizations

www.spaceclearing.com
Karen Kingston offers tips and advice, plus sign-ups for workshops.

www.clearclutter.com
Free clutter-clearing tips and a downloadable e-book for a fee.

www.messies.com
For the seriously clutter-impaired, this site offers advice, self-help, group help, books, and a free introductory newsletter.

www.clutterersanonymous.com
Local support groups for clutter bugs with tips for taming the mess.

www.http://groups.yahoo.com/group/thecompact/
"The Compact" is a site dedicated to discussion and tips for people who are determined not to buy anything new for an entire year (except food, medications, and toiletries).

Service Providers and Product Vendors

www.cluttercoach.com
Offers tips, products, and clutter-clearing services provided by professional organizer Jane Carroo.

www.clutterfreeforever.com
Offers a home coaching program dealing with "hidden emotional and psychological reasons why coping with clutter is so hard to do." The site also sells an e-book by clutter maven Stephanie Roberts with six weekly lessons and provides group support.

www.mindoverclutter.com
Provides some excellent articles, message boards, and other resources to help people lead clutter-free lives.

www.containerstore.com
The Container Store (various retail locations) is the superstore for products that contain your clutter in style.

www.stacksandstacks.com
Both the Web site and various retail locations offer a huge selection of storage and organizational products on the Web for home and office.

www.junkbusters.com
Everything you've ever wanted to know about getting off mailing and phone lists.

www.stopjunk.com
Tips for getting off junk-mail lists, plus offers a kit for sale that provides sample letters and other help to stem the tide of junk in your home.

• DISPOSAL OF HOUSEHOLD ITEMS AND TRASH (see also Recycling; Selling)

Books

See recommended books in the Clutter/Decluttering/Sorting section above.

Web Sites and Organizations

www.epa.gov/opp00001/regulating/disposal.htm

The EPA's Web site offers guidelines for safe disposal of toxic waste and lists agencies and associations dealing with solid waste.

Also call 1-800-CLEAN-UP to locate local solid-waste agencies.

Service Providers and Product Vendors

Check local telephone listings under "Waste Disposal" and "Cleaning Services"

www.1800gotjunk.com

Has franchises in forty-six metropolitan areas and will haul any non-hazardous material two people can lift for a fee.

www.cleaningassociation.com

The official referral network for house, office, carpet, and industrial cleaning services with an online locator for finding a cleaning company near you.

• DONATING AND RECYCLING HOUSEHOLD ITEMS

Books

Glovinsky, Cindy. *Making Peace with the Things in Your Life.* New York: St. Martin's, 2002.

Charitable Groups

For information about donating locally, look in telephone directory under "Salvage/Thrift Shops," or log on to the following Web sites:

www.ajli.org

Association of Junior Leagues International, founded in 1921, promotes volunteerism and projects through various enterprises, including consignment boutiques and e-stores that accept donations of various household goods and clothing. Check local chapter.

www.bbbsa.org

Founded in 1904, Big Brothers Big Sisters of America is the oldest and largest youth-mentoring organization in America. It seeks clothing, household items, furniture, office supplies, and exercise equipment.

www.goodwill.org

A nonprofit provider of education, training, and career services for people with disadvantages, Goodwill offers an online locator of its three thousand local outlets, which accept donations of household goods, clothing, etc.

www.salvationarmy.org

Accepts a wide variety of furniture, clothing, and household items, as above. To schedule pickup, call 800-95TRUCK.

www.svdpusa.org

Society of St. Vincent de Paul. Click on "stores" for state-by-state listing and type of goods accepted.

Charitable Oversight

www.charitywatch.org

A site that ranks charities by their willingness to provide basic documents, including an annual report, complete audited financial statements, and Internal Revenue Service form 990.

www.charitynavigator.org

A site that helps charitable givers make intelligent giving decisions by providing information on more than five thousand charities and by evaluating the financial health of each of these charities.

Selected List of Donation and Recycling Sites

General

www.earth911.org

Lists state by state, item by item resources for recycling and reuse.

Books

Contact your local library, hospital, hospice, veterans' hospital, or nursing homes regarding their need for used books.

www.booksforafrica.org

Accepts textbooks for primary, high school, and college levels, except American history, civics, and foreign languages. 651-602-9844.

www.booksforamerica.org

Accepts complete encyclopedia sets, general-interest books, CDs, VHS tapes, DVDs, video games. Items can be mailed through U.S. Postal Service book rate. 202-364-9737.

www.reachoutandread.org

Gives children's books to kids at doctors' offices. Consult Web site for guidelines and instructions.

Cars, Planes, and Boats

www.800charitycars.org

A nonprofit organization that provides free donated vehicles to struggling families willing to work and become self-sufficient.

www.donatcacar.com

Provides charitable organizations with a practical means of raising funds via donated vehicles. Site lists supported charities by state. 800-237-5714.

Cell Phones

www.charitablerecycling.com

This award-winning group refurbishes phones and ships them to emerging countries as well as within the United States. The Web site will provide a shipping label.

www.verizonwireless.com/hopeline

Provides a store locator where phones can be donated. Refurbished cells are given to victims of domestic violence.

Clothing

Also see national charities with local links listed above.

www.womensalliance.org

Provides links to local groups that give low-income women professional clothing as part of their "fresh start" efforts.

www.careergear.org

Provides men in New York City, Miami, Cleveland, and Houston with interview clothing, motivation, and follow-up support that helps them get and keep jobs.

www.glassslipperproject.org

Welcomes donations of formal dresses, shoes, evening bags, jewelry, and unused makeup to be given to young women for "Prom Night" in the Chicago area. Has links to similar organizations across the country, along with information about shipping the clothing.

Computers and Peripherals

www.pcsforschools.org

This nonprofit organization acts as a liaison between computer refurbishers and schools. Offers a locator service to find local donation sites.

www.worldcomputerexchange.org

Donations are accepted for *working* Pentium II and above desktop and laptop computers, along with desktop and laptop Macintosh G3 and above, including all iMacs, which are given to some fifty developing countries. Site gives instructions for data erasure, packing, and shipping.

www.crc.org

Computer Recycling Center, based in the San Francisco Bay Area, has recycled more than one million computers, both for reuse in schools and to rescue electronics from ending up in a landfill. The site provides useful tips about how to destroy your data on the hardware and what computer recyclers will *not* accept.

Eyeglasses

www.givethegiftofsight.org

Offers a list of eyewear retailers, including LensCrafters, PearleVision, and Sears Optical, where you can drop off old glasses that will help people in America and around the world have better vision.

www.lionsclub.org

Collects used eyeglasses for distribution to the needy in developing nations. Use the locator to find a local Lions Club that accepts eyeglass donations.

Food

www.secondharvest.org

Network of some two hundred food banks and food-rescue organizations that distributes two billion pounds of food and grocery products to hungry and needy Americans in communities across the country. Site locator finds organizations near you.

Furniture

See national charities listed above; also try local thrift shops.

Hearing Aids

www.sotheworldmayhear.org

Used hearing aids are accepted for distribution in America and abroad. Send to address listed on the site or call 800-648-4327 for mailing instructions.

www.latinhearing.org

Redistributes "gently used" hearing aids to poverty-stricken areas in Latin America.

Letters

Historical societies and libraries often will accept letters of local interest.

www.warlettersproject.com

This site is supported by the Legacy Project and seeks donated letters and e-mails from servicemen and -women writing during wartime. A feature also offers tips for properly preserving letters.

Linens

Fine linens are welcome donations at charity boutique, thrift, or salvage shops; clean-but-threadbare linens are often appreciated by your local vet or animal shelter.

Medical Equipment

Local Rotary and Kiwanis clubs often serve as collection points for workable used medical equipment. Check local listings and call for instructions.

www.nationalmssociety.org

The Multiple Sclerosis Society accepts medical equipment and loans it to those in need. Call 800-667-7131 to see if your local chapter is accepting donations.

www.medisend.org

This nonprofit gathers surplus medical, surgical, diagnostic, and therapeutic medical supplies and equipment and distributes them, free of charge, to qualified hospitals in developing countries. Click on "How to Donate."

Musical Instruments

Local schools, music academies, and regional orchestras often accept donations of instruments.

www.mustcreate.org

This organization dedicated to the arts accepts donated musical instruments.

www.oriscus.com

Dedicated to musical education, this group accepts donations of musical instruments by arrangement.

www.savethemusic.com

Inspired by the film *Mr. Holland's Opus*, this site will accept donated musical instruments. 818-784-6787.

Sporting Gear

Local school districts, private schools, and after-school programs sometimes accept gently used sporting gear.

www.bgca.org

Boys and Girls Clubs of America often accept donations of sporting gear. Click "Find A Club" or call 800-854-CLUB to locate a club near you.

• ELDER CARE AND SENIOR ISSUES

Books

Astor, Bart. *Baby Boomer's Guide to Caring for Aging Parents.* New York: Macmillan Spectrum/Simon & Schuster, 1998.

Durrett, Charles. *Senior Cohousing: A Community Approach to Independent Living.* Berkeley, CA: Ten Speed Press, 2005.

Gore, Willma Willis. *Just Pencil Me In: Your Guide to Moving & Getting Settled After 60.* Sanger, CA: Quill Driver Books, 2002.

Hetzer, Linda, and Janet Hulstrand. *Moving On: A Practical Guide to Downsizing the Family Home (How to Get Rid of the Stuff, Keep the Memories, Maintain the Family Peace, and Get on with Your Life).* New York: Stewart, Tabori & Chang, 2004.

Ilardo, Joseph A., and Carole R. Rothman. *Are Your Parents Driving You Crazy?* Acton, MA: VanderWyck & Burnham/Publicom, 2001.

Loverde, Joy. *The Complete Eldercare Planner,* sec. ed. New York: Random House, 2000.

Morse, Sarah, and Donna Quinn Robbins. *Moving Mom and Dad! Why, Where, How and When to Help Your Parents Relocate, Making It Easier for Everyone!* Berkeley, CA: Lanier, 1998.

Rhodes, Linda Colvin. *The Complete Idiot's Guide to Caring for Aging Parents.* Indianapolis, IN: Alpha Books, 2001.

Web Sites and Organizations

www.aarp.org

The American Association of Retired Persons' site features current and frequently updated information on all subjects of interest to America's aging population. 800-424-3410.

www.alz.org

The National Alzheimer's Association provides educational and resource information and chapter links. 800-272-3900.

www.aahsa.org

The American Association of Homes and Services for the Aging coordinates not-for-profit member organizations dedicated to providing a continuum of services for the aging such as adult day services, home health, community services, senior housing, assisted-living residences, continuing-care retirement communities, and nursing homes to provide "healthy, affordable, ethical aging services for America."

www.aoa.gov

The federal government's Administration on Aging site has state and area agency links, including an Eldercare Locator that directs you to local and regional agencies for senior services.

www.elderweb.com

Resources on aging, other Web sites, and news.

www.cohousing.org

The Cohousing Association of the United States (Coho/US) is dedicated to promoting the cohousing movement and committed to integrating the needs and hopes of all champions of cohousing. Offers *Cohousing Magazine* free online, reports on ongoing cohousing projects, keeps a database of those interested in cohousing, and provides links to cohousing organizations across the country.

www.elderspirit.net

A group dedicated to furthering senior cohousing efforts throughout the country.

Service Providers and Product Vendors

Caregivers

www.caregiver.org

A not-for-profit site sponsored by the Family Caregiver Alliance with resource information, an online expert, fact sheets, caregiving tips, chat rooms, and links.

www.careguide.com

A commercial site with caregiving information and tips, along with an extensive directory of agencies serving the elderly.

www.nfcacares.org

The National Family Caregivers Association offers lists of publications and provides resources for family caregivers.

www.nfivc.org

Maintained by the National Federation of Interfaith Volunteer Caregivers, this site offers help identifying local volunteers willing to help the elderly.

www.parents-care.com

A subscription-based service dedicated to providing information to adult children of aging parents.

www.strengthforcaring.com

A site sponsored by the Johnson & Johnson consumer products company offering a free caregiver manual, articles, information on health conditions, daily care, housing, money, and insurance matters.

Lawyers and Legal Information Sources

www.seniorlaw.com

Resources on the legal needs of seniors and other issues.

www.nolo.com

A provider of do-it-yourself legal publications for handling everyday legal matters — or learning enough to make working with a lawyer easier. Offers "plain-English" books, forms, and software on legal issues, including estate planning, retirement, elder care, Social Security, personal finance, taxes, housing, real estate, and divorce.

Senior-Move Managers Interviewed for Rightsizing Your Life

www.nasmm.com

A nonprofit site of the National Association of Senior Move Managers, a professional association of organizations and businesses dedicated to helping older adults and their families with the physical and emotional aspects of moving. A search feature helps to locate senior-move managers nationwide.

www.movingsolutions.com

Margit Novack, senior-move manager. Pennsylvania: 610-853-4300.

www.welcomehomelocation.com

Beth Warren, senior-move manager. Florida: 727-585-7271.

Senior Housing

www.cohousingco.com

The Cohousing Company, headed by architects Charles R. Durrett and Kathryn McCarmant, has spearheaded more than forty cohousing communities — both senior and multigenerational — nationwide. Durrett and McCarmant are credited with coining the term "cohousing" in the *Oxford English Dictionary*. Nevada City, CA: 530-265 9980.

www.carescout.com

A commercial site with fee-based information on U.S. nursing homes, plus free information on products and assessing and monitoring your parent's care in a nursing home.

www.hud.gov/senior

A federal government site with information on low-income housing for seniors, along with other services. 800-569-4287.

www.nahb.org

The National Association of Home Builders site features their 50+ Housing Council, with information, resources, publications, and news plus a directory of member builders and contractors certified by the

CAPS program: Certified Aging-in-Place Specialists who retrofit homes for safety and accessibility.

www.retirementmaps.com

A visual "yellow pages" that maps the location of various types of retirement communities across the country, plus provides e-guides on topics of related interest.

• HOME AND INTERIOR DESIGN, SPACE PLANNING, AND REARRANGING (see also Organizing Your Life and Possessions)

Books

Bertolucci, Marisa. *Living Large in Small Spaces: Expressing Personal Style in 100 to 1,000 Square Feet.* New York: Harry N. Abrams, 2003.

Brown, Azby. *Small Space: Stylish Ideas for Making More of Less in the Home.* New York: Kodansha, 1993.

Gallagher, Winifred. *House Thinking: A Room-by-Room Look at How We Live.* New York: HarperCollins, 2006.

——. *The Power of Place: How Our Surroundings Shape Our Thoughts, Emotions, and Actions.* New York: HarperPerennial, 1994.

Harwood, Barbara Bannon. *The Healing House.* Carlsbad, CA: Hay House, 1997.

Kodis, Michelle. *Blueprint Small: Creative Ways to Live with Less.* Layton, UT: Gibbs Smith, 2003.

Lawson, Todd, and Tom Connor. *The House to Ourselves: Reinventing Home Once the Kids Are Grown.* Newtown, CT: Taunton Press, 2004.

Madden, Chris Casson. *A Room of Her Own: Women's Personal Spaces.* New York: Random House/Clarkson Potter Publishers, 1997.

Serrell, Allison. *Nest for Two: Creating a Harmonious Home.* San Francisco: Chronicle Books, 2004.

Susanka, Sarah. *Not So Big Solutions for Your Home.* Newtown, CT: Taunton Press, 2002.

Susanka, Sarah, with Kira Obolensky. *The Not So Big House: A Blueprint for the Way We Really Live.* Newtown, CT: Taunton Press, 1998.

Susanka, Sarah, and Marc Vassallo. *Inside the Not So Big House: Discovering the Details that Bring a Home to Life.* Newtown, CT: Taunton Press, 2005.

Ward, Laura. *Use What You Have Decorating: Transform Your Home in One Hour with Ten Simple Design Principles — Using the Space You Have, the Things You Like, the Budget You Choose.* New York: Perigee Books/Penguin Putnam, 1999.

Wheatman, John, and David Wakely (photographer). *Meditations on Design: Reinventing Your Home with Style and Simplicity.* York Beach, ME: Red Wheel/Weiser LLC/Conati Press, 2000.

Web Sites and Organizations

www.asid.org

American Society of Interior Design — thirty-eight thousand members strong with a network of forty-eight chapters in the United States and Canada — maintains a locating service online.

www.interiorarrangement.org

The Interior Arrangement and Design Association (IADA, Inc.) is both a professional and career-training organization whose members specialize in providing a one-day interior makeover using homeowners' existing furnishings. The site offers a member locator for specialists in "design in a day," utilizing space and repositioning of furnishings that exist in your home already for a more practical and pleasing result.

www.weredesign.com

Interior Redesign Industry Specialists (IRIS) populate this Web site, which provides a locator feature to find one-day and speedy makeover designers for the home.

www.iald.org

The International Association of Lighting Designers provides education and networking for architectural lighting designers. The site has a "Find a Lighting Designer" locator.

www.notsobighouse.com

Architect-author Sarah Susanka's Web site offers ideas and tips for making the most of personal and interior space.

Service Providers and Product Vendors

Space Planning

www.splaceplanning.com

A site for professionals and would-be designers offering, among other products, the "Junior Residential Room Planner," with 270 scaled magnetic furniture representations for working up furniture plans and interior designs.

Construction

www.servicemagic.com

An on-line marketplace connecting homeowners to prescreened service professionals. Includes customer ratings of construction professionals obtained through the site.

www.nahb.org

An online locator directs you to members of the National Association of Home Builders who are home builders and/or licensed contractors.

Designers Interviewed for *Rightsizing Your Life*

bankslinda@aol.com

Linda Banks Interiors, interior design and rearranging. Nassau, Bahamas; Sausalito, CA.

mfarrell@unex.berkeley.edu

Marlene Farrell, ASID, IIDA, CID, interior design and interior architecture. San Francisco.

cynthia@agingbeautifully.org

Cynthia Leibrock, MA, ASID, Hon. IIDA, proponent of universal (accessible) design. Livermore, CO.

toni@conceptsbytoni.com

Toni Pearl-Chepin, interior design and rearranging. Sausalito, CA.

jhmjw@aol.com

Mary Jean Winkler, Sun Hill Designs. New York City and environs.

• MOVING

Books

Carlisle, Ellen. *Smooth Moves: The Relocation Guide for Families on the Move*. Charlotte, NC: Teacup Press, 1999.

Stephens, Richard. *Simply Essential Home Moving Kit*. Vancouver, BC, Canada: Self-Counsel Press, 2002.

Web Sites and Organizations

www.remodelormove.com

A great site to visit if you're wrestling with the decision whether to remodel your current home or move to a new one.

www.movingscam.com

A site highly critical of the moving industry, here you will find a list of something close to three hundred moving companies on its blacklist, along with movers who've gotten the "thumbs up" in recent months. This free Web site is a wealth of updated information and tips and even offers several helpful e-articles, including "How to Find a Reputable Mover," "Understanding Estimates," and "How to File Moving Complaints."

Service Providers and Product Vendors

Check local telephone listings for names of moving companies and then vet them at www.movingscam.com. Also, check with local shipping and mailing outfits and compare prices before buying moving supplies.

www.boxesdelivered.com

Offers packing supplies, moving boxes, and moving supplies in preconfigured packages delivered to your door.

www.moveout.com

Offers a "Moving Box Calculator" to help determine the amount of moving boxes and moving supplies you will need to keep your move organized. Also sells four different moving kits, depending on your size move.

www.movingsupplies.net

Offers an extensive assortment of corrugated boxes, wardrobe boxes, and other moving supplies for packing, storing, and organizing, plus other moving "tools." Free shipping nationwide on orders of $50 or more.

• ORGANIZING YOUR LIFE AND POSSESSIONS

Books

Editors of *Real Simple Magazine. Real Simple: The Organized Home.* New York: Time Inc. Home Entertainment, 2004.

Fleming, Ann Carter. *The Organized Family Historian: How to File, Manage, Protect Your Genealogical Research and Heirlooms.* Nashville, TN: Rutledge Hill Press, 2004.

Koll, Randall, and Casey Ellis. *The Organized Home: Design Solutions for Clutter-Free Living.* Gloucester, MA: Quarry Books of Rockport Publishers, 2004.

Morgenstern, Julie. *Organizing from the Inside Out: The Foolproof System for Organizing Your Home, Your Office, and Your Life.* New York: An Owl Book of Henry Holt, 1998.

Starr, Meryl. *The Home Organizing Workbook: Clearing Your Clutter, Step by Step.* San Francisco: Chronicle Books, 2004.

Web Sites and Organizations

www.napo.com

National Association of Professional Organizers trade group with a national directory of trained organizers.

www.lifeorganizers.com

Offers tips and "what to do first" guides about clutter clearing, plus links to a directory of professional organizers.

Service Providers and Product Vendors (see also vendors in **Clutter/Decluttering/Sorting** and **Home Interior, Design, Space Planning and Rearranging**)

www.organize.com

A leading online retailer of home storage and organizational products. The company operates a retail store in Riverside, CA.

www.organizeway.com

An online directory of products and services that can help with home organization.

www.juliemorgenstern.com

Features advice, tips, and products.

Clothing Selection and Closet Organization

www.easyclosets.com

Lets you design your own space and order closet organizers, shipped out the next business day.

www.closetfactory.com

With franchises in 117 territories, the site has a locator to find closet experts near you.

www.AICI.org

Association of Image Consultants International Web site that has a locator to find a clothing consultant.

www.lindadaniels999@comcast.net

Linda Daniels, wardrobe consultant.

www.brendakinsel.com

Brenda Kinsel, wardrobe and image consultant.

Photo Organization (see **Preserving and Conserving**)

Organizing Professionals Interviewed for Rightsizing Your Life

Michi Blake, The Organizing Coach, 805-882-2003
Gail John, Get It Done, 415-331-8543

• PRESERVING AND CONSERVING

Books

Clothing & Fabrics

Mailand, Harold F., and Dorothy Stites. *Preserving Textiles: A Guide for the Non-Specialist.* Indianapolis, IN: Indianapolis Museum of Art, 1999.

Documents

McClure, Rhonda. *Digitizing Your Family History: Easy Methods for Preserving Your Heirloom Documents, Photos, Home Movies.* Family Tree Books, 2004.

Sturdevant, Katherine Scott. *Organizing and Preserving Your Heirloom Documents.* Cincinnati, OH: Betterway Publications, 2002.

Furniture

Long, Jane S., and Richard W. Long. *Caring for Your Family Treasures: A Concise Guide.* New York: Harry N. Abrams, 2000.

Photographs

Taylor, Maureen A. *Preserving Your Family Photographs: How to Organize, Present, and Restore Your Precious Family Images.* Cincinnati, OH: Betterway Publications, 2001.

Tuttle, Craig. *An Ounce of Preservation: A Guide to the Care of Paper and Photographs.* Highland City, FL: Rainbow Books, 1995.

Wilhelm, Henry. *The Permanence and Care of Color Photographs: Traditional and Digital Color Prints, Color Negatives, Slides and Motion Pictures.* Grinnell, IA: Preservation Publishing, 1993.

Rare Books

Gandert, Slade Richard. *Protecting Your Collection: A Handbook, Survey and Guide for the Security of Rare Books, Manuscripts, Archives, Works of Art and the Circulating Library.* Binghamton, NY: Haworth Press, 1982.

Web Sites and Organizations

www.si.edu

The Smithsonian Center for Materials, Research, and Education has information on preservation of antiques, musical instruments, art, and books.

www.wilhelm-research.com

This site features information on the preservation of traditional and digital photographs and motion pictures.

www.bcin.ca
The Bibliographic Conservation Information Network advises on conservation, preservation, and restoration of books and other cultural items.

www.aic-faic.org
The American Institute for the Conservation of Historic and Artistic Works offers tip sheets about preserving various treasures as well as leads to finding professional conservators by their specialty and location.

www.warlettersproject.com
Offers tips for properly preserving any types of letters.

www.preservationdirectory.com
Resources and research tools for historic preservation and cultural-resource management in the United States. Lists preservation organizations and programs.

Service Providers and Product Vendors

www.homemovie.com
This site — for a fee — can facilitate editing, preserving, and transferring your 8 mm home movies to other formats, including VHS and DVD.

www.gaylord.com
Offers free pamphlets on paper and document preservation, along with information about proper care of archival materials. Available, too, are archival and conservation supplies.

www.universityproducts.com
Supplies archival-quality materials for conservation, restoration, and preservation of papers and documents. The "Astute Collection" link on the site deals with preserving everything from baseball cards to 78 rpm records to comic books and coins.

• SELLING ONLINE AND OFF

Books

Collier, Marsha. *eBay for Dummies*, 4th ed. Hoboken, NJ: Wiley, 2004.

Ellis, Ian C. *Book Finds: How to Find, Buy, Sell Used and Rare Books.* New York: Perigee Books/Penguin Putnam, 2001.

Nissanoff, Candiel. *FutureShop: How the New Auction Culture Will Revolutionize the Way We Buy, Sell, and Get Things We Really Want.* New York: Penguin, 2006.

Perdigo, Cathy, and Sonia Weiss. *Pocket Idiot's Guide to Garage and Yard Sales.* New York: Alpha Books/Penguin Group (USA), 2003.

Prince, Dennis. *How to Sell Anything on eBay . . . and Make a Fortune!* New York: McGraw-Hill, 2004.

General Web Sites about Selling Household Goods

www.consignmentshops.com
A map here facilitates the search for a consignment, resale, thrift, antique, or salvage shop nationwide.

www.narts.org
The National Association of Resale and Thrift Shops' official Web site for its one thousand members also offers under its "Shopping Guide" link tips on how to prepare items for sale and FAQs.

www.yardsalequeen.com
Excellent tips, advice for sign making, yard-sale etiquette, links, and a chat board.

• DO-IT-YOURSELF SELLING

Books and Printed Collections

Check telephone listings for used bookstores. Specialty libraries sometimes purchase books in their field — e.g., books on sailing might go to the library of a maritime museum.

www.alibris.com
Large collections only (five hundred books or more).

www.amazon.com
Has a service where you can sell individual books.

www.ecampus.com
Will take some textbooks.

www.elephantbooks.com
Contact only with quality, antiquarian, scholarly, or academic books or collections.

www.textbookx.com
For selling used textbooks.

Clothing, Home Furnishings, and Furniture

Yard sales, consignment shops, and online auctions are your likeliest avenues for selling goods that still have life in them (see Web sites in this section).

Computers

List computers and peripherals for sale on eBay or craigslist online or in local publications.

www.usanotebook.com

Buys computer equipment from private individuals, although their main business is buying off-lease and used computers from institutions.

Estate-Sale Professionals

Check local listings under "estate-sale professionals" or "auction houses."

www.google.com

Type "estate-sale professionals" or "auction houses" to find local companies, but ask for recent references of the places you contact.

Appraisers

www.appraisers.org

Members promise to abide by the Uniform Standards of Professional Appraisal Practice (UsPAP).

www.appraiserassoc.org

A professional association of appraisers of personal property recognized for setting standards for the profession. Offers a locator to find an appraiser either by specialty or location.

www.aoaonline.org

A not-for-profit international association listing personal property appraisers that offer online written appraisal reports.

Auctioneers

www.auctioneers.org

The site for the National Auctioneers Association that guides users to locate auctioneers by specialty and location.

Online Auction Sites and Trading Assistants

www.ebay.com

The granddaddy of online auction sites. On the home page click on "Help"; click on the letter T; then scroll down to "Trading Assistant" (experienced traders who can help you sell) — or sell your items as per instructions on the site. Hired assistants photograph, price, write descriptions, place your item online, and manage all aspects of the sale for a fee, which varies according to the type and price of the item.

www.craigslist.com

Now in most major metropolitan areas, craigslist will refer you to others happy to do the work of selling online.

www.auctiondrop.com

Affiliated with UPS stores, auctiondrop is likely to have a drop-off site close to home at some thirty-eight hundred storefronts. If the item you want to sell is worth more than $75, weighs less than twenty-five pounds, and is legal to sell on eBay, the company's trading assistant will accept it, charging a 20 to 38 percent fee, depending on sale price. Liquidation services are also available, though not through UPS-affiliated drop-off stores.

www.isoldit.com

This trading-assistant site for eBay has more than 170 drop-off locations open across the country and in Canada and the UK. Click on "Store Locations" and "How It Works" to see if this method of selling online is for you. Sliding fees depend on price and type of item to be sold.

www.quikdrop.com

With some eighty-six bricks-and-mortar franchises dedicated to providing a simple, fast, and convenient way to sell items and vehicles on eBay, this trading-assistant site has a locator and other tips, plus an explanation of fees for service.

www.snappyauctions.com

Fifty drop-off locations are established and more are on the way, Tells you the mechanics of having someone else take the drudgery out of online sales. Sliding commission scale of 15 to 35 percent.

• STORAGE AT-HOME (see also **Organizing Your Life and Possessions**)

Books

Blaine, Claudia, ed. *Complete Home Storage.* Menlo Park, CA: Sunset Publishing, 2003.

Fay, Martha, et al. *Pottery Barn: Storage and Display — Stylish Solutions for Organizing Your Home.* Menlo Park, CA: Oxmoor House/Sunset Books, 2004.

Hallam, Linda, ed. *301 Stylish Storage Ideas.* Des Moines, IA: Better Homes and Gardens/Meredith Books, 1998.

Ingham, Vicki Leigh, ed. *Clutter Cutters: Store It with Style.* Des Moines, IA: Better Homes and Gardens/Meredith Books, 2004 (see also **Clutter, Declutter, Sort**).

Javier, Nancy, and Barbara Finwall. *Small Space Survival Guide: Storage and Decorating Tips and Tricks.* Little Rock, AR: Leisure Arts, 2003.

Petrowski, Elaine Martin. *Design Ideas for Home Storage,* 1st ed. Saddle River, NJ: Creative Homeowner, 2006.

Tolpin, Jim. *Built-In Furniture: A Gallery of Design Ideas.* Newtown, CT: Taunton Books, 2001.

Service Providers and Product Vendors

www.bedbathstore.com

Online sales of portable storage closets and other items to contain your gear.

www.calclosets.com

Official California Closets site with locator link.

www.containerstore.com

Retail stores and a Web site offering a large and eclectic mix of some ten thousand products devoted to helping people simplify their lives.

www.easyclosets.com

You can order closet organizers direct and install them yourself if you are "comfortable using a few basic tools," potentially saving big bucks. Check out the design-your-own-closet feature, or you can request that professionals design a closet for you.

www.storage-and-organization.com

A division of the retailer StacksandStacks, the site features an assortment of more than four thousand organizers and storage items for all of the rooms of your home and office.

• STORAGE OFF-SITE

Web Sites and Organizations

www.selfstorage.org

The official industry site represents some six thousand members who own and operate some twenty thousand self-storage facilities in the United States, Canada, and sixteen other nations. The locator feature finds local storage facilities by zip code and offers consumer tips for proper storage procedures through "Library" and "General Information" links.

Service Providers & Product Vendors

www.doortodoor.com

This Seattle-based company in some two thousand cities brings storage units, which you fill, to your home. The square "pods" are picked up on a flatbed truck and secured in large commercial storage facilities. The site offers moving and storage tips and links to box sales for home delivery.

www.publicstorage.com

A well-organized commercial site with a zip code locater feature, checklists for proper storage, and a cost-comparison calculator.

www.shurgard.com

This company has storage facilities dotted around the globe. Targeting both home and business storage, a locator feature can determine if one of the six hundred–plus facilities is near you.

Author's Note and Acknowledgments

When a book is published, the author is usually the one to stand in the spotlight. Pull back the curtain, though, and you'll see an army of supporting cast members who made the production possible.

Center stage with me are all the stellar professionals at Springboard Press. Jill Cohen and Karen Murgolo conceived of an imprint that would, in the words of their mission statement, speak to baby boomers and others in ways that would "inform and inspire them on their quest for balanced, happy, fulfilling lives." When the proposal for this book crossed their desks and Jill and Karen gave it two thumbs up, the rest, as they say, was *her*story! I appreciate their vision and kindness more than I can say.

I am the author of five published works of historical fiction, but *Rightsizing Your Life* was my first, full-length nonfiction book in twenty-two years. Blessedly, into my life stepped one of the best "prescriptive nonfiction" editors in the business, Michelle Howry. This woman is so skilled and supportive that I want to take her with me wherever I go from here on out. Only writers understand the special talents and contributions of editors like Michelle, who are able to put forth suggestions in ways that prompt authors to race back to their keyboards fired with enthusiasm. When we follow the directives of these special guardians, we usually produce a vastly improved manuscript. I hope I have, and I am indebted to this editor as a total star in her field.

Matthew Ballast, directory of publicity, and his colleagues on the production side made this the happiest publication experience of my career, and they all have my thanks. The same holds true for my hardworking and talented agents, David Vigliano of Vigliano Associates and Celeste Fine, now at Folio Literary Management.

A book about people reinventing their lives requires scores of folks willing to talk candidly to a working writer. To everyone who paid me that honor, I extend my warmest thanks. There would have been *no* book without my gaining deep understanding from people in the throes of making sometimes difficult life transitions. To protect the privacy of those few interviewees who requested it, some names and identifying characteristics have been changed, although the vast majority made no stipulations whatsoever. To all of you, please accept my heartfelt appreciation for your gifts to me.

I am at my core, and by training, a reporter, not an "expert." I thank my fellow authors and the experts whose work in the fields of psychology, architecture and design, organization, relocation, preservation, and space planning bolstered my own knowledge and whom I have quoted, as indicated, throughout the book. These experts are also acknowledged in the Resource Directory, where I've listed helpful titles and Web sites so that readers can tap the source.

If writers are lucky, they have friends and families who make the experience of doing a book a lesson in gratitude. In my case the list is far too long to record each individual's name, but I include en masse my pals at the Sausalito Woman's Club, an institution approaching its one hundredth year and still going strong. The members know who they are, and I hope they realize the many ways they sustained me through this particular marathon, as did the members of Lane Driscoll's tap class!

My writer friends were always my best sounding boards, including my cousin-by-marriage, the hilarious and talented novelist Jane Heller; my critique partner, novelist Diana Dempsey; my cookbook pal and media sister, Diane Rossen Worthington; my fellow historical novelist Michael Llewellyn; Cavalier King Charles spaniel fancier and novelist Mary Alice Monroe; home-design editor extraordinaire Barbara Thornburg; and writer-turned-interior-designer Cynthia Challed. Author, neighbor, and "spiritual sister," the Reverend Bardet Wardell, and friend, the Reverend Diana Phillips of Cambridge, Massachusetts, provided key wisdom that helped me conceptualize some of the subtler underpinnings of this effort.

Web crawler par excellence Susan Wintersteen invariably spotted just the article I needed the moment I needed it. The same goes for the up-to-the-minute information that Dr. Diana Arsham passed along. I thank them both for their assistance and for their enduring friendships.

And then there's my kindred spirit, Gail Sheehy, whose e-mail reply accepting my invitation to write the foreword for *Rightsizing Your Life* came back to me in a nanosecond. We were spicy, young things when we worked together on the groundbreaking *New West Magazine,* founded some thirty years ago by her husband, the legendary editor and publisher Clay Felker. Personally, I don't think we've changed that much! Gail, I thank you for your stylish, truth-telling brand of nonfiction, which has been a source of insight and guidance for millions of readers such as I.

Deep appreciation goes, too, to the Monday Night Gals in Mill Valley, as well as to my two friends of longest duration from my youth in Carmel, Nicki Wilson McMahan and Diane Barr Young. I am also indebted to the attendees of the Tuesday morning W.I.S.E. gatherings. Every one of the aforementioned made a significant contribution to this effort, so bless you all.

My family was my other support system — especially husband, Tony Cook; son, Jamie; sister, Joy; and cousin, Alison Harris. Blood ties don't begin to account for their thoughtfulness, literary talents, and love.

I fully realize some people might think it strange (if not bizarre and *very* Californian) to thank one's pets, but I want to express my love and appreciation for Dandy Cat, who died prematurely and suddenly just a few days after the manuscript for *Rightsizing Your Life* was sent off to the publishers. He and our jaunty, economy-size dog, Ensign Aubrey, hung out with me every single day of my solitary confinement. If there's a kitty heaven, Dandy deserves to be let in despite his habit of snubbing certain family members on occasion. Aubrey, on the other hand, is already known by his legions of fans as a writer's angel and snoozes close by as I type this, keeping a sleepy eye on the word count.

Ciji Ware
Sausalito, California

Index

About the Author

Emmy Award–winning television producer, author, radio commentator, journalist, and home decorating veteran, **CIJI WARE** coaches people over fifty on the secrets of creating a simpler lifestyle through a step-by step process of freeing themselves from possessions and outsized households that don't suit them anymore. Ware's mantra? "Don't just downsize . . . *Rightsize!*"

An experienced public speaker, Ware teaches boomers, empty nesters, retirees, those embarking on second and third marriages, and the elderly what to keep, what to toss, and how to improve their surroundings in the process.

Over a span of twenty-two years, Ware became a seasoned health-and-lifestyle reporter for ABC, CBS, NBC, and PBS television affiliates in Los Angeles. During that period she also authored five published works of fact-based historical fiction, including the bestselling *Island of the Swans*, for which she received the 2001 Dorothy Parker Award for excellence in the "classics" category.

A native of Carmel, California, Ware graduated from Harvard University with a degree in history and is the first woman from Harvard College to serve as president of the Harvard Alumni Association worldwide. She is married to Internet executive Tony Cook and is the mother of editor, cinematographer, and producer Jamie Ware Billett.

Ciji Ware enjoys hearing from readers at ciji@rightsizingyourlife.com.